Play Like A Grandmaster

Play Like A Grandmaster

ALEXANDER KOTOV
Translated by Bernard Cafferty

B T Batsford Ltd, *London*

Symbols

+	Check
!	Good move
!!	Super move
?	Doubtful move
??	Blunder
W	White to move
B	Black to move

First published 1978
Reprinted 1980, 1982, 1984, 1986, 1987
© Alexander Kotov, 1978
ISBN 0 7134 1807 9 (limp)

Filmset by Willmer Brothers Limited, Birkenhead
Printed and bound in Great Britain by
Billing & Sons Ltd, Worcester
for the Publishers
B.T. Batsford Ltd,
4 Fitzhardinge Street, London W1H 0AH

BATSFORD CHESS BOOKS
Adviser: R.G. Wade
Editor: J.G. Nicholson

Contents

6 Contents

Preface

Friends and reviewers of the author's book *Think like a Grandmaster* took him to task for restricting his account to just one side of chess mastery—the calculation of variations. They felt that he had not touched upon much that was important and essential for a player who was aspiring to reach the top in chess.

Thus there originated the idea of this book *Play like a Grandmaster* which the author has been working on for some years. It is a continuation volume to *Think like a Grandmaster*, and deals with the most important aspect of chess wisdom, those laws and rules which have been developed by theoreticians of this ancient game of skill which includes elements of science, art and competitive sport. The book also contains the author's personal observations and the results of his study of the achievements of his fellow grandmasters.

In order to make the book a real textbook for players who have already mastered the elements and have some experience of play under competitive conditions, it contains several unusual but very important and recurring sections.

The sections headed 'Learn from the World Champions' show how various problems are solved by the kings of chess.

Then we penetrate the depths of a grandmaster's thought processes in the sections 'The Mind of a Grandmaster', in order to understand how he thinks and solves problems at the board, how his mind works.

Finally, 'How to Train' and 'Exercises' contain a description of methods of private study and training adopted by leading players in their time, as well as collections of relevant examples on various topics which will provide the reader with test material to work on by himself.

Will the reader of this book play like a grandmaster after he has worked through it carefully? It is hard to say; naturally this will depend partly on his natural gifts and his persistence in trying to achieve his objectives, as well as upon his personal qualities as a competitor. In any event the reader will certainly take a big step forward in his assimilation of chess theory, and will come to understand many fine points involved in thinking about his moves and in chess problem-solving. These are the factors which in the final analysis bring success in competitive play.

Acknowledgment

The author gratefully acknowledges the work of Jonathan C. Shaw and Leslie J. Smart in proof-reading this book, and of John G. Nicholson for his re-arrangement and editing of the manuscript.

RGW

1 Positional Judgement

The Three Fishes of Chess Mastery

In order to become a grandmaster class player whose understanding of chess is superior to the thousands of ordinary players, you have to develop within yourself a large number of qualities, the qualities of an artistic creator, a calculating practitioner, a cold calm competitor. We shall try to tell you about what a player needs in order to improve and perfect himself, and give advice on how to carry out regular training so that both your playing strength and style get better.

Of all the qualities of chess mastery three stand out, just as in the old myth the world stands on three fishes. The three fishes of chess mastery are positional judgement, an eye for combinations and the ability to analyse variations. Only when he has a perfect grasp of these three things can a player understand the position on the board in front of him, examine hidden combinative possibilities and work out all the necessary variations.

We consider it essential to start with the question of positional play. This is the basis of everything else. It is possible that because of your character you do not often play pretty combinative blows. There are players of even the highest standard in whose games the sparkle of combinative play is quite rare. On the other hand in every game you play, in every position you study, you have no choice but to analyse and assess the current situation and form the appropriate plans.

In order to provide the reader with a framework within which the fundamentals of positional play may be studied, we will first consider an important question which hitherto has not received the attention it deserves; namely, what are the basic types of struggle which arise in practical play?

A General Theory of the Middlegame

If a chess statistician were to try and satisfy his curiosity over which stage of the game proved decisive in the majority of cases, he would certainly come to the conclusion that it is the middlegame that provides the mose decisive stage. This is quite understandable, since the opening is the stage when your forces are mobilized, and the endgame is the time when advantages achieved earlier are realized, while the middlegame is the time when we have the basic clash of the forces, when the basic question, who is to win, is settled.

That is why it would seem that chess theoreticians should devote the maximum attention to the general laws of the middlegame. Alas, this is far from being the case. There are very many books devoted to the huge mass of possible opening variations, and a fair number of books on the endgame, but far less attention is paid to the systematic study of the basic part of the game.

Why is this? One reason is that experienced grandmasters do not have the time to devote to the difficult task of describing typical middlegame methods and considerations, and this work tends to fall to people who have not played in top class events and who therefore lack the requisite deep study of this question.

Apart from collections of combinative examples there are few books extant on the middlegame which can be wholeheartedly recommended.

What we now undertake is an attempt to fill this gap in chess literature, to describe the rules and considerations which a grandmaster bears in mind during a tournament game.

First of all we have to distinguish the different sorts of struggles which can arise. Let us consider two contrasting examples from grandmaster play.

Euwe–Alekhine, 19th game, match 1937.

1 d4 ♘f6 2 c4 e6 3 ♘c3 ♗b4 4 ♘f3 ♘e4 5 ♕c2 d5 6 e3 c5 7 ♗d3 ♘f6 8 cd ed 9 dc ♗×c5 10 0–0 ♘c6 11 e4! ♗e7 12 e5 ♘g4 13 ♖e1 ♘b4 14 ♗b5+ ♔f8 15 ♕e2 ♗c5 16 ♘d1 ♗f5 *(1)*

We can see that from the start the players have been making threats, their pieces have made raids into the enemy camp by crossing the fourth rank. It is a stiff fight getting tenser with each move.

17	h3	h5!
18	♗g5	♕b6
19	♘h4	

It would be bad to accept the sacrificed piece. After 19 hg hg 20 ♘h4 g3 21 ♘×f5 gf+ 22 ♘×f2 ♗×f2+ 23 ♕×f2 ♖h1+ 24 ♔×h1 ♕×f2 25 ♖f1 White should win, but Black has the stronger move 20 . . . ♗e4 with a very unpleasant attack.

19	. . .	♗e4
20	hg	♘c2

Black could have played 20 . . . hg transposing to the previous variation, but Alekhine considered the text stronger.

21	♘c3	♘d4
22	♕f1	

Not the strongest. 22 ♕d2 was better with the following variations:–

I 22 . . . ♘×b5 23 ♘×e4 de 24 ♖×e4

II 22 . . . hg 23 ♘×e4 de 24 b4!

III 22 . . . ♘e6 23 b4 ♗×b4 24 ♘×d5 ♗×d2 (or 24 . . . ♕×b5 25 ♕×b4 ♕×b4 26 ♘×b4 ♘×g5 27 f4) 25 ♗e7+ ♔g8 26 ♘×b6 ♗e1 27 ♘×a8 ♗c3 28 ♖c1 ♗×e5 29 ♖e1

IV 22 . . . ♘e6 23 b4 ♗d4 24 ♘×e4 de 25 ♗c4 ♘×g5 26 ♕×g5 ♗×f2+ 27 ♔f1 hg 28 ♘g6+

22	. . .	hg!

Not 22 . . . ♘×b5 23 ♘×b5 hg 24 g3 ♖h5 25 ♗e3 ♗×e3 26 fe! winning.

23	♘a4	♕c7

The only move, since if 23 . . . ♕×b5 24 ♕×b5 ♘×b5 25 ♘×c5 ♖h5 26 ♖×e4 de 27 ♘×e4 and White keeps the pawn on e5.

24	♖×e4	

It is clear that the position is not too nice for White, but taking the bishop is not the best line. Euwe considers that White would be able to defend the position after 24 ♘×c5 ♕×c5 25 ♗d3 ♘e6 26 ♗e3 ♗×d3 27 ♗×c5+ ♘×c5 28 ♖e2 ♖×h4 29 ♕c1.

24	. . .	de
25	♕c4	♖c8?

A serious mistake. 25 . . . ♞e6 26 ♞g6+! was also wrong. The only defence was 25 . . . ♛×c5 26 ♛×c5+ ♛×c5 27 ♞×c5 ♞×b5 and Black can hold the endgame.

26 ♖c1　　　　　　　　b6

26 . . . ♛×c5 would lose to 27 ♞×c5 ♛×g5 28 ♞e6+! with an attack on the black king.

27 ♞×c5　　　　　　　bc
28 ♝a6?

A decisive mistake. White would win after 28 e6 ♞×e6 29 ♞g6+ ♚g8 30 ♞e7+, or 28 . . . ♞×b5 29 c7+ ♚g8 30 ♛×b5. He could also continue the attack by 28 ♝e3. Now Black gets a draw by some fine moves.

28 . . .　　　　　　　　♛×e5
29 ♝×c8

Or 29 ♝e3 ♖×h4 30 ♝×d4 ♛h5 31 ♚f1 ♖h1+ 32 ♚e2 g3+

29 . . .　　　　　　　　♛×g5
30 ♛×c5+　　　　　　　♛×c5
31 ♖×c5　　　　　　　♖×h4

With the threat of repetition of moves . . . ♞e2+, ♚f1 ♞f4, ♚g1 ♞e2+ etc.

32 ♖c4　　　　　　　　♞e2+
33 ♚f1　　　　　　　　♞f4
34 ♚g1　　　　　　　　g3

A dubious attempt to play for a win. He should force the draw by repetition.

35 ♝a6!

After 35 fg Black gets the advantage by 35 . . . ♞e2+ 36 ♚f1 (36 ♚f2? e3+ winning the exchange) 36 . . . ♞×g3+ 37 ♚g1 f5

35 . . .　　　　　　　　gf+
36 ♚×f2　　　　　　　♖h6
37 ♖×e4

A final slip. After 37 ♖c8+ ♚e7 38 ♖c7+ ♚e6 39 ♝c4+ ♞d5 40 ♖×a7 the chances would favour White. Now it is a draw.

37 . . .　　　　　　　　♖×a6
38 ♖×f4 ♖×a2 39 ♖b4 g6 40 ♖b7 ♚g7 41 ♚f3 g5 42 b4 ♚g6 43 b5 f5 44 b6 ♖a3+ 45 ♚f2 a6 46 ♖b8 ♖b3 47 b7 ♚g7 48 ♖a8 ♖×b7 49 ♖×a6 ½–½

What happened in this game? We did not see any deep strategic plans or long range manoeuvring. From the very start the opposing forces flung themselves into a close order conflict and rained threats on the opponent's bastions. The whole game consists of sharp variations in which sacrifice followed sacrifice, and each tactical stroke met with a counter blow from the other side.

Quite a different type of game now follows.

1 d4 ♘f6 2 c4 g6 3 ♘c3 ♗g7 4 e4 0–0 5 ♘f3 d6 6 ♗e2 e5 7 0–0 ♘bd7 8 ♖e1 c6 9 ♗f1 ♖e8 10 d5 c5 11 g3 ♘f8 12 a3 ♘g4 13 ♘h4 a6 14 ♗d2 h5 15 h3 ♘f6 *(2)*

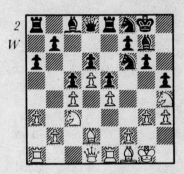

Taimanov–Geller, Candidates Tournament, Zurich 1953

Here the opposing pieces are a certain distance from each other, and there is no question of getting the sort of hand to hand tactical battle such as we saw in the previous game, at least for the moment. White quietly prepares to open files on the Q-side.

16	b4	b6
17	bc	bc
18	♖b1	♘6d7
19	♕a4	♗f6
20	♘f3	h4

This show of activity is out of place. Black should continue to manoeuvre with his pieces within his own camp while waiting to see what White will undertake.

21	♘d1	hg
22	fg	♘b8
23	♖e3	

Now White has a nice game alternating play on the b or f files as he chooses.

23	...	♘h7
24	♖eb3	♗d7
25	♕a5	♕c8
26	♘f2	♗d8

	27 ♕c3	♗a4

Black has been successful at defending himself on the Q-side so Taimanov now transfers his attention to the K-side.

	28 ♖3b2	♘d7
	29 h4	♖a7
	30 ♗h3	♕c7
	31 ♘g5	♘×g5
	32 ♗×g5	♗×g5
	33 hg	♔g7
	34 ♕f3	

With the simple threat of ♔g2, then ♗×d7 and mate by ♕f6+ ♖h1 and ♕h8 or ♖h8.

	34 . . .	♕d8
	35 ♖b7	

Now the outcome will be decided by this entry to the 7th rank. Note how effortlessly White has increased his advantage.

	35 . . .	♖×b7

36 ♖×b7 ♔g8 37 ♗×d7 ♗×d7 38 ♘g4 ♕×g5 39 ♖×d7 f5 40 ef ♖b8 and Black resigned. 1–0.

What strikes you when working through this game? The answer must be the absence of a tactical clash. For a very long time there were just strategical manoeuvres and re-forming ranks. Moreover there were practically no variations to consider as you can see from the notes to the game. When playing such a game an experienced grandmaster would never start working out variations. He would weigh up one or two short lines and that's it! In such positions general considerations prevail:– where should a certain piece be transferred to, how to stop some particular action by the opponent. Finally which piece to exchange, which one to keep on the board.

Hence we can draw a simple and clear conclusion. There are two main types of position, and resulting from that, two different kinds of struggle. In the one case we get a constant clash of pieces mixing it in tricky patterns, with tactical blows, traps, sometimes unexpected and shattering moves. In the other case it is quite different. The respective armies stand at a distance from each other, the battles are restricted to reconnaissance and minor sorties into the enemy position. The thrust of the attacking side is prepared slowly with the aid of piece regrouping and 'insignificant' pawn advances. We may call positions of the first type combinative-tactical, of the second type manoeuvring-strategical.

We have distinguished two types of position according to the presence or absence of sharp contact, critical moments and threats of 'explosions':

corresponding to this twofold division we get a marked difference in the working of the grandmaster's mind in each case. In the first case the player is always tensed up as he constantly examines complicated variations, takes account of tactical blows and tries to foresee and forestall deeply hidden, unexpected moves and traps. Little attention is given to general considerations since the player can hardly spare time for these in view of the time limit, and it is hardly necessary to bear them in mind in such positions. Sometimes he might just make some such general comment to himself as 'it would be nice to get a battery against f2 by ♕c5 and ♗b6', or 'watch out all the time for that open h-file', or 'try and get rid of that powerful bishop of his at e4'. However these are just short verbal orders to oneself, a formulation of the general ideas resulting from analysis. Obviously there are no such things as deep general plans, regroupings, manoeuvres. Concrete analysis, working out tactical strokes, spotting traps, anticipating cunning or surprising 'explosions'—that is what is called for in positions of the first type.

So in the first case the mind is kept on tenterhooks, and works in accordance with the slogan 'keep a close watch'; whereas in the second case the work of the mind is marked by calm, comparative slowness and the absence of nervousness. What is there to get excited about, when there can be no violent explosions, no unforeseen tactical strokes or tricky traps? The mind is occupied with formulating plans for regrouping and moving about with the pieces with the almost total absence of variations. Only at certain specific moments do tactics come to the surface, causing the grandmaster to work out a few variations before reverting again to general considerations.

We shall revert later to the question of the mind of a grandmaster, but I ask the reader to read carefully through these lines and grasp firmly the difference in thought patterns. This point is very important in clarifying the rules for thinking about moves and handling your clock properly. If you make plans in sharp tactical positions, you can easily fall into a trap that figures in the calculations you failed to make. Vice versa, if you are going to calculate variations in positions where you should be thinking about general planning, you will waste precious time and will not get the right orientation. So let us commit firmly to memory the fact that the mind of a grandmaster is principally occupied, in combinative-tactical positions, with the calculation of variations; in manoeuvring-strategical positions, with the formulation of general plans and considerations.

The two games we have just looked at are extreme examples of the types of struggle which can arise. To bring out the difference between them even more graphically, we shall try to indicate their course by a schematic diagram. On the diagram below we have the depiction of the Euwe–Alekhine game, a wavy line full of zig-zags (No. 1). Then in No. 2 we get an idea of the course of the Taimanov–Geller game, a simple straight line.

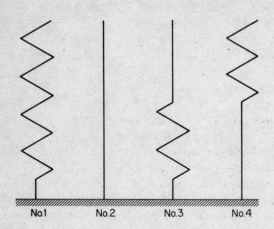

However in tournament play there are other types of game which have a mixed content. One such may start in the sharp combinative manner but then settle down into a calm course. Such a 'calm after the storm' is seen in the next game and we depict it in No. 3.

1 e4 c6 2 d4 d5 3 ♘c3 de 4 ♘×e4 ♘d7 5 ♘f3 ♘gf6 6 ♘×f6+ ♘×f6 7 ♘e5 ♗f5 8 c3 e6

A well-known variation of the Caro–Kann which normally leads to quiet play, but young players can find means of conjuring up terrific complications.

9	g4!	♗g6
10	h4	♗d6
11	♕e2	c5
12	h5	♗e4
13	f3	cd!

Pieces on both sides are en prise. Clearly a case of a combinative-tactical struggle, abounding in unexpected strokes and cunning traps.

14	♕b5+	♘d7
15	♘×f7!	

The position becomes even more complicated, particularly after Black's strong reply.

15 . . .	♗g3+
16 ♔c2	d3+
17 ♔c3!	♕f6
18 ♔×e4 *(3)*	

Karpov–A. Zaitsev   Kuibyshev 1970

Have you ever seen such a position for the king with all the pieces still on the board and only eighteen moves made? The position is most complex, and naturally no general considerations can help a player to find his way in such great complications. You simply must work out variations, and both sides have to make the great effort to seek the best line for each side by means of analysis of the many possibilities.

18 . . .	♕×f7
19 ♖h3	a6
20 ♕g5	h6?

This apparently threatening move loses the game, whereas there was a variation which would continue the attack and lead to victory—20 . . . e5! 21 ♖×g3 ♘c5+ 22 ♔c3 0–0 23 ♖h3 ♖ad8 24 ♗d2 ♘e4! 25 ♔×e4 ♕d5+ 26 ♔e3 ♕c5+ 27 ♔e4 ♖d4+. This is not easy to find as is shown by the fact that such an excellent tactician as the late Alexander Zaitsev missed it.

21 ♕e3!	e5
22 ♔×d3	♗f4
23 ♕g1	0–0–0
24 ♔c2	♗×c1
25 ♖×c1!	♕×a2
26 ♖h2	

The white king now feels safe after his risky expedition to the centre under the eyes of the enemy pieces. Note that the character of the play now changes, and the rest of the game is a typical manoeuvring-strategical one.

26	...	♖hf8
27	♖d2!	♛a4+
28	♔b1 *(4)*	

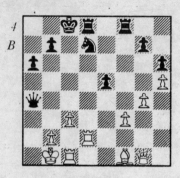

Let us assess the resulting position. White's pawn formation is better. He has no weak pawns while the pawn at e5 is isolated. There are also weak white squares in Black's position and this with White having a bishop on that colour. White's rooks are better mobilised, and the knight occupies a passive post at d7. All this indicates a positional advantage for White, and Karpov starts to exploit this in a methodical way without hurrying. The play changes character from complex clashes to quiet 'reasoned' manoeuvres.

28	...	♛c6
29	♗d3!	♔c7

Obviously not 29 ... ♛×f3 30 ♗f5 and the knight will be lost.

30	♗e4	♛b6
31	♛h2	♖dc8
32	♖cd1	♘f6
33	♗g6	♖e7
34	♖e1	

'Pile up on the weak pawn e5!' White's advantage becomes clearer. Note however that all this takes place without any clash of the pieces; it is all quite peaceful.

34	...	♛b5
35	♖de2	♘d7
36	♗f5!	♖×f5

A sacrifice of desperation. The e5 pawn cannot be held and **Black** tries to complicate matters by giving up the exchange, but without success.

37	gf	♛d3+

38	♔a1		♕×f5
39	♕h4!		♘f6
40	♕c4+		♔d8
41	♕c5		

and White won without any real trouble exploiting his material advantage.

Now examine a game in which the two parts came in the reverse order— the quiet part first, the complications later.

1	d4		d5
2	c4		e6
3	♘c3		c6
4	♘f3		♘f6
5	cd		

Such an exchange in the centre normally leads to stabilization of the position there, and to a consequent calming of the play. White will castle short and then advance with his pawns on the Q-side. Black normally restricts himself to slow manoeuvres on the K-side.

5	...		ed
6	♕c2		♘bd7
7	♗g5		♗e7
8	e3		0–0
9	♗d3		♖e8
10	0–0		♘f8
11	♖ab1		

A typical preparation in such positions for advancing b4 and a4, after which White will aim to weaken the c6 pawn and open lines on the Q-side.

11	...		♗e6
12	b4		♖c8
13	♘a4		

Another well-known device, transferring the knight to c5 from where it will press on Black's position on the Q-side.

13	...		♘e4
14	♗×e7		♖×e7
15	♘c5		♘×c5
16	♕×c5		b6
17	♕c2		♕d6
18	♖fc1		g6
19	♖b3		

Intending to treble the major pieces on the c-file. Note how quiet it is, with no tactics in sight.

19 ...		♘d7
20 h3		♘b8
21 a3		♗d7
22 ♖c3		♗e8
23 h4		

An important strategical device in such positions. White advances this pawn to h5 and exchanges on g6. That rules out a subsequent f6 by Black, since Black would not be prepared to weaken his g6 square further. Then the white knight will establish himself on e5.

23 ...		a6
24 h5		♖a7
25 hg		hg
26 ♘e5		a5
27 b5! *(5)*		

Kotov–Ragozin   USSR Championship 1949

A sharp change in the course of events. As if at a sudden signal the game moves into tactical complications. If Black replies 27 ... c5 then 28 dc! ♕×c5 (28 ... bc 29 ♖×c5) 29 cb ♖×c3 30 ba!! ♖×c2 31 ♖×c2! and wins.

27 ...		♖ac7

This simply leaves Black a pawn down, but the position remains tense.

28 bc		♔g7
29 ♕b1!		♘×c6
30 ♕×b6		♖b8
31 ♕×b8!		

The queen is given up for two rooks, but White had to calculate accurately the combinative possibilities which arise.

31 ...		♘×b8

32	♖×c7	♕×a3
33	♗×g6	♘c6!

It looks as if Black has tricked his opponent by this unexpected move, but White had taken it into account and a sacrifice of the exchange follows.

34	♖1×c6!	♗×c6
35	♖×f7+	♔h6
36	f4!	

This forces win of the queen or mate.

36	. . .	♕×e3+
37	♔h2	♕×e5
38	fe	1–0.

If we examine our earlier schematic diagram, we will see that the outline course of this game is shown in No.4.

Why have we made such a distinction? We wish to illustrate the nature of a grandmaster's thinking process during a game, and how the rhythm of this thinking changes in accordance with the nature of the position which lies in front of him. So we have established one of the major features that guides a grandmaster. If he faces a combinative-tactical position, he deals with it by working out variations, using general considerations only at certain rare moments. In manoeuvring-strategical positions he restricts himself to general considerations, though here too he has recourse at times to short analysis of variations. Finally he has the flexibility to change from one approach to another as appropriate.

Now what do general considerations consist of? We now devote a great deal of attention to this vital question which lies at the bottom of all positional play.

The Basic Postulates of Positional Play

The level of development of positional sense depends on many factors. Most of all it is shown in the ability of a player by dint of natural ability to determine swiftly, at one swoop, the main characteristics of a position. Chess history knows many examples of the ability to sniff out the essence of a position without the player having to trouble himself with wearisome analytical effort. Such cases reveal a real natural gift.

Yet the main thing that develops positional judgement, that perfects it and makes it many-sided, is detailed analytical work, sensible tournament practice, a self-critical attitude to your games an a rooting out of all the defects in your play. This is the only way to learn to analyse chess positions and to assess them properly. Mastery only comes after you have a wide experience of studying a mass of chess positions, when all the laws and devices employed by the grandmasters have become your favoured weapons too.

Positional sense is like the thread that leads you through the labyrinth in your tense struggle at the board from the first opening move to the final stroke in the endgame. When people come to say about you that you have a good positional sense, you will be able to consider yourself a well-rounded and promising player.

We shall now try to state in a systematic way all the postulates and rules of middlegame play that have been worked out by theoreticians over the long history of chess. They might appear elementary to the discriminating reader. Why bother to repeat what has long been known? Believe me, for all my long practical experience of play and writing, I have found it far from easy to reduce to a common denominator all that has been expressed so far in chess history. Moreover what is elementary? When I pose this question I call to mind Mikhail Tal. The ex-world champion has often commented that he regularly watches the chess lessons on TV meant for lower rated players. His idea is that the repetition of the elements can never do any harm, but rather polishes up the grandmaster's thoughts.

For greater clarity we shall try to express the concepts of middlegame theory in short exactly formulated points.

1. In chess only the attacker wins.

Of course there are cases where it is the defender who has the point marked up for him in the tournament table, but this is only when his opponent exceeds the time limit or makes a bad mistake—overlooks mate, or loses a lot of material. Moreover, if one follows strict logic, even after this loss of material the game could be played out to mate and in this case the final victory goes to the former defender who in the later stages, after his opponent's mistake, is transformed into the attacker.

The question then arises, which of the two players has the right to attack. Before the time of the first world champion Wilhelm Steinitz, who is the creator of modern chess theory, it was held that the more talented player attacked. Steinitz put it quite differently. The talent and playing strength of a chess player was a secondary consideration.

2. The right to attack is enjoyed by that player who has the better position.

If your position is inferior, even though you are a genius, you do better not to think of attacking, since such an attempt can only worsen your position.

3. The side with the advantage has not only the right but also the duty to attack, otherwise he runs the risk of losing his advantage.

This is another postulate of Steinitz, and practice knows very many examples confirming it. How often has temporising, missing the appropriate moment to press, losing a few tempi, led to the loss of advantage, often of great advantage? Attack is the effective means in chess, it is the way to victory.

Where does this leave the defender? Here too Steinitz has wise advice to give.

4. The defender must be prepared to defend, and to make concessions.

That means that the defender must try to repulse the attacker's blows, anticipate his intentions. Later theoreticians have added the rider to Steinitz that the defender must not leave out of his calculations the possibility of a counter strike, the chance to go over to counter-attack at the appropriate time. Defence thus means subjecting yourself for a time to the will of your opponent. From that comes the well-known fact that it is a lot harder to defend than to attack.

Then the question arises, what means of attack are at the disposal of a player, and what should be chosen as the object of attack?

5. The means of attack in chess are twofold, combinative and strategical.

As we have seen, attacks may develop with or without immediate contact between the forces.

Which method is appropriate? The answer is best indicated by the nature of the position you are dealing with. Often it depends on the nature of the opening you have chosen, on the style of the players, but the decisive say lies with the position. No temperament no matter how passionate can produce an 'explosion' in a stabilized position, and attempts to do this can only rebound upon the instigator.

Finally the question arises, where should the attack be made, and the answer is clear:

6. The attack must be directed at the opponent's weakest spot.

This almost goes without saying. Who would be foolish enough to attack a position at its strongest point? 'Why attack a lion when there is a lamb in the field?' The grandmaster seeks to direct his attack against the weakest, most sensitive, spot in the enemy fortifications.

So we see how many difficult problems pose themselves to the grandmaster in the middlegame. Should he attack or defend? To answer this he has to establish whether he or the opponent has the advantage, but that is not all. Even when you have settled the first question and established who has the right (and correspondingly) the duty to attack, you have to seek out the opponent's most vulnerable spot. The procedure to determine these questions is termed positional assessment, and we shall now consider this important topic in depth.

Positional Assessment

The player who wishes to improve, who wants to win in competitive play, must develop his ability to assess positions, and on that basis to work out plans for what comes next.

This work of analysis can be compared to that of a chemist who is trying to determine the nature of a substance. Once upon a time the process was carried out in rough and ready fashion by visual inspection. Then Mendeleyev discovered the periodic table of elements and after that the chemist merely had to break down the substance into its constituent elements in order to determine the exact nature of the substance before him.

That is the way chess players work now. About a century and a half ago the best players of the time solved their problems by visual inspection on the basis of their experience. There was no scientific method about this, but then came Steinitz's theory. Thereby the player gained a basis for rational analysis suitable for solving whatever problems were posed, no matter how intricate the position. Steinitz taught players most of all to split the position into its elements. Naturally they do not all play the same role in a given position, they do not have the same importance. Once he has worked out the relationship of the elements to each other, the player moves on to the process of synthesis which is known in chess as the general assessment.

When he has carried out the synthesis, has assessed the position, the grandmaster proceeds to the next step, when he draws up his plan for what follows. We shall deal with this later, and restrict ourselves to the statement that every plan is intimately linked with assessment. The analysis and assessment enables the player to find the weak point in the enemy camp, after which his thoughts will naturally be directed towards exploiting this weakness with the aid of a deeply thought out plan of campaign which takes account of the slightest nuances of the given position.

In defining the elements there is no perfect agreement amongst chess theorists. Each writer has his own list. It seems to us that the following 'Mendeleyev' table of chess elements will be sufficient to cover all those smaller parts out of which the analysis of a position is made up.

Table of Elements

Permanent Advantages

1 Material advantage.
2 Poor opponent's king position.
3 Passed pawns.

4 Weak pawns (of opponent).
5 Weak squares (of opponent)
6 Weak colour complexes (of opponent).
7 Fewer pawn islands.
8 Strong pawn centre.
9 The advantage of two bishops.
10 Control of a file.
11 Control of a diagonal.
12 Control of a rank.

Temporary Advantages

1 Poor position of opponent's piece.
2 Lack of harmony in opponent's piece placing.
3 Advantage in development.
4 Piece pressure in the centre.
5 Advantage in space.

We have already spoken of Steinitz's view that a win should not be played for if there is no confidence that the position contains some advantage or other. The question then arises, what does this advantage consist of? Steinitz gives the detailed and concrete reply, 'An advantage can consist of one large advantage, or a number of small advantages.' He then adds the important guide to further action: 'The task of the positional player is systematically to accumulate slight advantages and try to convert temporary advantages into permanent ones, otherwise the player with the better position runs the risk of losing it.'

This is a valuable piece of advice, stressing that elements vary not just in their importance but in the length of their lifetime. Some are long term or permanent, others are temporary and either change (becoming greater or smaller) or disappear altogether.

If we are a sound pawn up, or if the opponent's K-side is seriously weakened, then we enjoy a long term advantage. If, however, we have a lead in development or there is a badly placed piece in the enemy camp, then this is a short term advantage and can easily be dissipated in the subsequent play. Of course it is not possible to draw a fixed line between the twelve elements which we have defined as permanent and the five we give as temporary. For example an open file or diagonal can be closed by means of an exchange of pawns and material inequality can be restored to equality, but the division we have made is a sufficiently good guide in our judgement and decision taking processes.

This is the appropriate place to sum up Steinitz's positional rules in the form of short laconic summaries such as we encounter in mathematics, physics and other exact sciences. It is a matter of some surprise that no-one has done this before. We suggest the following form of words for them.

Steinitz's Four Rules.

1. The right to attack belongs only to that side which has a positional advantage, and this not just a right, but also a duty, otherwise there is the risk of losing the advantage. The attack is to be directed against the weakest spot in the enemy position.

2. The defending side must be prepared to defend and to make concessions.

3. In level positions the two sides manoeuvre, trying to tilt the balance of the position, each in his own favour. With correct play by both sides, level positions keep on leading to further level positions.

4. The advantage may consist of a large advantage in one form or element only, or of a number of small advantages. The task of the positional player is to accumulate small advantages and to try to turn these small advantages into permanent ones.

These four rules of Steinitz can be of great help and serve as a guiding thread for every player in his positional battles. However we should point out straight away the harm that arises if these rules are turned into strict dogmas: The Russian school, while recognizing the importance of Steinitz's teachings and the usefulness of his rules, always favours a concrete approach to assessment of a position with due regard for dynamic features.

One other practical point. We have enumerated seventeen elements of a chess position, but during actual play a player would not find it too easy to consider each of the seventeen at every point. The grandmaster is helped out of this dilemma by the fact that usually not all the elements apply to a given position. There might well be only five to seven of them relevant.

We recommend the following approach; as a rule consider a restricted number of grouped elements. The following is a grouping of elements that has been proved most useful in practice:–

1. Weak squares and pawns.
2. Open lines.
3. The centre and space.
4. Piece position.

The last named consists of such factors as king position, development, harmony of position, and the bad placing of one piece.

So in practice we need consider these four only, with the proviso that if we discern some other element, say the two bishops, then we add this to our assessment.

The Elements in Practice

Let us now take practical examples from actual play in which analysis and assessment were carried out. Normally there is a mixture of factors involved, an advantage in one element may be compensated for by the opponent enjoying an advantage in another element. All this has to be weighed up, comparing the significance of each element. However it may also be the case that one of the elements suddenly assumes decisive significance and confers a clear advantage. We shall start with such positions.

Weak Squares
Weak squares can be defined in essence as those squares which cannot be protected by pawns. Of course from a practical point of view we have a wider concept depending a great deal on the actual position: thus a square can sometimes be considered weak even when it can be protected by a pawn, but only with a serious weakening of position.

In assessing any position a grandmaster is bound to take account of weak squares, both his own and those in the enemy camp. Moreover it is often the case that he starts his assessments from here: a number of weak squares, or even a single weak square, can be the outstanding feature of the position. A piece that gets established on this weak point spreads confusion in the defence and decides the issue.

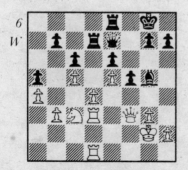

Botvinnik–Flohr, Moscow, 1936.

Even a first glance at diagram 6 will show that all other weak squares and other positional factors recede into the background by comparison with the gaping 'hole' at d6. Obviously a knight established there will play a decisive role, and Botvinnik plays to get his knight to the square he has prepared for it.

34	♘b1	♛f8
35	♘a3	♗d8
36	♘c4	♗c7
37	♘d6	♖b8
38	♖b1	

Relying on the beautiful knight at d6 White makes a Q-side thrust.

38	...	♛d8
39	b4	ab
40	♖×b4	♗×d6

The knight must be removed, but now White gets an advanced protected passed pawn, another great positional trump.

41	ed	♛a5
42	♖db3	♖e8
43	♛e2	♛a8
44	♖e3	♔f7
45	♛c4	

White misses a tactical stroke and thus makes his win more difficult. By playing his king first to g1 he could follow his plan without allowing any tactical tricks.

45	...	b5!

The point is that taking this pawn either on b5 or on b6 en passant would lose material to a discovered check.

46	♛c2	♖×d6

Flohr in his turn goes wrong. 46 . . . ♖a7 would put up a stiffer fight, though after 47 ab ♖a2 48 ♖b2 cb+ 49 ♔h3 the united passed pawns would guarantee a white victory.

47	cd	c5+

48 ♔h3 cb 49 ♛c7+ ♔g8 50 d7 ♖f8 51 ♛d6 h6 52 ♛×e6+ ♔h7 53 ♛e8 b3 54 ♛×a8 ♖×a8 55 ab ♖d8 56 ♖×b3 ♖×d7 57 b6 1–0.

Weak Pawns

There are many types of weak pawns: backward pawns, isolated pawns, doubled pawns, pawns far advanced and as a result cut off from contact with 'base'. All are spoken of as weak pawns, even though for the moment there is adequate protection from the pieces. After all the pieces might go away, leaving the pawn to its fate.

A pawn can be proved to be weak, however, only when it can be attacked. The reader should take particular note of the following comments by Bronstein when talking about the position of diagram 7, which arises in a well-known variation of the King's Indian Defence.

'It seems it is time to reveal here the secret of the pawn at d6 in the King's Indian Defence. Although this pawn is on an open file and is apparently subject to attack, yet it is still a tough nut to crack. It is hard to get at. What would seem easier than moving the knight at d4 away, but the point is that the knight is badly needed at d4. Its task there is to observe the squares b5, c6, e6, and f5 as well as neutralizing the bishop at g7. The knight can only move away from the centre after White has prepared to meet Black's various threats (a4–a3, ♗c8–e6, f7–f5) but during the time taken by these preparations Black will be able to reform his ranks.

Hence the weakness of the d6 pawn turns out to be imaginary.

Modern methods of playing the opening know of many such imaginary weaknesses, yet it was the supposed "permanent" weakness at d6 that long condemned the King's Indian Defence as "dubious".'

Hence we urge you to attack weak pawns, but at the same time you have to have a critical and creative attitude to even the most obvious pawn weaknesses!

Diagram 8 shows a critical moment in Gligorić–Szabo, Candidates Tournament, Zurich, 1953. Bronstein comments thus:–'Black has the advantage since the a5 pawn is weak, and the pawns at e5 and f4 limit the scope of the bishop.' There now came:

25	♘f3	♖fb8
26	♘fd4	♘c×d4
27	♘×d4	♘×d4
28	cd	♗b4
29	♖a1	♖b5

30	♖a4	♖ab8
31	♖fa1	♗c3
32	♖c1	♖b1
33	♖×b1	♖×b1+
34	♔f2	♖a1

Black's advantage increases move by move.

35	♖×a1	♗×a1
36	♔e2	♗c3
37	♔d3	♗×a5
38	h3	

White misses the chance of a study-like draw by 38 ♗d2 ♗b6 39 ♗b4! after which it is hard for Black to penetrate with his king to the centre.

38	...	♗e1
39	g4	g6
40	♔c2	♔f8
41	♔d1	♗g3
		0–1

Weak Colour Complexes

These arise when one side weakens a whole set of squares of one colour on which the opponent's pieces come to dominate. From the position of diagram 9, White made a heroic fight against a weak complex on the white squares.

White's king is in check. His best chance is 12 ♔f1 avoiding further weakening of the white squares, but Makogonov played 12 g3 after which Botvinnik immediately settled down to exploit the new weaknesses on the K-side.

12	...	♕h3
13	♔f2	♗×c3

Makogonov–Botvinnik, Sverdlovsk, 1943

14 bc	♗f5

A device which we advise the reader to remember. Try to exchange a bishop which defends the opponent's weak colour complex.

15 ♗×f5	♕×f5
16 g4!	

White tries at all costs to get some grip on the white squares on his K-side.

16 ...	♕e6

17 ♗a3! ♘e4+ 18 ♔f3 h5 19 h3 f6! 20 c4 hg+! 21.hg ♖×h1 22 ♕×h1 0–0–0 23 ♖d1 fe 24 cd cd 25 ♖c1+ ♔b8 26 ♕h4 ♖e8 27 f5 ♕f7 28 ♖c2 g6 29 ♗b2 a6 30 ♔e2 ♔a7! and Black won by means of a direct attack on the king.

Pawn Islands

There should be no need to stress that a comradely united pawn mass is the best sort of pawn configuration. Then every foot soldier senses the presence of his mate by his shoulder and receives the appropriate support and reinforcement when needed. It is a different state of affairs when the pawns are ripped into fragments. Then there is no hope of help since the other pawns cannot jump the ditch separating them. That is why the presence of a number of pawn islands is a serious drawback that can lead to defeat.

In assessing diagram 10 (Gligorić–Keres, 1953 Candidates Tournament) Bronstein wrote in the tournament book:

'White is well dug in, but Black's advantage is of a permanent nature and is expressed not so much in the active nature of this or that piece, but in his better pawn configuration. Concretely this consists of:–

a. All Black's pawns are linked in a single branch, while White's are weakened.

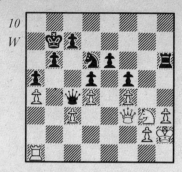

10
W

b. The pawns at d5 and f5 ensure Black's knight a post at e4. If White exchanges the knight on that square then a protected passed pawn ensues.

c. If Black can win the pawn at a4 then his own passed a- pawn will play through to queen unhindered. White already has a passed pawn at h3, but this cannot advance since White's pieces are not in a position to support it.

These principal features of the position are sufficient explanation of the fact that Black attacks all the time while White must merely repel threats. In such conditions White's defence must break down at some stage.'

40	♔g1	♛b3
41	♘e2	♛c2
42	g4	

The courage of despair. If Black is given time to go ♖g6 and ♘e4 then White would be ripe for resignation.

42...		fg

43 hg ♖h4 44 ♖c1 ♛h7 45 c4 ♖h3 46 ♛g2 ♛d3 47 cd ♘e4 48 de ♛e3+ 49 ♔f1 ♖f3+ 0–1

Open Files

It is hardly necessary to elaborate on the significance of open files and their influence on the course of play. The rooks and queen use them to attack weak pawns and to get into the heart of the enemy position. The control of an open file is a big positional plus.

Bronstein comments on the position of diagram 11, 'An open file is worth something when there are objects of attack on it, or when the line serves as an avenue of communication for transferring pieces, normally the rooks, to the main point of battle. In this case the f-file fits both criteria. The main point is that it is close to the king which is a cause of alarm for Stahlberg. In the diagram position Black has the choice of using his rooks

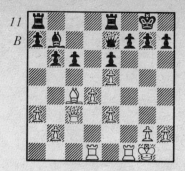

Keres–Stahlberg, Zurich, 1953

on either the c- or d-files, while White operates on the f-file. We get a sharp struggle and it gradually becomes clear that the f-file carries more weight than the two files open for Black's use.'

16 ...	c5
17 ♕e1	♗e4
18 ♖f4	♗g6
19 h4	cd
20 ed	♖ac8
21 ♕e2	♖c7
22 ♖df1	h5
23 ♖1f3	♖ec8
24 ♗d3	

Depriving the f7 point of the defence of the bishop. The rooks' pressure thus becomes more threatening.

24 ...	♗×d3
25 ♖×d3	g6
26 ♖g3	♔h7
27 ♖g5	♕f8
28 ♕c4	♕h6
29 d5	

It was even stronger to go 29 ♖f6 completely blocking the K-side with the heavy pieces.

29 ...   ed

30 ♕×d5 ♕f8 31 e6 ♕c5+ 32 ♕×c5 bc 33 ef ♔g7 34 f8 = ♕+ ♖×f8 35 ♖×f8 ♔×f8 36 ♖×g6 and White soon won the endgame. The final moves were 36 . . . c4 37 ♖g5 ♖b7 38 ♖×h5 ♖×b2 39 ♖c5 ♖c2 40 ♔h2 ♔e7 41 h5 c3 42 ♖c6 1–0

Open Diagonals

What has been said about open files applies by and large to open diagonals. They are weighty factors in assessing the chances in complex positions, and there are cases where a single diagonal proves decisive.

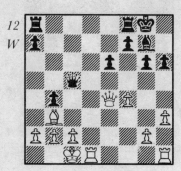

Medina–Botvinnik, Palma, 1967.

Botvinnik assessed the chances in diagram 12 thus, 'It is clear that despite the exchanges and material equality White is positionally lost, as he has no counter to Black's pressure along the a1/h8 diagonal. Black's main idea was based on a tactical finesse, namely that after 21 ♖d7 ♖ad8 22 ♖hd1 (or 22 ♖×f7 ♖×f7 23 ♕×e6 ♕f5) 22 . . . ♖×d7 23 ♖×d7 ♕g1+ 24 ♖d1? ♗×b2+ Black gets a material advantage. My opponent noticed this, but surprisingly enough, after 40 minutes thought he decided that he could not profitably avoid this. The point seems to be that the threat ♕-e7-f6 could not be met easily.'

21	♖d7	♖ad8
22	♖hd1	♖×d7
23	♖×d7	♕g1+
24	♔d2	♕f2+

After 24 . . . ♗×b2 25 ♔e2 and 26 ♖d1 Black would merely be a pawn up, whereas now he decides matters more quickly.

25	♔d3	♕f1+
26	♕e2	

Or 26 ♔d2 ♗×b2

26	. . .	♕×f4
27	♕f3	♕e5

and Black soon won.

Open Ranks

The importance of ranks is usually smaller than that of files and diagonals. Yet occasionally it is a rank which turns out to be the highway along which decisive manoeuvres are carried out.

Karpov–Hort, Moscow, 1971

Not only a superficial analysis but even a very attentive study of the position of diagram 13 might find it hard to spot the decisive positional element which guarantees the advantage for White. The point is that here White can make good use of the ranks.

22	♖g4!	♛f6
23	h4!	♛f5
24	♖b4	♝f6
25	h5	♞e7
26	♖f4	

These rook manoeuvres along the fourth rank make a strong impression and show what a depth of assessment the young world champion of our days is capable of. The simple, clear moves of the rook provoke a lack of harmony in the opponent's game and create a number of unpleasant threats.

26	...	♛e5
27	♖f3!	

This and the next few moves show that the main factor now is the third rank.

27	...	♞×d5
28	♖d3	♖×h6

28 ... ♞e7 29 ♝f4 with great advantage is no improvement.

29	♖×d5	♛e4

30 ♖d3 ♛h1+ 31 ♔c2 ♛×a1 32 ♛×h6 ♝c5 33 ♛g5 1–0

Passed Pawns

A passed pawn is one of the most important factors in the endgame, while its role in the middlegame can also be very significant. The presence of such a pawn can be the factor leading us to assess the position as favourable to its possessor, sometimes even as of decisive advantage.

Smyslov–Keres, Zurich, 1953

In diagram 14, White's advantage is undeniable, principally because of his lead in development. Almost all his pieces are in play while the enemy king is stuck in the centre. To exploit this there came:

14 d5!

The pawn cannot be taken and there is a threat of 15 de. This leaves Black with only one way of trying to hang on.

14 . . .		e5
15	bc	0–0
16	♘d2	♗e7
17	♘c4	a5
18	♘×e5	♘×e5
19	♕×e5	♗f6
20	♕g3	

White has got a threatening passed pawn in the centre, moreover it is an extra one. Smyslov advances the pawn as far as possible, not so much hoping to queen it as to induce panic in the enemy camp.

20 . . .		c4
21	♗a4	♕e7
22	♗f4!	

All to support the passed pawn. If Black decides to win a pawn back by 22 . . . ♕a3 then 23 ♗c6 ♗×c6 24 dc ♕×c3 25 ♕×c3 ♗×c3 26 ♖ac1 and 27 ♖×c4 with decisive advantage.

22 ...	♜fd8
23 d6	♛e4
24 ♖e1	♛f5
25 d7	h5
26 ♖e8+	♚h7
27 h4	♜a6
28 ♗g5	♖×d7

Resignation in effect. The advance of the passed pawn has been decisive.

29 ♗×d7	♛×d7
30 ♖ae1	

and White duly won.

The Two Bishops

Supporters of a concrete approach to the assessment of chess positions often deny the advantage of two bishops over bishop and knight or two knights. However this is not quite correct. It is certainly impossible to allege that the bishops are always an advantage in every position, but in the great majority it is better to have the two bishops: then when the position opens up, the bishops will get favourable diagonals and their significance can decide matters.

Diagram 15 may be considered a classical example of 'prelate power.'

Bogoljubow–Janowski, New York, 1924

In order to get the two bishops Black gives up a pawn.

1 ...	♞c5!
2 ♗×h7+	♚×h7
3 ♛h5+	♚g8

4	♕×e5		♗f6
5	♕h5		♗a4

The bishops start their threatening work. By occupying key diagonals they paralyse the action of almost all White's forces.

6	♖e1		♕d6
7	h3		♗c2
8	♕f3		

It was better to go 8 ♕e2 and if 8 . . . ♗a4 then 9 ♕h5 with repetition of moves.

8	. . .		b5
9	♕e2		♗a4!
10	♕f3		♖c4
11	♗a1		♖dc8
12	♖b1		e5
13	♘e2		♗c2
14	♖bc1		♗e4
15	♕g4		♗b7

This manoeuvre by the bishop is pretty. Now the bishops literally control the whole board.

16	♖×c4		♖×c4
17	f4		

Hoping to exchange one bishop, but this advance only weakens the K-side.

17	. . .		♕d2
18	♕g3		♖e4
19	♗c3		♕d5
20	♗×e5		♖×e3!

A small combination based on the strength of the Q-bishop.

21	♕g4		♗×e5
22	fe		♖×e5
23	♔h2		♕d2

White's position is hopeless. Although Black no longer has the two bishops, the excellent placing of his remaining pieces carries the day. Such a transformation of advantages is a common phenomenon in playing with the two bishops. In trying to cope with the bishops the defender makes many concessions in other elements.

24	♕g3		f6
25	h4		♗d5
26	♕f2		♗c4
			0–1

Space

This factor needs little stressing, and is a positional element that a grandmaster is bound to take into account when assessing the position. If one side occupies the greater part of the board, his men cramp the enemy forces and drive them to the edge of the board. Of course one has to take into account the possibilities of counter play, but if this advantage in space is consolidated it may lead to victory.

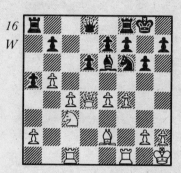

16
W

Smyslov–Golz, Polanica, 1968

In the position of diagram 16, White's pieces are active while the enemy's are pressed back to the last three ranks. Smyslov starts by a thrust in the centre which soon becomes a general advance all over the board: the main role in all this is played by pawns.

19 f5!

Smyslov comments, 'White's pawn foreposts on the flank cramp the enemy pieces. Black will have to go to a great deal of trouble to improve his position by transferring the knight to c5. In the meanwhile White can prepare an attack.'

19 ...	♗c8
20 ♖cd1!	♘d7
21 ♘d5	

Black hoped to go ♘c5, but the threat of f6 prevents this and provokes the following weakening.

21 ...	f6
22 b6	

Further cramping all over the board.

22 ...	♘c5
23 fg	hg
24 e5!	

Excellent! The frontal breakthrough is widened. The reply is forced

24	...	fe
25	♖×f8+	♛×f8
26	♕h4	♔g7
27	♖f1	♝f5

If the queen moves White takes on e7 with the knight.

28	g4	♝e4+
29	♔g1	♕d8
30	♘×e7	♘d7

The knight hurries back to the defence of the K-side. If 30 . . . ♕×b6? then 31 ♕f6+ ♔h7 32 ♕f7+ ♔h8 (32 . . . ♔h6 33 h4!) 33 ♘×g6+ ♝×g6 34 ♕×g6 ♘d3+ 35 ♔h1 ♘f4 36 ♕h6+ ♔g8 37 ♝f3 with a very strong attack (Smyslov's variations).

31 c5!

Once again an active pawn move. This time the aim is to get the bishop to the a2/g8 diagonal, if 31 . . . dc.

31	...	d5
32	♝b5	♘×c5
33	♕f6+	♔h7
34	♕f7+	♔h8
35	♖f3	1–0

Poor Position of a Piece

An active position for the pieces is one of the most important elements of the positional struggle, possibly the decisive one. That is why in assessing any position it is vital to assess the position of the pieces, and not just the overall placing of them, but each one considered separately. The following

17
W

Capablanca–Bogoljubow, London, 1922

example (diagram 17) shows how the position of just one piece can affect the course of the game.

This is how Capablanca assesses the position; 'Black's queen, rook and knight are aggressively placed, and compared to White's pieces have greater freedom. All White's pieces are defensively placed, and his c and e pawns are subject to attack. The only way to defend both pawns would be ♘d2, but then Black would reply ♕b4 and then he could advance his a pawn with no difficulty.

So far everything has been in Black's favour, and if there were no other factors in this position White's position would be lost. However there is a feature which is very much in White's favour, namely the position of the bishop at h7. This bishop is not only completely cut off from play, but, even worse, there is no way of bringing it into play. Hence White is playing, as it were, with an extra piece.'

36	♘d4	♕×e3
37	♖×e3	♖b8
38	♖c3	♔f7
39	♔f3	♖b2
40	♘ge2	♗g8
41	♘e6	♘b3

Exchanging knights on e6 would leave the bishop no hope of ever getting out of the mousetrap at g8 and h7. Nor is 41 . . . ♘×e4 42 ♔×e4 ♖×e2+ good. After 43 ♔d3 ♖h2 44 ♔d4 h5 45 c5 a pawn plays through to queen, since support for the advance comes from two extra pieces—the white king and knight, whose opposite numbers are huddled in the corner.

42	c5	dc

43 ♘×c5 ♘d2+ 44 ♔f2 ♔e7 45 ♔e1 ♘b1 46 ♖d3 a3 47 d6+ ♔d8 48 ♘d4 ♖b6

49	♘de6+	♗×e6

At last the bishop does something, but only to leave White with unstoppable passed pawns.

50	fe	♖b8
51	e7+	♔e8
52	♘×a6	1–0

Lack of Harmony in Piece Placing

Having just seen an example of one badly placed piece affecting the outcome of the game what of those cases where this applies to a number of pieces? Of course this is a serious disadvantage, often a losing one.

We shall come across a number of such cases later on, but let us consider the play from diagram 18, a particularly instructive example.

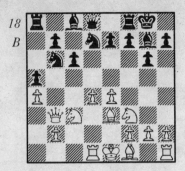

Botvinnik–Yudovich, USSR Ch. 1933

Clearly Black has placed his pieces badly. His bishop at c8 has not yet moved, and the knights hinder his own development. Only the other bishop is well placed, firing along an open diagonal, but what can it do on its own? At the same time White's pieces can boast of their excellent placing and his pawns are particularly proud, ready to advance and cramp Black even more. It takes only a few moves for Botvinnik to demonstrate the advantage of his forces by carrying out a nice concluding attack.

11	...	♛c7
12	♗e2	♛d6
13	♘a2	

Not allowing the queen to get to b4.

13	...	e6
14	0–0	h6
15	♖c1	f5
16	♘c3	♚h7
17	♖fd1	fe

Otherwise Black will not be able to disentangle the bunched up pieces, but lines are now opened and the enemy king comes under withering fire.

18 ♘×e4   ♛b4
19 ♛c2 ♛×a4 20 b3 ♛a3 21 ♘h4! ♛e7 22 ♘×g6! ♚×g6 23 ♗h5+!
1–0

The Centre

The importance of this element is such that it deserves a section to itself: to a great extent the position in the centre determines the advantage of one side and the future course of events. Right from the start the beginner has it dinned into him that he should seize the centre and try to hold it with all his forces. This applies, he is taught, right from the opening, through the middlegame, down to the endgame.

Later on we learn that only with a firm grip on the centre do we have the right to start active play on the wing, otherwise we run the risk that the opponent might be able to produce an unexpected counter-strike in the centre, after which our attack will become pointless. We are told by theoreticians about the various problems involving the centre, how the old masters considered every pawn centre good, whereas the hypermoderns of early this century declared that piece pressure on the centre could be more effective than occupying it with pawns which might become weak and need defending.

We shall soon deal with this problem, but first let us note the axiom that the reader must understand and assimilate: the pawn formation in the centre determines the general nature of the whole struggle.

Theory recognises five sorts of centre:–
1 A Pawn Centre, 2 A Fixed Centre, 3 An Open Centre, 4 A Closed Centre, 5 A Centre under Tension. Let us examine these in turn.

The Pawn Centre

When we have two or more pawns in the centre and the opponent does not have any, we are naturally justified in seeking to advance these pawns and sweep away the opponent's fortifications. He in his turn will put obstacles in our way, possibly attacking the pawns with his pieces so that our pawns may become weak or be removed from the board altogether. Hence we get the problem of piece pressure on the centre—the chief hobby horse in the teachings of the chess Hypermodernists.

The resolution of this problem depends on concrete assessment: if the central pawns are strong and well supported then the pawn centre gives us a positional advantage, but if the pawns are weak then they are a serious drawback.

From diagram 19, White got his centre pawns moving.

16	e4	♘c4
17	♗c1	cd
18	cd	de
19	fe	♘e5
20	♕d2	♘g6

White's centre is soundly guarded, and this gives him the advantage. In accordance with Steinitz's first rule White goes for an attack on the K-side and in the centre.

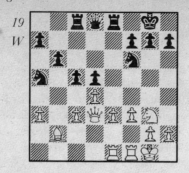

Furman–Lilienthal, USSR Ch. 1949

21	e5!	♘d5
22	♘f5	♖e6
23	♕f2	♕d7
24	h4!	

A typical attacking device. A wing pawn makes a lightning dash towards the enemy camp where it spreads confusion in the ranks.

24 ...   f6

25 ♕g3 fe 26 de ♘de7 27 ♘d6 ♖×c1 28 ♖×c1 ♘×e5 29 ♕f2 h6 30 ♕f8+ ♔h7 31 ♘f5 ♘×f5 32 ♕×f5+ g6 33 ♕f8 ♖e8 34 ♕f4 h5 35 ♖c3 ♖e7 36 ♖e3 1–0

The Fixed Centre

If there is no pawn movement in the centre, then both sides will try to establish their pieces on squares defended by their pawns. This sort of play

Botvinnik–Sorokin, USSR Ch. 1931

based on building up centralised pieces followed by extending the scope of these pieces on the flank as well was particularly well mastered by Botvinnik.

In diagram 20, the pawns are jammed up against each other at e4/e5. If we examine in turn the role of each piece we come to the conclusion that of Black's pieces only the queen is active. White hurries to exchange this piece and at the same time he makes a safe defence for his d4 square.

20	♕e3!	♕×e3
21	fe	♗g4
22	a5	♘c8
23	♖c1	♗×f3
24	gf	♘e7
25	♘d5	

White creates a base for his operations at d5, occupying it first with knight and then bishop with its long-range action.

25	...	♘c6
26	♘×f6+	gf
27	♖d7	♖ab8
28	♔f2!	

With the threat of 29 ♖g1+ winning the f7 pawn. Black is gradually driven into making concessions.

28 ...   ♘×a5
29 ♖cc7 ♖bc8 30 ♖×f7 ♖×c7 31 ♖×c7+ ♔h8 32 ♗d5 b5
33 b3

White has an overwhelming position, and wins by simply bringing up his king to the enemy monarch.

33	...	♖d8
34	♔g3	f5
35	♔h4	fe
36	fe!	

The right way! The important thing is not how nice the pawns look, but the operation point at d5.

36 ...   ♖d6
37 ♔h5 ♖b6 38 h3 ♖d6 39 h4 ♖b6 40 ♔g4 ♖f6 41 ♖a7 ♖b6 42 ♖c7
♖d6 43 ♖c7 ♖f6 44 ♖a7 ♖b6
45 ♖c7

White has been repeating moves to win time—a common device in competitive play during time trouble.

45	...	♖f6
46	♔h5	♖d6

47 ♗f7!

Preparing a mating net by ♗g6.

47 ...   ♖f6

48 ♗g6 ♘xb3 49 ♔xh6 ♖f8 50 ♖h7+ ♔g8 51 ♖g7+ ♔h8 52 ♗f7
♖xf7 53 ♖xf7 ♔g8 54 ♔g6 ♘d2 55 ♖d7 1–0

The Open Centre

This is the case when there are no pawns on either side in the squares d4, d5, e4, e5, or possibly there might be one pawn in this area. In view of the open terrain the whole emphasis is on piece play. Bear in mind that in such cases flank attacks with pawns are ruled out. With an open centre, the likelihood of an enemy central strike is so great that a flank pawn advance is equivalent to suicide.

So, with the stress on piece play, we have many examples to choose from.

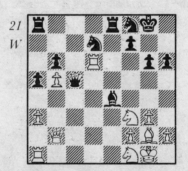

Reti–Capablanca, New York, 1924

Diagram 21 shows an open centre. White has seized control of the d-file, while the black queen is on the c-file. With a few energetic moves the talented Czech maximizes his mobilization and overwhelms Black's pieces.

1 ♖ad1   ♖a7
2 ♘e3   ♕h5

To meet the grave threat 3 ♘g4.

3 ♘d4   ♗xg2
4 ♔xg2   ♕e5
5 ♘c4   ♕c5

The queen has to cope with the weaknesses all on her own: Black's rooks and knights are passive onlookers.

6 ♘c6   ♖c7
7 ♘e3   ♘e5

8 ♖1d5!   1–0

The queen is trapped and could only be released by 8 . . . ♞c4 but then White wins material by 9 ♖×c5 ♞×b2 10 ♖c2 ♞a4 11 ♞d5, so Black resigned.

The Closed Centre

This type of centre is marked by pawn masses jammed up against each other closing the files and cutting off diagonals. As the centre cannot be broken open the players prepare to by-pass it, manoeuvring and pressing on the flank. With the centre closed and no risk of a quick counter there, the bold advance of wing pawns is quite safe. Diagram 22 is an instructive example:

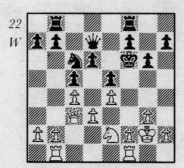

Reti–Carls, Baden-Baden, 1925

Having earlier foreseen the coming of a closed centre position, White is first to get in with an advance on the K-side.

20 f4	♔g7
21 f5	f6
22 ♕d2	g5?

A serious mistake. Black had to restrict himself to playing on the other side with . . . b5. The pawn move in the vicinity of the king is weakening, and Black should have remembered the rule confirmed in so many games: 'Don't make pawn moves where you are weaker.'

23 g4	b5
24 h4!	h6
25 ♖h1	bc
26 dc	♞d4
27 ♞c3	♖h8

28	♖h3	♖bg8
29	♖bh1	

Now an entry by the white major pieces on the h-file is inevitable.

29	...	♛d8
30	♘d5	gh

Capitulation, but there was no defence against the threatened capture on g5.

31	♖×h4	♔f7

32 ♔f2 ♛f8 33 ♖×h6 ♖×h6 34 ♖×h6 ♛g7 35 ♛a5! 1–0

A decisive irruption, and once again on the flank, though this time it is the other side.

The Centre under Tension

This is sometimes called a fluid centre: the tension may be resolved at any moment. If the two sides remove all the centre pawns then we get an open centre; if the pawns get jammed then we have a closed centre. Sometimes we may get a fixed centre, rarely a mobile one. The policy of the players in a fluid situation is to manoeuvre and wait for a suitable opportunity to turn the centre into one of the other four forms in the hope that this will turn to their own advantage.

Boleslavsky–Keres, Candidates Tournament 1953

Diagram 23 shows a fluid centre. It would be hard to talk about weaknesses or an advantage for either side here: it is still a book position given in any work dealing with the Ruy Lopez. Keres prepares a known method of liquidating the centre pawns which turns out very effectively in this game.

12	...	♖d8!
13	♘f1	d5

It is in Black's favour to open the centre as his pieces are well mobilized.

14 ed

14 de de 15 ♘3d2 was better.

14	...	ed
15	cd	♘×d5
16	♕e2	♗b7
17	♘g3	cd
18	♘×d4	

The centre has been cleared, and now we have an open centre. As we have already said, this leaves it all to the pieces as the pawns play no part.

18	...	g6!
19	♗h6	♗f6
20	♘b3	♘c4
21	♘e4	♗×b2

Black already has a material advantage.

22	♘bc5	♗×a1
23	♖×a1	f5!
24	♘×b7	♕×b7
25	♘c5	♕c6
26	♘d3	♘c3
27	♕e1	♕f6

Black has both material and positional advantages and exploits this accurately.

28	f4	♘e4!

29 ♔h2 ♕c3 30 ♕b1 ♘cd2 31 ♕c1 ♖×d3! 32 ♗×d3 ♕×d3 33 ♕c7 ♘f3+! 0–1

The Clash of Elements

We have examined several examples in which each time the decisive role was played by one of the elements of position. The player who had an overwhelming advantage in this element gradually increased it, transformed it into other benefits and finally won.

In practice it is more often the case that we have to deal with positions in which there is no clearly marked plus in any one element: each player stands better than his opponent in one respect, but worse in another. So we get a clash of elements with plusses in some elements being compensated for by minuses in others, and there is a tense struggle to accumulate small advantages.

The practical player thus needs not only attentiveness and the ability to analyse a position, but must also show considerable objectivity in assessing the elements of the position. If you are going to consider your plusses as a real treasure house and denigrate those of the opponent, you are heading for catastrophe. Objectivity in your approach to the position is a most important quality so that you can properly orientate yourself in the tasks of analysis, assessment, and finding the right plan.

A grandmaster pays attention to every slight detail and tries not to miss the slightest nuance, the least factor which might affect the assessment. Here are examples of such scrupulous care:

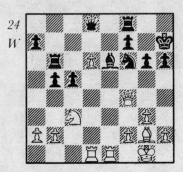

Euwe–Keres, Candidates Tournament 1953

Bronstein wrote this about the position of diagram 24: 'Every positional achievement, in this case the pawn at d6 which engages the attention of the black pieces, is important not in itself but in its link with other combinational factors. In this position the factors for White are:–
1 The unguarded pawn at c5.
2 The weakened cover of the black king.
3 The constant possibility of advancing the pawn to d7.
4 Control over c7 and e7, combined with the attempt to control the e- or c-file.
For Black the factors are:–
1 The chance to surround the d6 pawn from three sides.
2 The attack on the Q-side by a majority of pawns.
3 The possibility ♘h5 to drive the queen from her strong post.
By comparing and weighing the chances for each side the masters normally reach more or less objective conclusions which are called the assessment of the position.'

Euwe now played 22 a3 which Bronstein criticized as not corresponding to the demands of the position. He recommends instead 22 b3 to put a brake on the advance of the Q-side pawns, or 22 ♖×e6!? fe 23 ♕e5 with active play against Black's many weaknesses that would be full compensation for the exchange.

After 22 . . . ♖e8! 23 ♘c4 ♘×e4 24 ♖×e4 ♕d7 25 ♕e5 ♖d8 26 ♕×c5 ♖×d6 the players agreed a draw.

Smyslov–Botvinnik, USSR Absolute Ch. 1941

Botvinnik assesses diagram 25 :- 'A quick glance is sufficient to note the weak side of White's position. His bishops are not very active, Black has a good base for operations at f5. Moreover one should not omit to note an organic defect of White's pawn formation—his Q-side can communicate with the K-side only via the c1 square.'

We may comment that it is no simple thing to spot such a 'trifle' which turns out not to be a trifle!

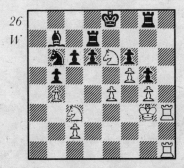

Lasker–Capablanca, St. Petersburg, 1914

Let us assess diagram 26, a position from a famous game. Material is level, but White has a marked advantage chiefly because of square weaknesses in Black's position. White has weak squares too, at c4, f4 and h4, but these have little influence on the play since the enemy pieces cannot get at them.

Black has gaping weaknesses at e6 and g6, while a5 and h5 are also weak. The weak pawn at f6 may become an object of attack, and this would soon prove telling. Another significant factor is White's advantage on the open files. His rooks are well established on the h-file and can be transferred quickly to the a-file. Another minus in Black's position is the passive position of the bishop at b7, and there is no active diagonal to which it could be transferred. The active position of the white rooks means that they can at any moment get on to the poorly defended 7th rank.

Also White has an undoubted advantage in space due to the advanced pawn at f5, and the knight at e6 is firmly stuck in the heart of the enemy position. All White's pieces are actively placed, whereas the black men laze about on the back two rows. Although White has some weak points, White's plusses in various respects give us the right to make the assessment that White has a won position.

By the laws of strategy, White is here under an obligation to attack, otherwise he risks losing his advantage. If White were to do nothing here then Black would go ♞–c4–e5, then ♖e7 and ♗c8 to drive out or exchange the intrusive knight and the position would become quite defensible.

The great strategist Lasker uses the advantages of his position to start the decisive thrust.

1 e5!

The idea is clear. He activates his knight at c3 and starts an attack on the weak pawn at f6. After the capture on e5 the knights get access to c5 from where they become dominating. The pawn sacrifice is temporary, as White can visualize that Black will soon have to lose material.

1 ...	de

Capture by the other pawn would lead to the early loss of the g5 pawn and the formation of united passed pawns for White at f5 and g4.

2 ♞e4	♞d5
3 ♞6c5!	

Strong and simple. The rook cannot move from d7 since ♞d6+ would win the bishop, so the exchange is lost.

3 ...	♗c8
4 ♞×d7	♗×d7
5 ♖h7	♖f8
6 ♖a1!	

The last two moves exploit the small advantages already mentioned—the chance to take the 7th rank, and the chance to swing across to the other open file.

6 . . .		♔d8
7	♖a8+	♗c8
8	♘c5	1–0

Black has no defence against the mating threats 9 ♘e6+ or 9 ♘b7+.

Learn from the World Champions

We will now study some examples of assessment by the kings of chess.

A method of assessing positions is frequently found in Capablanca's notes both to his own games and to others.

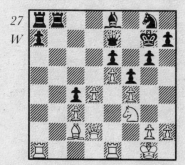

Bogoljubow–Wahltuch, London 1922

Capablanca wrote of diagram 27, 'It is not hard to assess this position. Force is equal, but Black has three weak pawns—the a, c, and e. The a7 pawn would be strong and a source of worry to White if there was the time to advance it far down the board safely, but this is not the case, so it is merely a weakness. The only positive feature of Black's position is the fact that his rook occupies an open file. If the bishop could be transferred from e8 to d5 via c6 it would defend two weak pawns and exert pressure on the long diagonal. Then Black's position would not be too bad. However this is not feasible as White will play ♗a4 as his first move.

White has no weak points. His wedgelike pawn formation is very aggressive, and he has adequate space for piece manoeuvres. So it is clear that White must have the advantazge. As we have already said, his first move will be ♗a4 to exchange the enemy bishop and prevent it moving to d5, so that it could defend the weak pawns at c4 and e6. Moreover this first move makes way for the queen, which will penetrate into Black's position via a2.'

The reader will note some features of the Cuban champion's method of assessment. He does not go through the elements we had in our table, but only deals with the main ones which determine the nature of the position and the development of subsequent events.

Nor does he restrict himself to a static statement, as is shown by his inclusion of the move ♗a4, and he puts the final touch to White's stated advantage by indicating the possible lines for both sides—Black's advance of the a-pawn and White's penetration with his queen via a2.

Here is an exact and clear verbal assessment of diagram 28 by Smyslov.

Smyslov–Golombek, USSR–GB match, 1954

'White's advantage is minimal, and consists of the strong king position in the centre, while his bishop is more active than Black's which is rather shut in at b8. The slight separation of the pawns at e6, g6, h7 makes Black's task more difficult.'

White played 33 ♘d1 and Smyslov makes a more exact assessment by linking it with White's plan. 'The c3 square is freed to let the bishop take the important diagonal a1/h8, while the knight sets off to g4 to attack the enemy pawns. White does not fear e5 since he would answer f5 and then find it easier to create a passed pawn on the flank. Moreover Black's central position would thereby be weakened—the d5 square.'

33 ...	♗d6
34 ♘f2	♘d8
35 ♗c3	♘f7
36 ♘g4	h5
37 ♗f6+ !	

'An important intermediate move. In order to exploit a pawn weakness you have to fix it. With this aim White establishes his bishop on f6 where it will anticipate a possible active line by Black based on g5.'

37	...	♔d7
38	♘f2	♗c7
39	♘d3	♔c6
40	♘e1!	

Another fine manoeuvre—the knight sets off for h4 to attack the weak pawn at g6.

40	...	♘d6+

41 ♔d3 ♘f5 42 ♘f3 ♔d7 43 ♔e4 ♘d6+ 44 ♔e3 ♘f5+ 45 ♔f2 ♗d6 46 h3!

Having fixed the weaknesses at e6 and g6 Smyslov now settles down to the culmination of the attack on the K-side pawns.

46	...	♗c7
47	g4	hg
48	hg	♘h6
49	♔g3	♘f7
50	g5!	

Black's position is now indefensible since if 50 ... ♘d6 then 51 ♘e5+ .

50	...	♗d8
51	♔g4	♗×f6
52	gf	♔d6
53	♘e5!	1–0

In his notes to games Robert Fischer normally gives more interesting variations than verbal reasoning, but this certainly does not mean that in thinking about his moves during actual play he avoids general considerations and overall assessments. Possibly these are simply less necessary for him in view of his intuition and the immense analytical effort which he put in at the time of his passionate enthusiasm for the game. However in his notes too you can find valuable general assessments.

The eleventh world champion wrote of diagram 29 thus; 'Petrosian and Tal both happened to stroll by the board at this instant. Petrosian made a wry face which looked to me like "Can Black do this and live?". Black's ugly defence is based on sound positional considerations; once he can consolidate there is a strong potential in the two bishops coupled with his beautifully posted knight and compact pawn mass. These assets in the long run, hopefully, should outweigh the temporary weakness of his king and the immobile target on e6.'

14	♘ce2!	♔h8
15	♘f4	♖g8

Gligorić–Fischer, Candidates Tournament, 1959

16	♖g1	d5!
17	fe	de
18	♘d5	♕c5
19	♘×e7	♕×e7
20	♘f5	♕×e6
21	♕h6	♗d7
22	♖d6	♘×g4!

After a lot of complications Black has achieved a marked advantage, but then played inaccurately and the game ended in a draw.

When we considered Steinitz's rules we noted that the Soviet school, while recognizing his teaching, also puts a high price on a concrete approach to each position. Diagram 30 is one example that could be quoted from very many.

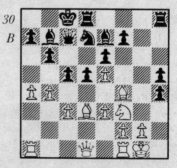

Spassky–Petrosian, World Ch. match 1966

Petrosian played 17 . . . c4 here and later wrote about it: "Right after the game I found out that this move had surprised the audience. Indeed its drawback is obvious—the square d4 becomes White's domain. But I hasten to add that this is only so in words. After all White will not be able to derive any benefit from having a queen, or say, rook on d4. As for the knight which it is normally advantageous to place on such blockading squares, its main care here is to guard the e5 pawn. Hence Black has his hands untied so that he can now operate on the g-file.'

The subsequent play confirmed the correctness of this concrete assessment.

18 ♗e2

As Petrosian pointed out 18 ♗f5! was better, when it is bad to take the bishop, but Spassky was worried about playing his bishop to h3 where it would just be a 'big pawn'.

18 . . .   a6!

Once and for all preventing White developing an initiative on the Q-side, and transferring the action for both sides to the K-side.

19 ♔h1   ♖dg8

20 ♖g1 ♖g4 21 ♕d2 ♖hg8 22 a5 b5 23 ♖ad1 ♗f8 24 ♘h2 ♘xe5! 25 ♘xg4 hg 26 c4 ♗d6 27 ♕e3 ♘d7 28 ♗xd6 ♕xd6 29 ♖d4 e5 30 ♖d2 f5 and Black won by a direct attack by all his forces on the K-side and in the centre.

In the play of the current world champion Anatoly Karpov an immense role is played both by assessment of the position and verbal summaries of his conclusions. At the same time the reader will see how concrete is the approach of the champion to assessing a position. He has no dogmatic preconceptions, everything is based on deep analysis of the specific features of the given position.

Karpov–Spassky, USSR Spartakiad, 1975

Karpov comments on diagram 31 thus:–

'When e3 has been played in such positions the point f2 is often subjected to attack. With the pawn at e2 it is harder to carry out this attack, and the knight would always have a supported square at d3. Here however one senses a certain weakness on the K-side and Spassky plays on this.

There is the threat of ♘×f2. It can be anticipated by 20 ♗×e4 ♕×e4 21 ♖d4 (essential, otherwise d4) 21 . . . ♕c2. Now White wins the d5 pawn, but it is not clear whether he would win the game. The alternative is the sharp variations arising after 20 ♕×a7. I considered this move for quite a long time and concluded that I would get the advantage. It looks as if the queen goes far away from the main scene of action, but a more careful examination reveals that she can soon be exchanged for her opposite number which is on the same rank.'

20	♕×a7	♘×f2
21	♘×d5	♗×d5
22	♕×e7	

'If Spassky were simply to recapture on e7 then after 23 ♖×d5 ♘g4 White could play to keep the pawn by 24 e4, or, even stronger, 24 ♗h3 ♘×e3 25 ♗×c8 ♘×d5 26 ♖d1. The endgame would be bad for Black. The bishop would certainly be much stronger than the knight and the black king would be a long way from the Q-side where White has a pawn advantage. So Spassky decided to sacrifice his queen.'

22	. . .	♘×d1
23	♖c1!	

A nice tactical decision underlining once again how concrete is Karpov's assessment. Even such unexpected moves are brought in to help solve general strategic problems. Now Black is forced to remain with rook and knight for the queen.

23	. . .	♖b8

24 ♕b4 ♗×g2 25 ♔×g2 ♘e3+ 26 ♔g1 ♖e6 27 ♕f4 ♖bd8
28 ♕d4!

White's task is to exchange a pair of rooks after which Black's power to resist is greatly reduced. You can't help recalling here the words of Karpov's trainer Furman who once said of the very young Karpov, 'Tolya knows which piece to exchange, and which to leave on.'

28	. . .	♖de8

29 ♕d7 ♘g4 30 ♖c8 ♘f6 31 ♖×e8+ ♖×e8 32 ♕b7 ♖e6
33 ♕b8+   ♘e8

Black's pieces are pressed back to the edge of the board. White soon won by advancing his Q-side pawns.

The reader will see that the world champion not only works out his assessments on the basis of the elements which we enumerated, but links them organically with the concrete features of the actual position.

The Mind of a Grandmaster

The time has come to deal with the question of when a grandmaster carries out his analysis and assessment of the position, and how this process takes place in his mind.

The first crucial moment is normally when we come to the end of the opening and start the middle game. After a theoretical variation has been played, or when the pieces have been mobilized in accordance with our own ideas, the time is ripe for the first overall assessment.

It is at this point that a grandmaster spends a great deal of time, since it is from here that the whole future course of the game may be mapped out. We recommend that at this point the whole position is considered from the point of view of the elements and their influence on the play.

The main question to answer is, who stands better. Obviously, as laid down in Steinitz's rules, the player with the better position will have to attack and the inferior side will have to defend.

Then must be established where the weakest enemy point is, since this is the place where we will direct our attack.

Next it is time to form a plan for the next few moves, a point we shall deal with later. With his general problems settled the grandmaster then normally begins the analysis of concrete variations, their depth depending on the nature of the position. A sort of interior dialogue takes place each move, a dialogue of the following sort:– 'I go knight to e5, he retreats the queen. I advance the pawn to d5. He can't take it since then the centre is opened. He has to reply c6–c5. Then I play c2–c4. What a fine knight I have in the centre, and a protected passed pawn into the bargain.' Thus it goes every move, with each new problem to be solved. Examine the notes of the best grandmasters to their games and you will find both deep general assessments, and routine small assessments at nearly every move.

There are other times too when a general assessment will be needed—at the transition from the middle game to the endgame, or when combinational storms end. At such times the position has to be looked at afresh and a new assessment formed.

We recommend you to try and divide the playing time into 'my time' and 'his time' and follow the golden rule that when your clock is going you restrict yourself to the analysis of variations, while when the opponent's clock is going you consider general questions to do with the position—overall assessment and planning. Of course there are exceptions, if it is a question of a tactical struggle with one main line that must be probed deeply. Then there are those grandmasters who like to walk around when it is not their turn to move.

However there is the example of Botvinnik (and Fischer) who rarely get up from the board, but sit there all the playing time. I tried to follow Botvinnik's example, and found it hard since I am not that sort of character. However when I managed it my results greatly improved.

Of course there is the complication that 'my time' is controlled by me, whereas I have no control over how long or short a time the opponent thinks with his clock running. Thus it may be that general considerations may have to be thought about during 'my time', especially if you are up against a quick player. Nevertheless try and follow the rule given above. Go through detailed variations in your own time, think in a general way about the position in the opponent's time and you will soon find that you get into time trouble less often, that your games have more content to them, and that their general standard rises.

How to Train

In striving to train, to improve in positional judgement, you should bear in mind the two sides of it:– training at home, and training during an actual competition game.

As regards the former, you have to analyse many games and positions and try to divide them into types according to the different elements mentioned in our 'Mendeleyev' table. You should be aiming for a thorough understanding of each element and its link with the others. It would be useful if the results of this home training were written down in special notebooks, with each element being allotted an appropriate amount of space.

In studying the interaction of the elements, there are few better ways than going through notes to games by theoreticians who do not give just a list of variations, but provide a systematic explanation of the ideas of each game and how they are linked with the concrete variations. The author can recommend a few books of this sort, notably the three volume collection of Botvinnik's games and Bronstein's book 'The International Grandmasters Tournament' on the 1953 Candidates Tournament.*

*Tr. Note. The best of Botvinnik's notes to his games have been translated into English, notably in "One Hundred Selected Games" (MacGibbon and Kee) and "Botvinnik's Best Games 1947–1970", Batsford, 1972. Unfortunately the 1953 Candidates book is not yet available in any language other than Russian.

After this, attention should be concentrated on the link between overall assessment and the lesser assessments made each move. Once again grandmasters' notes to games will be a guide. Notice how at a critical point the annotator will enumerate all the elements of a given position and describe their interaction, working out the relative worth of each. Then you will see that he goes on by giving short variations at each move accompanied by verbal assessments. These short comments are a result of the overall assessment and of the analysis of the factors brought about by the opponent's last move.

While seeking improvement along these lines, be aiming to cultivate the knack of seeing at a glance which of the elements are crucial to a given position, which are irrelevant and play no part.

Training is also possible during actual play. Observe yourself from the side, as it were, and check whether you are able to discipline yourself to useful work at the board. This applies particularly to our recommendation about the different nature of thought according to whether it is our clock or that of the opponent that is going. Avoid the criminal waste of time that arises from the confusion of these two types of thought and that can easily lead to time trouble. Observe too how the stronger players behave at the board, how they suddenly fall into deep thought as they carry out a general assessment, how they still sit at the board thinking when it is not their turn to move. We know what they are doing—they are solving general problems, formulating verbal summaries of the position and planning ahead.

EXERCISES

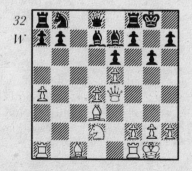

32
W

Analyse and assess the position. Find Black's most vulnerable point. Indicate how the next few moves are likely to go.

33
B

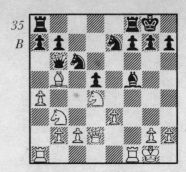

35
B

Give a verbal assessment. Indicate the weak points for each side. Make a few moves for each side which arise logically from the position.

Black played 14 . . . ♞×d4 here. Assess the move. What positional factors are changed by this exchange in the centre? Which weaknesses does White thereby get rid of? Does the move give White the advantage? If so, formulate exactly what this consists of.

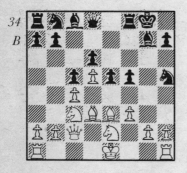

34
B

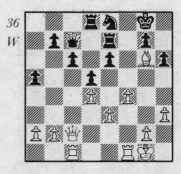

36
W

What is the way for Black to get full control of the black squares in the centre? How will play develop?

Analyse and assess. What should White be aiming for with his next few moves? Which moves will enable him to achieve this aim?

Where is Black weakest? Which diagonal particularly interests White? How can White exploit his opponent's weaknesses, which moves will he play?

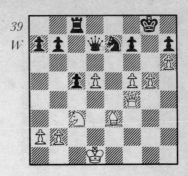

What is the strength of White's position? What moves will exploit Black's weaknesses? Indicate how the play should go.

Which of the lines (file, diagonal, rank) on the board is White's weakest? How can Black exploit this? Indicate the way the play will go.

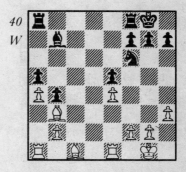

Make a detailed verbal summary of the position. What plusses does White enjoy? And Black? How do you think the play will go?

Does White have the advantage here? Indicate Black's weak point. Show in a concrete fashion how to exploit this.

Analyse and assess. Who has the advantage and what does it consist of? What plan would you form for Black?

Analyse and assess. What does White's advantage consist of? What plan would you choose for White? Indicate the next few moves.

2 Planning

Types of Plan

Once assessment has been carried out the aims of each side become clearer. The player will work out what he must undertake in the next few moves, which manoeuvres he must make and where, which regrouping is called for. In short, we are now in the phase of planning.

The nature of the position will suggest the sort of thought processes that will be necessary. If there is a combinational-tactical position, then we will normally make some such formulation as, 'I must attack on the K-side.', or 'I must undermine the enemy pawn chain at all costs.' Then this is backed up by more detailed analysis of concrete variations. If we have a manoeuvring-strategical position, then concrete variations are reduced to a minimum and the main emphasis is put on as detailed a plan as possible.

One absolute rule may already be stated:– it is impossible to play chess without a plan. One chess sage put it thus, 'A sound plan makes us all heroes, the absence of a plan—idiots.' Another commented, 'Better a bad plan than no plan at all.' Yet another, 'The player who will lose is the one without a plan. It is better to have a shallow or even faulty plan than just make moves not knowing what you are doing.'

Planless play is thus fatal, as we can prove by a host of examples. Here is just one *(44)*.

Bronstein commented here, 'The opening is over and both sides have to form a concrete plan. Yet instead of doing something active, White starts running on the spot and tries for "pressure" on the backward pawn by not letting it advance to c5.

Yet the real point is that Black does not intend to advance this far since on c6 the pawn will be guarded by just one bishop, while White will be putting it under pressure all the time with two rooks. As a result Black gets superiority of force at those parts of the board where the real battle is to be decided.'

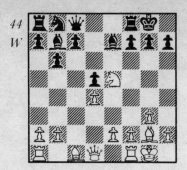

Lundin–Botvinnik, Groningen, 1946

11 ♕b3

The right plan was to open the centre after 11 ♗f4 ♕e6 12 ♕c2 c6 13 e4! with advantage to White. The loss of time leads White into great difficulties.

11 ...		♕e6
12	♘d3	♖d8
13	♗e3	c6
14	♖fd1	♘d7
15	♖ac1	♘f6

By building up his forces on the K-side Botvinnik prepares a fierce attack there. Meanwhile White just runs on the spot without sensing the danger.

16	♖c2	♘e4
17	♖dc1	♖ac8
18	♘f4	♕d7
19	♕a4	a5!
20	♕b3	b5
21	♕d3	g5!
22	♘h5	f5

Black has a formidable position and soon got ecisive advantage. Despite inventive defence the Swedish master was forced to resign.

What is a plan? Even nowadays you can read in some books that a plan in chess is something that the grandmaster thinks up almost from the first few moves (certainly immediately after the 'book' moves are finished) and realizes right up to the last few moves. This is quite mistaken.

We shall see later that in exceptional circumstances it is possible to create and carry out such a plan 'from first to last', but in the majority of cases the grandmaster does not do this, in fact he simply cannot.

Here is a definition which correctly reflects the course of thought and action of a grandmaster:– 'The plan in a game of chess is the sum total of successive strategical operations which are each carried out according to separate ideas arising from the demands of the position.'

Does a plan depend on our will, is it the fruit of our burning fantasy? Can I do as I like with my pieces on my board (or on my half of it)? No, that is a quite mistaken concept. As Steinitz pointed out almost a century ago every plan must have its justification, and this justification lies not in the personality of the player, but in the position lying before him. This is a very valuable definition which indicates to the player the way he has to go. 'The plan is based on assessment.' Hence it is not fantasy, but creative work that creates the plan.

There seem to be two sorts of plan in practical play. To make this clearer we start with elementary endings *(45)*.

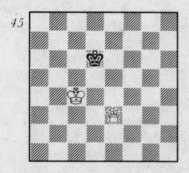

45

Even a queen up you can't win unless you proceed according to plan. Here it runs thus, 'White with the aid of both pieces drives the king into a corner, or to the edge (but be careful not to give stalemate!) and then mates with the queen either guarded by the king or checking along the last line of the board.'

Winning the endgame with bishop and knight against lone king is more complicated and it is no accident that there are cases where a master has not found the right way *(46)*

The win can only be forced by playing to a strict plan consisting of three stages:

1. All three pieces co-operate to drive the king to a corner opposite to the colour of the bishop.

2. All three pieces again drive the king to the corner of the same colour as the bishop, taking care that the king does not slip out en route.

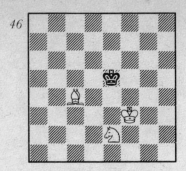

46

3. While preventing the king from getting out of the corner, the three attacking pieces are re-arranged to create one of several mating positions.

In the first case the plan has only one stage. In the second there are three stages. It is best to speak of two sorts of plan generally—the single-stage plan and the multi-stage plan. This distinction is confirmed as a useful one by the examples we shall consider.

First, though, another theoretical distinction. In the end-game mates, the player knows not only what will happen in the first stage but in all subsequent stages. Of course he may not be able to say on which square mate will be given, but the general outline is clear all the way. It is useful to divide multi-stage plans into three types. The first is when the maker of the plan can state the tasks and aims of each stage. This is called the plan when 'everything is clear to the end.' Then there is the plan when the future is glimpsed but dimly as if through a smoke haze. This we call the plan when 'something can be seen;' and finally there is the plan when only the first stage is at all clear, when it is not known what will happen at the second and subsequent stages. This third type is named 'subsequent darkness'. We feel that this division will help the reader to follow more easily our account of planning in chess.

One-Stage Plans

First we consider one-stage plans, which tend to occur in positions where each side has a clear aim and tries with all his might to carry it out.

Realizing material advantage
It has been known for a long time that material advantage can only be exploited by goal-directed, planned play. We have seen this already with the endgame examples. In more complicated examples, victory can only

be achieved by assessing the position correctly and forming a plan that arises from it.

Botvinnik–Tal, world title return match 1961.

Consider diagram 47. White is a pawn up, but it is hard to make it tell. How many endgames with opposite coloured bishops have ended in a draw! The win can be achieved here only by a deeply thought out logical plan based not only on the exploitation of material advantage but also positional plusses.

Botvinnik wrote as follows about his plan. 'White intends to open the K-side hoping that he will either penetrate with his rooks into the opponent's rear, or create another passed pawn.'

28 g4		♖ab8
29 h4		♖c6
30 h5		

'White's plan becomes clear: play e5, exchange on f6 then the advance of the f and g pawns will enable him to achieve his objective.'

30 ...		♖bc8
31 e5		g6

This only helps White, but it is well known that Tal is never keen on passive defence. He prefers active lines, even if they are dubious.

32 hg+		♔×g6
33 ♖3c2		fe
34 de		♖h8
35 ♖h2		♖6c8
36 ♔d2		♗b3

Now the pawn gets to a7 which makes Black's position hopeless. After other moves White would double rooks on the h-file, and play ♗e3 which would force Black to station his rooks at h7 and h8. Then the white king could penetrate along the black squares on the Q-side which would win.

| 37 a6 | ♗c4 |
| 38 a7 | ♖h7 |

39 ♖a1 ♖a8 40 ♗e3 ♖b7 41 ♖×h6+ ♔g7 42 ♖ah1 ♖b2+ 1–0

Botvinnik here had a one-stage plan—to break through on the K-side, and he would have carried it out if Black had not made it easier for him by letting the passed pawn get to a7. Clearly in such cases it is quicker and better to abandon the initial plan.

Realizing Positional advantage

A one-stage plan is often called for in order to make a positional advantage count. As in the previous example, the player with the initiative envisages a favourable regrouping and carries out the necessary manoeuvres.

Karpov–Polugayevsky, Candidates Match 1974

The grandmasters in the press centre were having a lively discussion about the possibility of an exchange sacrifice on f6 in diagram 48 and decided that White would have a dangerous attack.

'Sacrifice? Why?', was Karpov's reaction when he came into the press centre straight after the game. 'There is a regrouping available that underlines straight away the hopelessness of Black's position.' Then he indicated the plan which leaves Black with no hope—♗f4 to make room for the queen, which reaches g3 via f2, then ♘f5 and doubling the rooks on the f-file. Black simply cannot withstand this massive pressure. The game saw the realization of this one-stage plan.

| 27 ♗f4! | ♖a8 |
| 28 ♕f2 | ♖ad8 |

29	♕g3	♛c3
30	♖f3	♛c2
31	♖df1	♝d4
32	♗h6	♞c6
33	♞f5	♛b2

If 33 . . . ♝e5 then Karpov has prepared the pretty 34 ♗×g7! ♗×g3 35 ♖×g3 h5 36 ♗f6+ ♔h7 37 ♖g7+ ♔h8 38 ♖×f7+ ♔g8 39 ♞h6 mate.

34	♗c1!

Simple and convincing. White wins the exchange, then goes on to reap the rewards arising from his one-step plan.

34	...	♛b5

35 ♞h6+ ♔h8 36 ♞×f7+ ♖×f7 37 ♖×f7 ♝f6 38 ♕f2 ♔g8 39 ♖×f6 gf 40 ♕×f6 1-0

Karpov carried out an original one-stage plan in this next example *(49)*.

Karpov–Andersson, Madrid, 1973

In this apparently simple position Karpov spotted the strategically correct plan which is as follows:- exploit the weakness of the enemy Q-side by placing his bishop on a6 and the queen on b5. Black is then tied down so that White can advance his pawns to create a passed pawn on the wing. With better placed pieces the threat to advance this pawn proves decisive.

19	♗b7!	♖c7
20	♗a6	♖c6
21	♕b3	♛b8
22	♕a4!	♖c7

The threat was 23 ♖×d7 and 24 ♕×c6.

23	♕b5	♞f6

24 f3 d5 25 c5! h5 26 a4! ♖e8 27 cb ab 28 a5 ♖×c1

29 ἁ×c1	♛e5

Black realized that the ending after 29 . . . ba 30 ♛×b8 ἁ×b8 31 ba was hopeless for him, since the passed pawn becomes too strong after the exchange of rooks. Hence he tries a desperate attack·on the other side, but White's well placed forces repel this unsupported sally.

30 ♛×b6	d4

31 ♔h1 ♛e3 32 ἁf1 e5 33 ♗d3 h4 34 gh ♛f4 35 ἁg1 ♛×h4 36 a6 g6 37 a7 ♔g7 38 ♗×g6 1–0 (If 38 . . . fg then 39 a8 = ♛ ἁ×a8 40 ♛b7+).

No less important than forming a plan is sticking to it. After all the opponent will try to anticipate your intentions, foresee what your next moves will be. Naturally he will seek the earliest possible opportunity to branch off into something you have not expected in the hope of gaining from this unexpected turn.

50
W

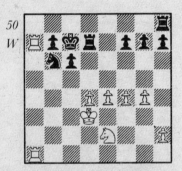

Kotov–Eliskases, Stockholm, 1952

White envisaged an effective plan from diagram 50 along these lines:– To strengthen my position I have to provoke weakness on the K-side in the enemy pawn formation, since only then will a pawn advance by me find something to 'latch on to'. So the rook has to slip back to the K-side, force one or two pawns to advance, then play back to the a-file and follow up with a K-side pawn advance.

25 ἁ7a5!	ἁhd8
26 ἁg5	f6
27 ἁga5	♞c8!

Black has worked out what White intends and hurries to put pressure on the pawn at c4 so as to tie White down. Yet White still has a way to reach his objective.

28 f5

An inaccuracy in carrying out the plan. The preliminary 28 h4 ♘d6 29 ♘c3 would rule out Black's following move and let White proceed along the lines laid down, whereas now the play goes in another direction.

28	...	g5!

Robbing White of f4 for his knight which could then play into e6 with great effect. Taking en passant would ruin the cohesion of White's pawn mass.

29	h4	h6
30	hg	hg
31	♖h1	♘d6
32	♖h6!	

Fortunately for White he has a striking combination which enables him to get an unusual sort of rook ending. The fact that there was such a combination indicates that he had a number of sound positional factors in his favour, but the diversion from his plan is still apparent.

32	...	♖e7
33	♘c3	♖de8
34	e5! (51)	

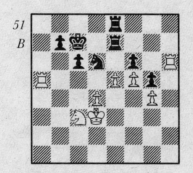

34	...	fe
35	♘d5+	cd
36	♖c5+	♔b8

36 ... ♔d7 37 ♖×d5

37	♖×d6	ed

By advancing the pawn to e4 Black could make it even more difficult for White to win, though even now it is hard to see a way to victory. At first sight the position looks quite level.

38	♖c×d5!	♖e3+
39	♔c4!	

Black had not taken account of this finesse. Now the f5 pawn has decisive force especially as its advance is supported by the king.

39 . . .	♖c8+
40 ♔×d4	♖g3
41 f6	♖×g4+
42 ♔e5	♖f4
43 ♖d8!	

It is important to exchange a pair of rooks so that Black will not have a chance to attack the white king.

43 . . .	♖×d8
44 ♖×d8+	♔c7
45 ♖g8	♔d7
46 ♖g7+	♔e8

Or 46 . . . ♔c6 47 ♖×g5 ♖f1 48 ♔e6 ♖e1+ 49 ♔f7 b5 50 ♖g7 ♔b6 51 f7 ♖e7 52 ♔g8 ♖×f7 53 ♔×f7 ♔a5 54 ♔e6 ♔a4 55 ♔d5 b4 56 ♔c4 winning.

47 ♖×b7!

If Black could get rid of the g-pawn he would reach a book draw. The fine point is the fact that this pawn will hinder his own rook in checking the king.

47 . . .   ♖f2

48 ♔e6 ♖e2+ 49 ♔f5 g4 50 ♔g6! ♖f2 51 f7+ ♔d8 52 ♖b8+ ♔e7 53 ♖e8+ 1–0

Planning for the Defender

We have already commented that it is harder to defend than to attack. It is no easy matter to have to fall in with the opponent's intentions, and that is why the defender's plan, just like his tactical operations, have to be very exact.

Alekhine–Bogoljubow, World Ch. Match 1934

The great master of defence, Lasker, commented thus on diagram 52:–
'White has difficulties. The centre is closed and so here the knights are
stronger than the bishops.'

Alekhine played 15 ♘h4, which Lasker assessed as follows:–
'When Alekhine recognizes the weaknesses in his position he has a
tendency to become very aggressive. Patient defence is not for him if he can
see the slightest chance of creating an attack. Yet sound strategy often
demands that you submit to the opponent's will so as to strengthen your
weaknesses and get rid of defects in your game. The right plan here was
♔h1, ♘g1 so as to defend h3; then g3, f3 and ♖f2. In that way all the K-
side squares would be defended, including the fourth rank. If Black
prepared an attack by f7–f5 then White in his turn could play f3–f4 or take
on f5. White should be reconciled to the fact that Black had the initiative.
Striving to take this initiative from Black is the least appropriate way to
play.'

(The game continued 15 ♘h4 g5 16 ♘f5 ♘xf5 17 ef e4 18 ♗e2
♗xf5 19 h4 ♘h7 20 g4 e3! 21 ♕xf5 ♖e5! 22 ♕d3 ed with good
winning prospects for Black. Tr.)

There are many games which have been saved, or even won, by clever
defence. In my early days of learning the game I was greatly impressed by
the defence put up by White in this position *(53)*

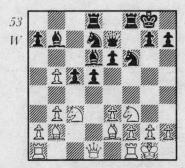

Tarrasch–Alekhine, Pistyân, 1922

Black has given up a pawn in the Blumenfeld Counter Gambit to get a
strong centre and attacking chances on the K-side. White has to consider
the pressure along the f-file, especially against f2. There are also nasty
threats along the h2/b8 diagonal.

Tarrasch thought up an excellent defensive plan to guard f2 and h2. The queen goes to c2 keeping an eye on f2 but allotting the main defence of that point to a knight on d1. Defence of h2 is the task of the other knight which goes to f1 via d2.

13	♕c2!	e5
14	♖fe1	e4
15	♘d2	♘e5
16	♘d1	♘fg4
17	♗×g4	♘×g4
18	♘f1 (54)	

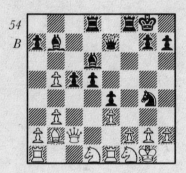

White has carried out his plan, but even the finest play cannot save a bad position, especially against such a fine attacker as Alekhine. Black's next move indicates that not all the points in White's camp are defended and that there is the irreparable drawback for White in that he cannot hold back the opponent's central pawn mass.

18	...	♕g5!

The second stage of the attacking plan, aiming at g2 which is defended only by the king. Black will bring up his reserves by ♘–h6–f5–h4. White still makes some defence against this but then another attacking trump is played—the central pawn advance.

19	h3	♘h6
20	♔h1	♘f5
21	♘h2	

White is ready to defend g2 with his rook, but at this moment when White's forces are somewhat distant from the centre comes the breakthrough there.

21	...	d4!
22	♗c1	d3
23	♕c4+	♔h8

24 ♗b2	♘g3+!

A formidable attack. The knight cannot be taken because of the catastrophe at h2 after 25 fg ♕×g3.

25 ♔g1	♗d5
26 ♕a4	♘e2+
27 ♔h1	♖f7
28 ♕a6	h5!

Preparing the final combinative stroke. Even White's inventive defence has merely served to prolong the game.

29 b6	♘g3+!
30 ♔g1	ab
31 ♕×b6	d2
32 ♖f1	♘×f1
33 ♘×f1	♗e6!
34 ♔h1	♗×h3!
35 gh	♖f3
36 ♘g3	h4
37 ♗f6	♕×f6
38 ♘×e4	♖×h3+
	0–1

In some games a sound defensive plan leads to positions in which the defender can go over to the counter attack. This possibility may form part of the plan from the start, in other cases it is a long-term prospect.

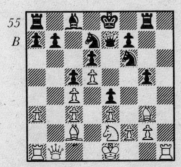

Williams–Karpov, Nice Olympiad, 1974

In diagram 55, White has prospects of pressure on the b-file and enjoys more space. However a deeper study of the position reveals Black's chances of counter attack by ♘f6–g4, f7–f5, ♘f8–g6 and f4.

Karpov forms the deep plan whose first stage is to put his king into safety on a7, where it will not interfere with or be endangered by his counter attack.

15 . . .		♔d8
16	a4	a5!
17	♖a2	♔c7
18	♖h6	♖a6!

Careful play, defending d6 and preparing to exchange a pair of rooks which will reduce White's chances on the b-file.

19	♕b5	♔b8
20	♖b2	♔a7

Now the king is out of range of White's minor pieces, and the enemy queen and rook can do him no harm either. There is a threat of 21 . . . ♘b6 and then 22 . . . ♗d7 so that the a-pawn will become indefensible. So White hurries back with his queen.

21	♕b3	♘g4
22	♖h1	f5!
23	♔d1	

White's king too decides to flee from the danger zone in the face of the long envisaged counter attack, but it is too late.

23 . . .		♖b6
24	♕a2	♖×b2
25	♕×b2	b6!

Before carrying out his operations on the K-side Black strengthens the position of all his pieces.

26	♗b3	♗a6
27	♘c1	♘de5
28	♕e2	♘g6
29	♔d2	♘f6
30	♕d1	f4! (56)

56
W

White resigned here, since great material loss will follow Black's central breakthrough, especially in view of the fact that the king has not yet managed to hide in the corner.

Multi-Stage Plans

We have already defined three sorts of multi-stage plan: when all the features are apparent to the planner; when only some details can be seen; and when nothing is clear after the first stage. Now we will consider each type in detail.

Everything is clear to the end
There are rare examples when a player can envisage all stages of his plan to the very end. The stages dovetail into each other, the aims are clear and the means also—which pieces are to be exchanged, which regrouped, which pawns to be advanced.

Alekhine–Chajes, Carlsbad, 1923

Alekhine outlined his plan from diagram 57 as follows:–

The first stage is to bring the king to the centre, so that in the event of the exchange of major pieces it can threaten a quick penetration at a5. This will inevitably induce Black to bring his king over, especially since it is needed to defend e6 and c6.

The second stage is to force Black's pieces one by one to leave the K-side by tactical threats to the king and to the enemy pawns (see the 39th and 41st moves). The threat of ♘e5 will tie the enemy knight to d7, which will hinder still further the mobility of Black's pieces which are already lacking in space.

The third stage is to double rooks on the h-file at a time when Black's forces are farthest away from the K-side. Then after an exchange of queens and bishops, the rooks will force an entry into the rear of the enemy position.

As Alekhine pointed out, no less than 28 moves were needed to bring the whole plan to fruition!

33 ...	♘g6
34 ♘d3	

34 ♔e2? e5!

34 ...	♗e8

35 ♔e2 ♔f8 36 ♔d2 ♖b7 37 ♗f3 ♔e7 38 ♖he1 ♘f8 39 ♘b4 ♔d8 40 ♔d3 ♖ge7

41 ♕d2!	

Indicating to the opponent his intention, if possible, to penetrate the Q-side by ♘a6 and ♕a5.

41 ...	♖a7

42 ♖h1 ♖ec7 43 ♖h2 ♗g6 44 ♕e3 ♔c8 45 ♖ch1 ♔b7 46 ♔d2 ♖e7 47 ♘d3 *(58)*

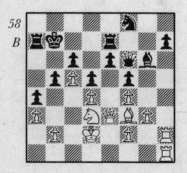

58
B

White has carried out the first two stages. Black's pieces have been diverted to the Q-side by the need to defend against various threats there. This has left the K-side without adequate defence.

47 ...	♘d7
48 ♗h5!	♖a8
49 ♗×g6	hg
50 ♖h7	♖ae8
51 ♘e5!	♘f8

Not 51 ... ♘×e5 52 fe ♕f8 53 ♕g5 and the queen dominates the black squares.

52	♖h8!	♖g7
53	♘f3	♖b8
54	♘g5	♖e7
55	♕e5!	

The black queen has a vital defensive role to play, whereas White's queen is not a very active attacker here. So the exchange of queens favours White. The reader will have noticed already that the choice of which piece to exchange and which to leave on the board is an important factor in good play. The judgement about when to exchange is developed by practical play and analysis of master games.

55	...	♕×e5
56	fe	♔a8
57	♖g8	

Decisive. The rooks have had their power reinforced by the disappearance of queens and now take the last rank with mating prospects. In reply Black makes a desperation sacrifice of a pawn in the hope of slipping throughthe Q-side with his king.

57	...	b4
58	♖hh8	♖ee8
59	ab	♔a7
60	♔c3	♔a6
61	♘f7!	

White has maximum mobility for his pieces and uses it to weave a mating net.

61	...	♖a8
62	♘d6	♖eb8
63	♖h1!	♘d7
64	♖a1!	1-0

From the position of diagram 59, Smyslov carried out a multi-stage plan to exploit his extra pawn, which is doubled, but central. Black's advantage consists of his control over the central squares d4, d5, c5, f4 and f5. White has control of the Q-file and a pawn majority on the Q-side which provide him with counter chances.

Smyslov's plan consisted of these stages:–

1. Exchange one pair or rooks at once, and leave the other on, ready to counter White's Q-side pawns and to attack the pawns at c4 and e4.

2. Use the threat of creating a distant passed pawn to divert the enemy rook to the h-file, and use his rook on the d-file.

3. Undermine the support of the e4 pawn by g7–g5–g4.

4. Tie down White's pieces by attacking the e4 pawn.

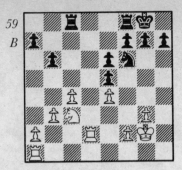

Gligorić–Smyslov, Candidates T. 1953

5. Play the king over to capture the enemy pawns.

20 ...		♖fd8
21	♖ad1	♖×d2
22	♖×d2	♔f8
23	f3	♔e7
24	♔f2	h5!
25	♔e3	g5

Admirable consistency. The threat of a passed pawn after h4 induces White to move his rook off the d-file, so that Black can occupy d4 with his own rook.

26	♖h2	♖d8
27	♖h1	g4
28	fg	♘×g4+
29	♔e2	♘f6

Third stage completed. Now to attack e4.

30	♔e3	♖d4
31	♖f1	♘g4+
32	♔e2	♔f8

Fourth stage completed. White's pieces are tied down to the defence of e4, so the time has come to play the king to g6 for a decisive attack on the enemy pawns.

33	♖f3	♔g7
34	♖d3	

This speeds up defeat. After other moves Black would advance his king as far as possible towards the g3 pawn then play f5.

34 ...		♔f6
35	♖×d4	ed
36	♘b5	♔e5

37	♘×a7	♚×e4
38	♘c8	d3+

Not falling into the trap 38 . . . e5?? 39 ♘d6 mate.

39	♔d2	♚d4
40	c5	bc
41	♘d6	♘e5
		0–1

Something can be seen
In multi-stage plans of this sort, only the first stage is clear. What comes later cannot really be discerned by the player. He merely understands the general drift of the play that will ensue, the typical manoeuvres and some of the tactical possibilities. Where the plan will end, how it will end, that is just a matter of supposition, perhaps a vague outline. Study Karpov's plan in diagram 60.

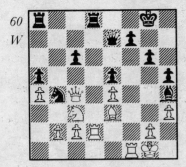

60
W

Karpov–Spassky, Candidates Match, 1974

White has two important strategical objectives. He must drive the active knight from b4 to a6, and drive the other minor piece from h4 where it prevents doubling of rooks on the f-file.

Karpov finds a curious way of achieving this by a knight retreat, though the idea is not new. The retreat ♘b1 enables c3 to be played and then ♘b1–d2–f3 will eject the bishop, though care must be taken to play ♔h2 as well so as not to let it settle at g3.

The first stage then is clear. Did Karpov look into the details of the subsequent play? Hardly. He probably envisaged the outlines of pressure on the f-file after he had doubled rooks there. ♘g5 might be possible to intensify the pressure. If Black goes f6 then there is a nice square for the queen at e6. However it is hardly possible to be more precise, since there are so many lines which Black may choose.

24 ♘b1!	♛b7
25 ♔h2!	♔g7
26 c3	♘a6
27 ♖e2	♖f8

Seeing that the doubling of rooks is coming, Spassky takes measures to defend f7.

28 ♘d2	♗d8
29 ♘f3	f6

White's objectives have been achieved. Now he has to look for the follow-up, and he can form the new plan: get the queen to e6 and operate on the d- and f-files.

30 ♖d2	♗e7
31 ♛e6	♖ad8
32 ♖xd8!	♗xd8

Not 32 . . . ♖xd8 33 ♘xe5 with disaster for Black on f7.

33 ♖d1	♘b8
34 ♗c5	♖h8
36 ♖xd8!	1–0

A simple but decisive combination which is the logical culmination of his new plan of play on the d- and f-files. After 36 . . . ♖xd8 37 ♗e7 Black suffers great losses.

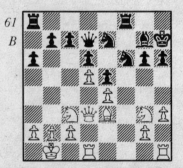

61
B

Neyshtadt–Kotov, USSR Ch. ½-final 1956

Black forms a plan in diagram 61 whose main aim is to open the long black diagonal for his bishop. The main stages are:–

1. Play b7–b5–b4 to drive the knight from its control of d5 and e4.

2. Play c6 and exchange on d5 to open the c-file.

3. Play d5 to get rid of the e4 pawn. Then e5–e4 will bring the bishop to life.

The plan is fully carried out and White in playing for some activity reinforces its effect by carelessly opening the b-file.

19 . . .	b5
20 ♘f1	b4
21 ♘e2	c6!
22 c4	

22 dc ♕×c6 23 ♕×d6 ♕×d6 24 ♖×d6 ♘×e4 25 ♖d7 ♘f5 also favours Black.

22 . . .	bc

23 dc ♕×c6 24 ♘×c3 ♖ab8! 25 ♘g3 ♖b4 26 ♖d2 ♖fb8 27 ♖c1 ♕b7

28 ♖cc2	d5!

Black finally gets to the third stage.

29 ed	e4
30 ♕e2	♘e×d5
31 ♘d1	♘d7
32 ♖c4	♖×c4
33 ♕×c4	

All stages of the plan have been carried out: the bishop at g7 now plays a big part, and the speed with which Black wins indicates that his plan was based on valid factors in the initial position.

33 . . .	♘×e3
34 ♘×e3	♗×b2

35 ♕b3 ♗g7 36 ♖×d7 (exchanging queens leaves Black a win too) 36 . . . ♕×d7 37 ♕×b8 ♕d3+ 38 ♔c1 (38 ♘c2 ♕d1 mate) 38 . . . ♕×e3+ 0–1

Subsequent Darkness

It can happen that a grandmaster forms a plan, but the subsequent play is quite unclear to him. If we compare planning to climbing a long staircase then it is a case of the top steps being unlit, so that one has to feel one's way.

Diagram 62 is not easy to assess. Neither side has any marked weakness; control of open lines is also about level. Flohr formed a long plan whose main aim was to get his knight to e4. Then he envisaged co-ordinating his pieces for an attack on the K-side.

A verbal summary would be:–

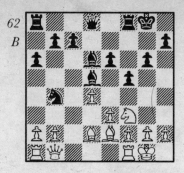

Feigin–Flohr, Kemeri, 1937

1. Go ♞b4–c6–b8–d7–f6–e4
2. Strengthen the knight on that square by the exchange of bishops on d5. Then attack on the K-side.

But what sort of attack? What regrouping will be involved, what manoeuvres? That is quite unclear.

15 ...		♞c6!
16 ♝c3		♛e7
17 ♖d1		♞b8!

18 ♞d2 ♞d7 19 ♝f3 ♞f6 20 ♛d3 ♞e4 21 ♛e2 ♞g5 22 ♝×d5 ed 23 ♞f3 ♞e4 *(63)*

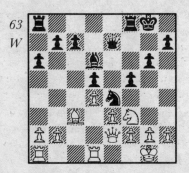

What a fine position for Black! Black's sound position in the centre now lets him attack by the advance of the K-side pawns.

23 ♖ac1	c6

24 ♝e1 ♖ae8 25 g3 ♛d7 26 ♛f1 g5! 28 ♖d3 f4 29 ef gf 30 ♞h4 ♚h8

Another aim has been achieved—the g-file is open for the use of the major pieces.

31	♕g2	fg
32	hg	♘g5
33	f3	♘h3+
34	♔h1	

34 ♔h2? ♘f4! 35 gf ♖×f4 is bad, but White does not have much hope after the text either.

	34 ...	♗e7

35 ♗d2 ♗×h4 36 gh ♕f5 37 ♖b3 ♖g8 38 ♕h2 ♖e6 39 ♖f1 ♘f2+!
0–1 (40 ♖×f2 ♕b1+, or 40 ♕×f2 ♕h3+)

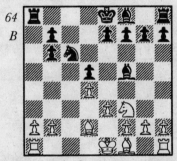

Janowski–Capablanca, New York, 1916

The great Capablanca probably only saw the vague outlines of subsequent events when he made his plan to regroup his pieces in diagram 64, a position from a famous game.

The plan was as follows:– Withdraw the bishop to d7 to support the advance b5. This pawn will provide excellent back-up to the knight which will play to c4. This square will be seen to be very important for Black. If White tries b3 to eject the knight he will have a hole at a3 and a backward pawn at a2. However White will probably not be able to stand the knight for long and will play ♗×c4. Then Black gets rid of his doubled pawn and can make a general pawn advance on the Q-side.

Did Capablanca examine the position further, and is it necessary to do this? Hardly. His experience and intuition will have suggested to him that victory is to be forced in such situations by further measures such as play on both sides of the board so as to stretch the defender's resources, but the details of these further measures have to be left till later, all depending on how the opponent reacts.

11 ...	♗d7!
12 ♗e2	

Janowski fails to anticipate the opponent's plans otherwise he would have played 12 ♗b5. Then the exchange of bishops would weaken the effect of Black's Q-side operations and the king would have had a useful post at e2.

12 ...	e6
13 0–0	

And here 13 ♘e5 was strong radically hindering Black's plan. The reader might be sceptical about the value of this game, objecting that by simple moves White could have spoiled Black's whole concept. However chess is many-sided and at any point (except for cases of forced lines in a combination) the opponent can diverge, can choose from several different lines. What is important, however, is to form a correct plan arising from the demands, the features, of the position. If our plan is good then we can feel confident that any divergence will not be to our disadvantage. Had Janowski chosen either move that we indicated as better, there is no guarantee that we would not have had an equally instructive outcome but along other lines.

13 ...	♗d6
14 ♖fc1	♔e7
15 ♗c3	♖hc8
16 a3	

Janowski still fails to see Black's plan otherwise he would have refrained from this move that makes the knight transfer to c4 more effective, and weakens the Q-side so that Black's subsequent pawn advance will work better.

16 ...	♘a5
17 ♘d2	f5
18 g3	b5
19 f3	

Missing the last chance to hinder Black's scheme by 19 ♗×a5! ♖×a5 20 ♖×c8 ♗×c8 21 ♖c1 ♗d7 22 ♘f3 or 22 ♘b3. Does this cast doubt on Black's plan? No, everything is all right since even in this better defence Black has his chances based on the two bishops, the possibility of getting rid of the doubled pawn by b4 and the distance of the enemy king from the centre.

19 ...	♘c4
20 ♗×c4	bc
21 e4	♔f7
22 e5	

A fresh inaccuracy. 22 ef ef 23 f4! intending a later ♘e5 was correct.

22 ...	♗e7
23 f4	b5 *(65)*

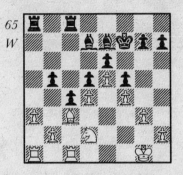

The kind of position Black was striving for when he played ♗d7. Now is the time to form the next stage. He will force b4 by moves such as ♖a6 and ♖ca8, but this in itself is not enough to force victory. That is why Black gets the idea of opening the g-file for his rooks so as to have combined play on both wings.

24 ♔f2	♖a4

25 ♔e3 ♖ca8 26 ♖ab1 h6 27 ♘f3 g5 28 ♘e1 ♖g8 29 ♔f3 gf 30 gf ♖aa8 31 ♘g2

Hoping to block the pressure on the g-file by his knight at g2, but the pin on the knight soon has grave consequences.

31 ...	♖g4
32 ♖g1	♖ag8
33 ♗e1	b4! *(66)*

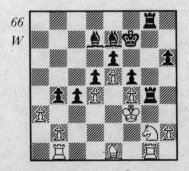

The culmination of the second stage. If White now exchanges bishops on
b4 then h6–h5–h4–h3 will be decisive since h3 to prevent the advance
would weaken g3 too much.

34	ab	♗a4
35	♖a1	

The fact that 35 ♖c1 loses to 35 . . . ♖×f4+ means that the bishop forces its
way to e4.

35	. . .	♗c2
36	♗g3	♗e4+

37 ♔f2 h5 38 ♖a7 ♗×g2 39 ♖×g2 h4 40 ♗×h4 ♖×g2+ 41 ♔f3 ♖×h2
42 ♗×e7

Or 42 ♖×e7+ ♔f8 43 ♗f6 ♖gh8! and wins.

42	. . .	♖h3+

43 ♔f2 ♖b3 44 ♗g5+ ♔g6 45 ♖c7 ♖×b2+ 46 ♔f3 ♖a8 47 ♖×e6+
♔h7 0–1

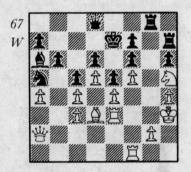

Kotov–Arnlaugsson, Amsterdam Olympiad, 1954

White has a slight advantage in diagram 67 in the possession of greater
space, while Black has some weak points e.g. h6. Admittedly White has a
weakness at c4, but this is a traditional weakness in the Nimzoindian
Defence and White has often been successful with this pawn formation.

If White is playing to win he will have to work hard to find a point of
entry in the black formation. There are two possibilities—along the g-file,
or via the transfer point h5. But it is not clear where the knight should go to
from h5, or how the bishop and queen will be employed.

Without looking too far ahead White formed this multi-stage plan.

1. Exchange a pair of rooks to help ease operations on the K-side.

2. Free the queen from the defence of c4 by playing the knight to e3.

3. With the help of the queen, offer the exchange of the second pair of rooks. As White's queen is more active than her opposite number Black will probably refuse the exchange and White's rook will get control of the g-file.

43	♖ff3	♖hh8
44	♗e2	♛e8
45	♖g3	♖×g3+
46	♖×g3	♖g8
47	♖f3	

White wants to exchange rooks at the most favourable moment, that is when his queen can take over the g-file.

47 ...	♛d8

48 ♘g3 ♛e8 49 ♗d3 ♛d8 50 ♘f1 ♛e8 51 ♘e3 ♛d8 52 ♛c2 ♛f8

53	♖g3	♖h8

After the exchange of rooks, Black's weak pawns at f6 and h6 would become exposed to attack and the white queen would easily get to the important square h5.

54	♛e2	♗c8

55 ♛g4 ♗d7 56 ♗c2 ♗c8 57 ♛f3 ♗a6 58 ♗d3 ♗c8 59 ♖g4 ♗d7 60 ♗c2 ♛e8

61	♖g7 *(68)*

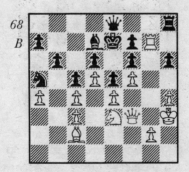

White has taken the g-file and so carried out all three stages of his plan. What next? White has to find a way of penetrating deeper, and formed this plan.

1. Free the knight from the defence of c4 by playing the king to d3.

2. Then play the knight back to h5. Then with the rook on g7 there would be the grave threat of ♛g6 winning the pawn on f6.

Without thinking about what would happen next, leaving all that 'in darkness' White pushed on.

61 ...	♕f8
62 ♕g3	♔d8
63 ♗d1	♗e8
64 ♔h2	♔c8
65 ♖g4	♔d8

Just as before Black sticks to passive waiting, since he has no alternative but to be prepared to defend.

66 ♔g1	♗d7

67 ♖g7 ♗e8 68 ♔f2 ♔c8 69 ♔e1 ♔d8 70 ♔d2 ♔c8 71 ♔d3 ♔d8 72 ♘f1 ♔c8

73 ♕g4	h5

At last White has provoked a weakening of the position. If Black had waited till the knight had got to h5 and then gone ♕f8–e7 White would win material by ♖g8..

74 ♕g3	♔d8

What next? A new plan was formed based on the fact that ♗×h5 was feasible at once since if ♖×h5 then ♖g8. However it seemed advisable to have the pawn at h4 well guarded so it was decided that first the king should return to h3. Then it should be plain sailing with the win of a pawn. However, the reader should prepare himself for some amusing turns yet in this game. It was played out over a number of morning adjournment sessions, and it is a convention that a team member who has morning play in the Olympiad should not normally have to begin a fresh game in the afternoon. My team colleagues, who were beginning to have extra burdens because of this long drawn out game, started to look at it with a jaundiced eye.

75 ♘e3	♘b7

76 ♔d2 ♘a5 77 ♔e1 ♘b7 78 ♔f2 ♘a5 79 ♔g1 ♘b7 80 ♔h2 ♘a5 81 ♔h3 ♘b7

82 ♗×h5	

Here I breathed a sigh of relief and expected an early resignation. Black calmly took the bishop.

82 ...	♖×h5
83 ♖g8	♕h6
84 ♘g4 *(69)*	

Having made this move I went for a stroll. When I came back to the board I did not understand at first what was happening.

84 ...	♕g5!

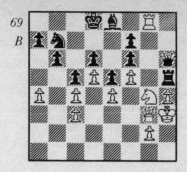

85	♖×g5		fg
86	♕e3		♖×h4+
87	♔g3		♖×g4+!!
88	♔×g4		f6

Now I looked at the board in dismay. How was I going to win? Where could I force an entry? The king was shut out and the queen could not do it all on her own, I sat there for about a quarter of an hour, and then formed yet another plan, the fourth so far! I was not put out by the pitying glances from my fellow team mates. My only concern was to find a win, otherwise I would have been labouring for days in vain.

The new plan to win was:–

1. Play the queen to h8 to limit the mobility of the enemy pieces as much as possible.

2. By a5, to open lines on the Q-side even at the cost of a pawn.

3. Combining threats by the queen on the h-file and on the queen side, White will finally force the bishop to quit e8 and then the white king will enter via h5.

Here is the conclusion of this epic game which is so instructive from the point of view of planning.

| | 89 ♕h3 | | ♔e7 |

90 ♕h7+ ♗f7 91 ♕h8 ♗e8 92 ♕g8 ♘d8 93 ♕h7+ ♗f7 94 a5! ba 95 ♕h1 a4 96 ♕b1 ♗e8 97 ♕b8 a5 98 ♕a7+ ♗d7

| | 99 ♔h5! | | |

The king has been waiting a long time for this!

| | 99 ... | | ♘f7 |

100 g4 ♘d8 101 ♔g6 ♘f7 102 ♔g7 ♘d8 103 ♕×a5 ♘f7 104 ♕b6 ♗e8 105 ♕b1!

Now just two long jumps are needed to get to grips with the pawn at f6.

105	...	♘d8	
106	♕h1	1–0	

The reader must be bound to agree that White was 'in the dark' about the many developments which came after his first plan. As for the sceptical reader who doubts whether such detailed planning was feasible, I must remind him that the game was adjourned several times and I had perfect freedom to examine all this at leisure, though I feel the planning would not be too much to expect at the board too.

As we stressed at the outset, a plan for a whole game is very rare. It can happen in one of two cases; either when the opponent fails to put up much resistance and all the play is 'at one end'; and when certain factors give a fixed form to the position that cannot be changed in the normal course of play.

1	c4	c5
2	b3	♘f6
3	♗b2	g6
4	♗×f6!	ef *(70)*

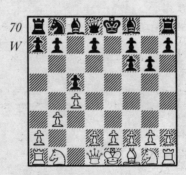

70
W

Karpov–Browne, San Antonio, 1972

The pawn formation is now determined for a long time to come and White can plan to exploit his 'permanent' square at d5, with the long term aim of using his superiority in pawns on the Q-side. Naturally such a plan calls for great technical ability which Karpov demonstrates over more than fifty moves.

5 ♘c3   ♗g7
6 g3 ♘c6 7 ♗g2 f5 8 e3 0–0 9 ♘ge2 a6 10 ♖c1 b5 11 d3 ♗b7 12 0–0 d6 13 ♕d2 ♕a5

14 ♖fd1

Black was forced into ♕a5 to guard his b-pawn, but White can now make a giant step forward by moving towards an ending by exchanging queens.

14 . . .		♖ab8
15 ♘d5		♕×d2
16 ♖×d2		b4

Forced in view of the threatened 17 cb ab 18 d4! with advantageous complications in the centre.

17 d4

Karpov considers this position strategically won for White, pointing to his grip on d5. Black's K-side pawns are immobile, White has in effect an extra pawn on the Q-side.

17 . . .		♖fd8
18 ♖cd1		

Karpov regarded this move as dubious, preferring 18 dc dc 19 ♖cd1

18 . . .		cd
19 ed		♔f8
20 c5		

And this is a mistake according to Karpov, who gives 20 ♘e3 as better.

20 . . .   ♘a7!

21 ♘e3 ♗×g2 22 ♔×g2 dc 23 dc ♖×d2 24 ♖×d2 ♖c8 25 ♘d5 ♖×c5 26 ♘×b4 a5

27 ♘d5		♖c6

A serious mistake letting White's pieces become active again. 27 . . . ♘c6 was better.

28 ♘e3		♖c5
29 ♘f4		♗h6
30 ♖d5		♖×d5
31 ♘f×d5		♗×e3

The losing mistake. By keeping the bishop on Black could hope for a draw, but now the extra pawn (in effect) gives White good winning chances.

32 ♘×e3		♔e7
33 ♘c4		♘c6
34 ♔f3		♔e6
35 ♔e3		♔d5
36 a3		

To prepare ♔d3, not playable at once because of the knight check at b4.

36 . . .		♔e6

37 ♔d3 ♚d5 38 f3 h6 39 ♔c3 h5 40 ♔d3 f6
41 f4! *(71)*

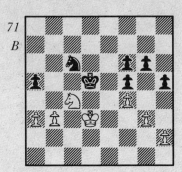

71
B

The culmination of the plan to 'kill' Black's K-side pawns, while White has a 'runner' on the other side.

41 ...	g5
42 ♘e3+	♚e6
43 h4	gh
44 gh	♘e7
45 ♔c4	♘g6

Black tries to get a passed pawn of his own, but it is too late.

46 ♘g2	♚d6

47 ♔b5 ♚d5 48 ♔×a5 ♚e4 49 b4 ♚f3 50 b5 ♚×g2 51 b6 ♘f8 52 ♔b5 ♘d7

53 a4

The knight unaided cannot stop two united passed pawns, as White's Q-side plan reaches its final stage.

53 ...	♘×b6

54 ♔×b6 ♚f3 55 a5 ♚×f4 56 a6 ♚e3 57 a7 f4 58 a8=♕ f3 59 ♕e8+ 1–0

Here is a game where an advantage achieved in the opening was exploited by a plan for the whole game, with the help of mistakes by the opponent.

1 ♘f3	d5
2 e3	♘f6
3 b3	♗g4
4 ♗e2	♘bd7
5 ♗b2	♗×f3

Such an exchange of bishop for knight is made only in exceptional circumstances when there are strong arguments in favour. In this case it just gives White the advantage.

6	♗×f3	e5
7	d3	c6
8	♘d2	♗d6
9	0-0	♕e7
10	a4	0-0

With the opening over and pieces developed, the stage has come for planning. Each side will try to clarify the pawn position in the centre in a way favourable to himself.

11	g3	♖ad8

12 ♗g2 ♖fe8 13 ♕e2 ♕e6 14 e4! ♘f8 15 ♖fd1 ♘g6 16 ♘f1 ♗c5 17 ♘e3 ♗×e3

18	♕×e3	d4?

A bad positional mistake. Black loses the chance of doing anything active, while White has clear prospects of opening the K-side and building this up into.a powerful attack. He had to maintain the tension in the centre.

19	♕e2	♘d7
20	♖f1	♕d6
21	♗a3	c5

This is even worse, as the ♕-side is finally blocked and White can confidently concentrate on the K-side.

22	♖ae1	♘b8
23	♗c1	♘c6 (72)

Romanovsky–Vilner, USSR Ch. 1924

At this point White formed a plan that covers the rest of the game.

Exploiting the closed nature of the centre and the absence of counter play on the Q-side, White plays his K-side pawns forward. This cramps his opponent and lets White force a way into the enemy camp via the g- and h-files. In effect Black's weak play has let White do largely as he pleases.

24	f4	f6
25	f5	♘f8
26	g4?	

Carelessness. The simple 26 ♕h5! would prevent king flight and greatly increase the effect of the line opening on this side.

26	...	♔f7!

27 g5 ♔e7 28 ♖f3 ♔d7 29 ♖g3 ♔c8 30 gf gf 31 ♗f3 ♘d7

32	♕g2	a5?

A fresh unnecessary weakening.

33	♗h5	♖e7
34	♗h6	♘b6
35	♖g8	

The first penetration. Black can do nothing to oppose the active play of his opponent. A correct plan leads to victory despite the inaccuracy at move 26.

35	...	♖c7

36 ♖d1 ♔b8 37 ♖d2 ♔a7 38 ♕g3 ♘b4 39 ♖g2 ♘c8 40 ♕f2 ♘c6 41 ♖2g3 ♔a6 42 ♕g2 ♖cd7 43 ♗e8 ♖c7 44 ♗f8! ♘6e7 45 ♗f7! ♕b6 46 ♗×e7 ♖×e7 47 ♖×d8 ♕×d8 48 ♖g8 ♕c7 49 ♗e6 ♘a7 50 h4 ♘c6 51 h5 ♔a7 52 h6 ♘d8

53	♗d5	

Another inaccuracy. 53 ♗c4 would rob Black of his last counter chance.

53	...	♘f7

54 ♕g7 ♕b6! 55 ♗×f7 ♕b4 56 ♕×f6! ♕e1+ 57 ♔h2 ♕f2+ 58 ♖g2 ♕f4+ 59 ♔h3 ♕f3+ 60 ♖g3 ♕h1+ 61 ♔g4 ♕d1+ 62 ♔h4 ♕h1+ 63 ♔g5 ♕c1+ 64 ♔h5 ♕h1+ 65 ♕h4 1–0

Learn From The World Champions

The holders of the world title have always been marked by their ability to plan positional games and foresee the development of affairs. This feature was particularly marked in Capablanca, Lasker and Botvinnik, while in our days Karpov shows this admirable trait of seeing, well before the opponent does, the outlines of the coming battle, and taking the necessary measures.

A striking example, despite the apparently routine nature of the

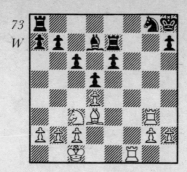

Lasker–Pillsbury, Paris, 1900

position *(73)*. Believe it or not the one-stage plan leads almost by force to the win of the b7 pawn! Yes, this pawn is to fall to the frisky white knight which starts its run by a retreat to b1 (the same move as in Karpov–Spassky, page 83).

The drawback to Black's position is the backward pawn at e6. Black will try at all costs to advance it, and White plans to exploit this by the knight manoeuvre ♘–b1–d2–f3–g5–f7–d6×b7!

22	♘b1		♖ae8
23	♘d2		e5

Otherwise 24 ♘f3 would prevent the advance for ever.

24	de		♖×e5
25	♘f3		♖e3

Other rook moves leave Black badly placed too, e.g. 25 . . . ♖5e7 26 ♘g5 ♗e6 27 ♖e1 with no answer to the two threats 28 ♖ge3 and 28 ♖×e6 ♖×e6 29 ♘f7 mate.

26	♘g5		♖×g3

27 hg h6 28 ♘f7+ ♔g7 29 ♘d6 ♖e7 30 ♘×b7 and with the end of the plan it was merely a matter of technique, in which Lasker was a past master.

Spassky planned to exploit his passed pawn in diagram 74, which is already well supported by the rooks. The plan is to advance it to the 7th rank ignoring the possible loss of the a-pawn. Once on the 7th it will tie down Black's forces. Then a combination of threats—queening the pawn, mating the king—will decide.

19	. . .		♕c2
20	♕f4!		

Avoiding the exchange of queens since White's threats need the

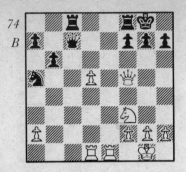

Spassky–Petrosian, World Ch. match, 1969

strongest piece on the board. The loss of the a-pawn plays no real part since Black's pieces will soon be forced to occupy very passive positions, and White can get the material back if he wishes.

20	. . .	♛×a2
21	d6	♜cd8
22	d7	♛c4
23	♛f5	h6

23 . . . ♛c6 24 ♘e5 ♛e6 is no improvement since after 25 ♛c2 there is a threat of 26 ♛c7 and then 27 ♘g6 ♛×g6 28 ♛×d8

24	♜c1	♛a6
25	♜c7	b5
26	♘d4	♛b6

A mistake that loses the game, but Black's position was very difficult. White has carried out the right plan and now reaps the fruits. 26 . . . ♛d6! would put up a better fight.

27	♜c8	♘b7
28	♘c6	♘d6
29	♘×d8!	♘×f5
30	♘c6	1–0

The passed pawn has carried the day.

White has the advantage in diagram 75 with well mobilized pieces and no weaknesses. Black's central pawns are rather rickety, particularly d6. In accordance with Steinitz's teaching that the position should be attacked at its weakest point, Tal concentrates his fire on d6. He plans to force the pawn to advance while hindering the advance of the e6 pawn. Then Black's pawns will be on white squares, the same colour as his bishop so that the black squares will be very weak. White's pieces will occupy the

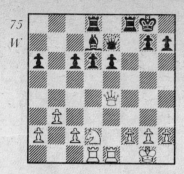

Tal–Byrne, Alekhine Memorial, Moscow, 1971

weak squares. There are three attacks to come on d6 (♘c4, ♕g3, ♖d1) and Black does not have time to bring up three defenders.

	18 ♕d3!	♕f7

Black has no time for 18 ... e5 19 ♕×a6 ♖a8 20 ♕c4+ ♗e6 21 ♕×c6 ♖×a2 22 c4 and White is a pawn up.

	19 ♕g3!	♕f5
	20 ♘c4	d5

Black would be in a bad way after 20 ... ♕×c2 21 ♖d2 and then 22 ♘×d6.

	21 ♘e3	♕f4
	22 ♘g4!	♕×g3
	23 hg	♔f7
	24 c4	♗e8
	25 ♖d4	c5

This attempt to activate himself leads to even greater difficulties for Black. After other moves White could achieve a complete blockade of the pawn centre and then decide matters by pressure on the flank (c5 and ♖a4 etc.).

	26 ♖d2	d4
	27 ♖de2	♖d6
	28 ♘e5+	♔e7
	29 ♘d3	♖f5
	30 g4	♖g5
	31 ♘e5	

The rook is trapped. The correct plan has driven Black's pieces into a critical position from which there is no escape.

	31 ...	d3

32 ♖d2 ♖d4 33 g3 h5 34 f4 ♖×g4 35 ♘×g4 hg 36 f5 ♗c6 37 ♖×e6+ ♔d7 38 ♖g6 ♗e4 39 ♖×g7+ ♔d6 40 f6 1–0

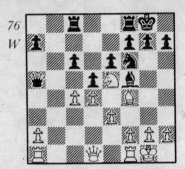

Botvinnik–Pomar, Amsterdam, 1966

In the position of diagram 76 white has the initiative, but what does his advantage consist of? More active pieces and the chance to take the only open file. Botvinnik forms this laconic plan, 'White's plan is simple. Play the pawn to c5, then exchange the bishop on g6 and take over the b-file. Will Black be able to find any counter play?'

        14 g4!   ♗g6

        15 c5   ♘e4

Black too has a plan—transfer the knight to c4 to divert White from the exchange on g6.

        16 f3   ♘d2

        17 ♖f2   ♘c4

        18 ♘×c4   dc

        19 ♗d6   ♖fe8

        20 e4

Even energetic measures have not helped Black. He has kept his bishop, but White still has the b-file and the pawn at c4 will need defending.

        20 . . .   f5

Black makes every effort to free the bishop, but the text leads to an advantageous opening of the f-file for White.

        21 ♕c2   fe

22 fe ♕a3 23 ♖e1 ♕h3 24 ♖g2 ♖cd8 25 ♖g3 ♕h6 26 ♕×c4 ♕d2 27 ♕c3!

The strongest, since if Black exchanges queens he has a lost ending not so much because of the pawn down as due to White's command of the b-file.

Pomar prefers the middle game.

27 ...			♛×a2
28 ♖g2			♛a6
29 h4!			

White now changes the direction of the game, leaving his plan of using the b-file in favour of a quick K-side attack. Where is the logic? The answer lies in the fact that the move f7–f5 has opened Black's K-side and an attack there by advancing the K-side pawns is the quick way to win.

29 ...		♖d7

30 h5 ♗f7 31 ♖a1 ♛c8 32 ♛f3! ♛d8 33 g5 g6 34 h6 e5

35 ♗×e5		♖b7

Black finally has control of this file, but at a time when it is no use to him. 35 ... ♖×d4 is bad—36 ♖×a7 ♖d7 37 ♖×d7 ♛×d7 38 ♛f6 ♛d1+ 39 ♔h2 ♛h5+ 40 ♔g3.

36 ♛f4		a5

37 ♖f2 ♗b3 38 d5 cd 39 c6 ♖a7 40 c7 ♛e7 41 ♗d6 1–0

Now three examples of the champions defending. First, a brilliant defensive plan by Euwe from the position of diagram 77.

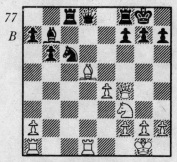

Alekhine–Euwe, World Ch. match, 1937

Black has to form a plan to counter the concentration of force aimed at his poorly defended king. The queen has to move and then White will go ♘g5 attacking f7 three times and hoping to assault h7 too. The attack can be supplemented by ♖–d3–h3.

The plan is to exchange bishops and get the knight over to the defence of the K-side.

16 ...		♛e7
17 ♘g5		♘e5!

The threat was to capture three times on f7 and then play ♖d7+. Black also had to see his intermediate move to save the knight.

18	♗×b7	♘g6
19	♕f5	♕×b7
20	♖d7	♕a6!

Another finess that had to be forseen—the queen threatens ♕×a2 as in the variation 21 ♖×f7 ♕×a2 22 ♖×f8+ ♘×f8.

21	h4	♖c5!

The last link in the plan. White has to exchange rooks as 22 ♕g4 ♘e5 23 ♕h5 h6 or 22 ♕h3 do not appeal to him.

22	♖d5	

Here the Dutchman went wrong by 22 . . . ♖×d5 giving White a powerful passed pawn, though the game still ended in a draw. The flexible 22 . . . ♕c8 would have led to complete equality.

As Botvinnik has pointed out Petrosian has a striking natural talent, developed by much analytical work, for 'placing his pieces in such a way that they defend each other with maximum security.' Hence there are many of his games where we find sound defensive plans. The next example *(78)* is of his favourite device of sacrificing the exchange.

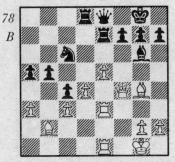

78
B

Reshevsky–Petrosian, Candidates T. Zurich, 1953

Black has a difficult position. White's centre pawns look ready to advance and sweep everything from their path, supported as they are by well posted pieces. Black's pieces are cramped on the back three rows. His main strength lies in the Q-side pawns. For the moment the enemy centre pawns have a black square orientation which suggests that it would be well to blockade them by a knight on d5. But this post cannot be reached since the square e7 is occupied by a rook. Well then, give up the rook so that the knight can reach d5 and be supported by a pawn at e6.

25 ...	♖e6!!
26 a4	♘e7!

Avoiding the cunning line offered by White's last move—26 . . . b4 27 d5! ♖×d5 28 ♗×e6 fe 29 ♕c4 and White will win.

27 ♗×e6	fe
28 ♕f1	♘d5
29 ♖f3	♗d3

Black's pieces have become active and the absence of the exchange is not felt. White therefore hurries to give it back and equalize.

30 ♖×d3	cd
31 ♕×d3	b4
32 cb	

Probably the only sound line. After 32 c4 ♘b6 33 ♖c1 ♘×a4 34 ♗a1 ♕c6, or here 33 d5 ed 34 c5 ♘×a4 35 ♗d4 ♖c8 36 ♕f3 ♕e6 Black has nothing to fear since he has blocked the enemy pawns.

32 ...	ab
33 a5	♖a8
34 ♖a1	♕c6
35 ♗c1	♕c7
36 a6	♕b6

White is trying to use his passed pawn, but Black can use his pawn too. The game is even despite the extra pawn, and the knight which was moved in such timely fashion to d5 dominates the scene.

| 37 ♗d2 | b3 |

38 ♕c4 h6 39 h3 b2 40 ♖b1 ♔h8 41 ♗e1 ½-½

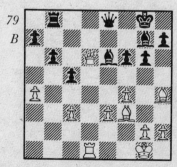

Taimanov–Fischer, Candidates Match, 1971

Black's position in diagram 79 looks dubious in view of the threats 27

♗c6 and 27 ♕c7. Even when Black meets this there is the prospect of White advancing his centre pawns.

Fischer draws up a plan which brings all these possibilities to naught. He regroups his rook to c8, the queen goes to f7, and the bishop from g7 to e7. This neutralizes White's chances along the d-file.

26 ...	♖c8!
27 a5	

27 ♗b7 ♗f8 28 ♕d2 ♖b8 gets nowhere.

27 ...	♗f8
28 ♕d2	♗e7!

This threatens ♖d8 and has firmly controlled any point of entry on the d-file. It is curious how the whole plan of regrouping has involved short moves to an adjacent square.

29 ♗d5	

Posing new problems of a queen entry, but the American copes again with short moves!

29 ...	♕f7
30 ♗×e6	♕×e6
31 ♕d7	♔f7!
32 ♕×a7	ba
33 e4	♕c6!

Another fine defensive move, with the threat 34 ... ♖a8, whereas 33 ... ♕×e4? loses to 34 ♖e1 ♖a8 35 ♕c7.

34 ♖d7	♕×e4
35 h3	a4

It is still not too easy for Black—35 ... ♖a8? 36 ♖×e7+, while if 35 ... ♔f8 then 36 ♖d1 with the two threats 37 ♕d7 and 37 ♖e1.

36 ♗f2	♔f8
37 c4	a3!

38 ♕×a3 ♖a8 39 ♕b2 ♔e8 40 ♕b5 ♔f8 41 ♖d1 ♕×f4 42 ♗×c5 (The sealed move) 42 ... ♗×c5 43 ♕×c5+ ♔g7 44 ♖f1 ♕e4 45 ♕c7+ ♔h6 46 ♖×f6?? ♕d4+ 47 ♖f2 ♖a1+ 0–1

Now two examples of cramping plans:

Black has an advantage in diagram 80 based on two bishops, which means that he will be able to generate pressure on both wings. He has a two-stage plan, the first part of which is to cramp White's minor pieces as much as possible by the advance of his pawns. The advance of the a-pawn will drive the knight to c1, the advance of the K-side pawns will limit the mobility of the bishop. The same effect arises if White tries to make more room by playing f4.

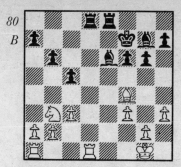

Englisch–Steinitz, London, 1883

The second part is nothing like so clear, but when it come to the decisive moment something must exist for Black.

22 .. .		g5!
23	☒×d8	☒×d8
24	♗e3	h6!

To advance . . . f5.

25	☒e1	f5
26	f4	

This advance cuts down the scope of the bishop, but other moves were no better.

26 .. .		♗f6
27	g3	a5!
28	♘c1	a4
29	a3	

At least White can block the advance a3 which would ruin his -side pawns.

29 .. .		♗c4
30	♔f2 *(81)*	

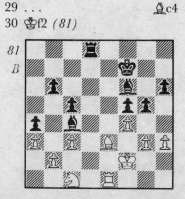

The first part is completed. The knight is on the back row and cannot become active. Now for the second stage. Black has two choices. He can put the rook on d5 and push forward the b-pawn with the hope of getting a passed pawn on the Q-side. The bishops would help to queen such a pawn.

The second choice illustrated in the game continuation is based on the idea of exchanging black square bishops, when it will be hard for White to stop the enemy rook penetrating to the two back ranks.

    30 ...   gf!
    31 ♗×f4
31 gf? ♗h4+.
    31 ...   ♗g5
    32 ♗×g5

Steinitz's idea is clearly seen after 32 ♔e3 ♖e8+ 33 ♔f2 ♖×e1 34 ♔×e1 ♗×f4 35 gf ♔e6 and ♔d5 followed by ♔e4 or ♔c4.

    32 ...   hg
    33 ♔e3   ♔f6
    34 h4

White is in Zugzwang since if he moves the rook Black strengthens his position further by ♔e5.

    34 ...   gh
35 gh ♖e8+ 36 ♔f2 ♖×e1 37 ♔×e1 ♔e5 38 ♘e2 ♖×e2! (The pawn ending is a win) 39 ♔×e2 ♔f4 40 c4 ♔g4 41 ♔e3 f4+ 42 ♔e4 f3 43 ♔e3 ♔g3 0–1

Karpov–Unzicker, Nice Olympiad, 1974

In diagram 82 Black controls less space, and his pieces are passively placed, particularly the knight at b7. Karpov formed this three point plan.
1. White closes the a-file by ♗a7, and under its cover concentrates his

major pieces on this file. Black has no counter to this and must wait passively.

2. White exploits Black's passivity by f4, and then f5. . . . e×f4 is not possible as White would reply ♘-d4-c6.

3. If Black plays passively White will concentrate his forces on the files opposite the enemy king, penetrating at f6, g6 or h6. If Black goes g5 then this penetration will take place on the weakened white squares.

At all stages of the plan Black has to take account of White coming in on the a-file after moving the bishop away from a7.

24	♗a7!	♘e8
25	♗c2	♘c7
26	♖ea1	♕e7
27	♗b1	♗e8
28	♘e2	♘d8
29	♘h2	

The last two moves are the preparation for stage two which Black cannot hinder.

29	. . .	♗g7
30	f4!	f6
31	f5	g5

Black decides to remove the tension from the pawns on the K-side, but now Karpov can use h5 as a transfer point.

32	♗c2	♗f7

33 ♘g3 ♘b7 34 ♗d1 h6 35 ♗h5 ♕e8 36 ♕d1 ♘d8 37 ♖a3 ♔f8 38 ♖1a2 ♔g8

39	♘g4!	♔f8

Taking twice on h5 would lose the queen to 41 ♘×f6+.

40	♘e3	♔g8
41	♗×f7+	♘×f7
42	♕h5	♘d8
43	♕g6!	♔f8

After the exchange of queens the pawn at g6 supported by ♘f5 would soon force a win.

44	♘h5!	1–0

Practical Advice

As the reader gets stronger, questions of planning will figure more prominently in his thinking, and he will start to come up against those problems which forever torment the strong player. We shall try to give some advice and warn the reader against typical mistakes in planning.

The first piece of advice is, 'Don't lose contact with the actual position!' As we shall see, even strong grandmasters can go badly wrong in this respect. Your plan must be subordinated to the demands of the position, must arise from it.

When you are looking for the best move you take into account many factors:—does it correspond to your aim, will it produce any drawback in your position, will the opponent be able to exploit the weak side of it? Only when you feel confident that you have weighed all these factors will you actually make the move.

In particular you have to take account of the fact that every plan produces a change in the position of the pieces and pawns, so you have to consider the fresh position arising after the plan has been carried out. Does this new position offer chances to the opponent that he did not have before? The next example *(83)* shows a faulty plan.

Szabo–Botvinnik, Amsterdam Olympiad, 1954

White has to take account of the weaknesses in Black's position, most of all the square c5 and the weakened K-side. The half-open c-file on which White has already begun operations also has significance. There is the possibility of Black's K-side pawns becoming active. Considering the position of the pieces, one concludes that both sides have positioned them well, especially the knight at d5 which has influence on both sides of the board.

White came to the conclusion that the position was about level and then considered his plan. The plan involving f3 was soon rejected—don't make pawn moves in the area where you are weaker. It is more logical to play on the Q-side. It would be nice to get rid of the knight at d5, but how? It would not be advantageous to give up the good bishop at e2.

So Szabo planned to undermine the support of the knight by ♕a2 and ♗b3 with pressure on the a2/g8 diagonal. Then double rooks on the c-file after which there is a threat of ♘–a5×b7, and if ♕d7×b7 then ♖×c6 and the strong point at d5 falls, and with it the whole enemy K-side is in danger.

Unfortunately, though this plan seemed sound—the knight sacrifice for two pawns would only be made when all preparations had been completed—there is a flaw. The white pieces leave the king unprotected and Black can storm that side. If Szabo had weighed this up he would probably have chosen another plan. The idea of undermining d5 is right, but was carried out wrongly. There were much better chances in a pawn advance by ♖b1, a4 and b5 striving to create a weak pawn on c6 and then operating on both the b- and c-files.

1	♕a2	a6
2	♗d1	♗f8
3	♗b3	♖e8
4	♖c2	h5!

Before White can complete his plan Black begins his assault which shows that White would be better off with his bishop at e2. Thus if now 5 h3 then 5 . . . h4 6 ♗h2 g4 with an attack.

5	h4	gh?

A tactical oversight that allows White back into the game. 5 . . . ♕g4! (Possible because there is no bishop at e2!) would give Black a powerful attack e.g. 6 ♗d6 gh 7 ♗×f8 ♖e×f8 8 ♘d6 ♖g7, or 6 hg h4 7 ♗h2 h3 8 ♗g3 ♖h7. Botvinnik further points out that 6 ♘d6 ♗×d6 7 ♗×d6 gh 8 ♔h2 ♖g7 leaves Black with an extra pawn and a growing initiative.

6	♗×h4	♕g4
7	g3!	

This calm reply makes the conduct of Black's attack difficult. Thus the apparently strong 7 . . . ♖g7 is simply met by 8 ♗×f6. Realizing that his previous move was wrong, Botvinnik takes speedy measures to prevent an explosion on his b7 and c6 squares.

7	. . .	♕d7!
8	♘a5	♔g7
9	♖fc1	♖e6

Now c6 is safely guarded and there is no way to undermine the knight at d5. After 10 ♗a4 ♘b6 11 ♗b3 ♘d5 with repetition of moves a draw was agreed.

Although chess is a creative game in which talent, inventiveness and fantasy play a big part, no less a role is played by knowledge based on the study of the play of the grandmasters of the past. When you examine these games you notice that many plans repeat themselves, and you will naturally hope to apply these recurring plans in your own games. The study of typical plans is something that the leading grandmasters devote a great deal of time to. I would say that the most far-seeing of them devote as much time to this as to the study of openings.

Botvinnik–Ragozin, Training game, 1947

The weakness of the black squares on the Black king side in diagram 84 is immediately apparent. Black's possesion of the d- and c-files is no compensation in view of the fact that White's active pieces do not let him use these files.

White's plan is simple. He will increase the pressure on the weakened black squares aiming for a bishop sacrifice on g6 so that his queen and rooks can get a mating attack. There are also knights on the board, but they will soon be exchanged since White's knight will be too strongly posted at f6. When you follow how precisely Botvinnik carries out the plan of exploiting the black squares, you are full of praise, but . . . 'To be fair we must note that it was not so hard for White to find the right plan here; all he had to do was to copy the play of Lasker against Capablanca at Moscow 1935.' (Botvinnik)

Naturally the reader would like to see the 'precedent' *(85)*:

The 67 year old ex-champion attacks the king with youthful vigour. Note the similarity of pawn structures.

24	♕c1!	♖ad8
25	♖1e3	♗c8
26	♖h3	♔f8
27	♕h6+	♖g7

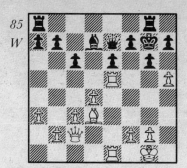

Lasker–Capablanca, Moscow, 1935

| 28 | hg | hg |
| 29 | ♗×g6! | |

Having taken control of the black squares, White makes this programmed sacrifice. Now 29 . . . fg is bad; 30 ♕h8+ 🏰g8 31 🏰f3+.

| 29 . . . | ♕f6 |

30 🏰g5 ♚e7 31 🏰f3 ♕×f3 (No other defence) 32 gf 🏰dg8 33 ♚f1 🏰×g6 34 🏰×g6 fg 35 ♕h2 and White forced a win with his material advantage.

Botvinnik followed this analogy. He exchanged knights, posted his pieces for the attack on the black squares and then sacrificed on g6. From diagram 84:

| 27 | ♘f6 | ♘e7 |

To exchange the knight before White goes 🏰–e3–h3–h7.

| 28 | 🏰e3 | ♘g8 |

29 ♘×g8 ♚×g8 30 ♕e7 ♗c6 31 🏰be5 🏰d7 32 ♕h4 ♕h8 33 ♕f4 ♕g7 34 🏰g3 ♗d5

| 35 | 🏰eg5 | 🏰×c3 *(86)* |

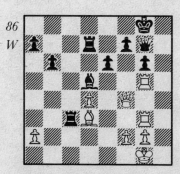

The concentration of force on g6 has been achieved and the explosion follows.

36	♗×g6!	♖×g3
37	♗×f7+	♔f8

Or 37 . . . ♖×f7 38 ♕×g3 forcing the win.

38	♖×g7	♖×g7
39	♗×e6+	1–0

However I must advise the reader to have a critical approach to examples of planning from the play of the grandmasters. Just as in the opening variations there is sometimes a move which can radically alter the assessment, so too there may be improvements in middlegame plans. The following game is an instructive example of a middle-game improvement, and a very fine achievement of planning.

1 d4 ♘f6 2 c4 e6 3 ♘f3 b6 4 a3 ♗b7 5 ♘c3 d5 6 e3 ♘bd7 7 cd ed 8 ♗e2 ♗d6

9	b4	0–0
10	0–0	

White's previous move revealed the outline of subsequent play. Spassky's plan has been tried many times before. White sees that Black aims at the K-side and intends to exchange the principal piece in this build-up—the bishop at d6. To achieve this he will play b5, a4 and ♗a3. Then White's major pieces get the attractive prospect of attacking the backward pawn at c7. Black realizes this and tries first of all to stop the pawn advance.

10	. . .	a6
11	♕b3	♕e7!

Preventing a4 and calculating that after 12 b5 ab 13 ♘×b5 c5 14 ♘×d6 ♕×d6 Black has a dangerous initiative which fully compensates for the lack of a black squared bishop.

12 ♖b1

Now even if White gets his pawns forward he will not have ♗a3. Black's correct preventative plan has taken the sting from White's standard plan.

12	. . .	♘e4
13	a4	♘df6
14	b5	♘×c3
15	♕×c3	♘e4
16	♕c2	♖fc8
17	♗b2	c6

Practically forcing an exchange on c6, otherwise Black will go c6×b5 and a5 with an excellent Q-side formation.

18	bc	♗×c6
19	♕b3	♕d7
20	♖a1	b5
21	a5 *(87)*	

A serious mistake. Spassky thought he could not afford to go into the endgame after 21 ab ♗×b5 22 ♗×b5 ♕×b5 23 ♕×b5 ab 24 ♖×a8 ♖×a8 25 ♖a1 ♖×a1+ 26 ♗×a1, but as was shown by subsequent analysis the endgame is drawish.

87
B

Spassky–Petrosian, 11th game, Match 1969

The tension on the Q-side has eased, and assessment shows that Black has the advantage. Black's knight is centralized, his rook at c8 occupies the open file, and his pawn structure is impressive, particularly with the outpost at c4 which Black now plays to exploit. One plan would be b4 followed by ♗b5 when c4 is very weak. However Petrosian prefers another one involving his favourite device of sacrificing the exchange:–

1. A queen sally aided by knight and ♗d6 will provoke white square weaknesses on White's K-side.

2. ♖c4 and pressure on the c-file will finally force White to take on c4 and open the long white diagonal after d5×c4.

3. Knight and queen will be brought into operation on the weak white squares.

21	...	♗b7
22	♘e5	♕d8
23	♖fd1	♕h4!
24	g3	♕e7
25	f3	

The last two moves and subsequent pawn moves on the K-side play into

Black's hands, but what was White to do? He should have just manoeuvred quietly, but this is not easy for an energetic player.

25 ...		♘g5
26 h4		♘e6
27 f4 *(88)*		

The white squares have been weakened and Black has to choose the most appropriate time to go ♖c4. First he re-arranges his pieces so that they attack the white squares to the maximum extent possible; f6 will drive back the enemy knight and prepare ♘–d8–f7–d6 so that it can go later to e4 or f5.

27 ...		f6
28 ♘f3		♘d8
29 ♔f2		♘f7
30 ♘d2		♖c4!

White refuses to take the exchange at once, since the long white diagonal worries him. So Black has to force acceptance by pressure on the central white squares.

31 ♕d3		♖e8
32 ♗f3		♗b4!

To exchange the defender of the white squares, and to make way for ♘d6. White prefers to offer a bishop exchange.

33 ♗a3		♗×a3
34 ♖×a3		♘d6
35 ♖e1		f5
36 ♖aa1		♘e4+
37 ♗×e4		fe!

This was the point of playing f5. Now the queen gets chances on the c8/h3 diagonal.

38 ♕b1   ♛d7 *(89)*

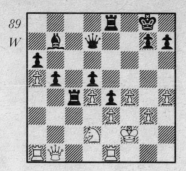

The beginning of the end.

    39 ♖a2   ♖ec8
    40 ♘×c4

Probably despair—if we are going to lose then at least be material up. The final phase of Black's plan now comes into operation.

    40 ...   dc
    41 d5

To open some prospects for the rooks.

    41 ...   ♗×d5
    42 ♖d1   c3!
    43 ♖c2   ♛h3
    44 ♖g1   ♛g4
    45 ♔g2   ♛f3+
    46 ♔h2   ♛×e3

The king has finally found a comparatively safe spot, but Black's pawns have grown too strong.

    47 f5   ♛c5
    48 ♖f1   b4
    49 f6   b3
    50 ♖cf2   c2
    51 ♔c1   e3

52 f7+ ♔f8 53 ♖f5 b2 54 ♕×b2 c1 = ♕ 55 ♕×g7+ ♔×g7 56 ♖g5+ 0–1.

The Mind of a Grandmaster

The right moment for making a plan is after a wide-ranging general analysis and assessment of the position. How far do we plan? To the point where we reckon we shall have reached our objective. In other words the plan starts with our laying down our objective and ends with its achievement.

In which cases should we aim for a one-stage plan, in which many-staged? It all depends on the concrete position we are dealing with, on the aim which we set ourselves. If the aim can be achieved in a few moves, if it is achieved without a number of steps then our plan is of the one-stage sort. If the distance to the aim consists of many moves, if we need several 'jumps' to reach it then it is a question of a many-staged plan with intermediate, subsidiary aims.

In whose clock time does the grandmaster think out his plan? As we have stressed already, everything that is expressed in words rather than variations should be thought out when the opponent's clock is ticking, as far as is possible.

How does the idea of a plan arise in the mind of a grandmaster? The process is a creative one, but it is inextricably linked with the assessment. One of the tasks of the assessment is to establish where the weak points lie in each camp, and the plan must be linked with these weaknesses.

Do not forget to devote some time to considering what plan the opponent has formed, or will form. The example of the Szabo–Botvinnik game showed us the consequences of ignoring the opponent.

Moreover, know your own capacity and do not try to overburden your mind with plans you cannot cope with. There are some players who, to judge by what they say after a game, are bubbling over with all sorts of ideas and plans. When you look into them you find that many of these ideas are not linked with the position, are superficial, unreal. You have to have realistic aims that you can cope with and that you can fit into a plausible plan.

Work hard at your planning, and always bear in mind Lasker's aphorism, 'To find the right plan is just as hard as looking for its sound justification.' This stresses what cannot be repeated too often, that assessment and planning are inextricably linked.

How to Train

Once again we divide this into two parts. Training at home, and training during a game.

For home training, the best thing is the study of well-annotated games. Once again we have to say that although there are many books on chess, there are few with the sort of thing the student needs. The modern grandmaster prefers to restrict himself to variations on the whole, but the student should look for games with verbal statements as well as variations. If such 'prose' is missing, don't despair, but try and find out on the basis of just the moves at what point the assessment and planning took place. The effort to work this out will repay you.

Training during a game should begin with simple plans. The most useful and necessary things are such as, which piece to exchange and which to leave on. This is a key question in many positions, and can form a plan in itself.

Another basis can be the regrouping of pieces, or of just one piece. Achieving harmony in your position may be very necessary when it is not clear what else you should be undertaking.

Always remember the value of analogies. The player who has 'collected' in his memory a number of sound plans will often find the opportunity to apply them, so easing the burden on himself: that is why the reader has been offered a large number of examples in this section.

One final point. Be sure that you formulate your plan in words (of course to yourself in internal monologue—you will be able to share them with others later when you write notes or demonstrate the game). A schoolteacher of mine used this method to establish whether we knew the meaning of a word. If we could give a succinct definition then we knew the word. If we floundered about, we didn't know it. It is the same with plans. Consider that you have a plan only when you can formulate it in words in your mind. Otherwise there is no plan.

EXERCISES

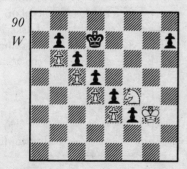

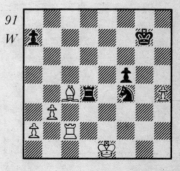

90
W

91
W

Find the four stage plan of realizing White's material advantage.

Formulate a plan for realizing the extra pawn. State which positional factors help this plan.

92
W

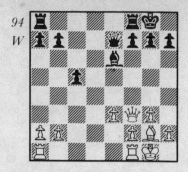

94
W

Assess the position. Formulate the positional elements which play the main part. State the steps of the winning plan.

Assess. Find a plan for each side. Indicate what moves Black will play if faced with passive play.

93
W

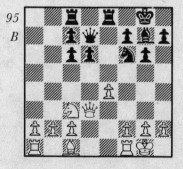

95
B

Assess. What does White's advantage consist of? Form the plan to realize these factors.

Form a plan for Black for the next few moves. Indicate the appropriate moves.

Assess. Find the best plan for Black.

Assess. Find a defensive plan for the weaker side.

3 Combinational Vision

Training Combinational Vision

The audience at an international tournament is like a theatre audience. Their gaze is fixed on the stage, but not so much at the 'actors', as at the demonstration boards. The comparative quietness of the audience is normally disturbed only when a surprising move is played, say when a piece is placed en prise. Sometimes someone will wave to the game demonstrators to indicate that he thinks they have put up the wrong move. But no! This time there is no error. The opponent replies, accepts the sacrifice, and a series of moves follow. Only then does the audience come to realize what is going on. A combination·has been played, a sacrifice made, and admiration is the order of the day.

Why was the grandmaster confident he saw the future whereas the audience thought it a mistake? The simple answer is that the grandmaster has a well developed combinational vision, the audience is less well qualified.

Is this a natural gift? Not really, otherwise the great players would have seen such combinations when they were very young. We know that child prodigies have played good chess, but rarely produced outstanding combinations. The marvellous productions of such combinational experts as Morphy, Alekhine and Tal came in their more mature period as a result of hard work and study. Of course a genius will master the subject better and quicker than one less well gifted, but we conclude that study and hard work will enable anyone interested in the subject to develop his eye for combinations.

The question might be posed whether a player cannot get by without a thorough mastery of this art. After all there are grandmasters in whose play you will not find complicated combinations and sacrifices. Their games do not figure in the anthologies of brilliancies, they play without putting anything en prise, not minor pieces, not even

122

pawns. They carry out quiet positional plans, and if they attack then they try to do it without sacrifices.

However, this point of view is not quite correct. Even if our positional master does not carry out startling sacrifices, he has to be aware of combinational ideas and foresee short simple combinations if only to circumvent them on the part of the opponent.

Elementary combinations are the basis of the whole chess struggle, and are the inevitable accompaniment of both strategical plans and tactical battles, such as one finds in pretty well every game.

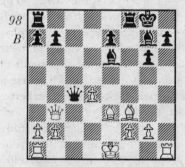

Smyslov–Botvinnik,
World Ch. match 1958

Botvinnik commented on the position of diagram 98, 'Here White offered a draw, and after White's last move 16 ♕d1–b3 it was accepted—but wrongly! From my old friend A. Model I learned that after 16 ... ♖×f3! 17 gf ♕c6 18 ♕d1 ♗d5 19 ♖h3 (19 ♖c1 ♕e6

20 b3 ♖f8 also favours Black) 19 ... ♕e6 Black would win the a2 pawn for the exchange. Then by forming on the Q-side a second passed pawn and combining this with an attack on the weakened refuge of the king Black would have excellent winning chances. I examined this sacrifice at the time, but my old failing—a weakness of combinational vision—told. I missed after 17 ♕×c4 the intermediate move 17 ... ♖×e3+.'

If we leave on one side the excessive modesty of a player who had been world champion for ten years at that time, we must note that even a player of Botvinnik's strength had to take account of combinational vision and try to improve it.

How does one improve in this respect? By analysing at home complicated positions. Just as a pianist practises the most complicated pieces to improve the technique of his fingers, so too a grandmaster must keep his vision in trim by daily analysis of positions with sharp possibilities, and this applies whether he prefers such positions in his play or not.

So we conclude that whatever your inclinations you must have combinational vision and keep it in regular trim by practising analysis of positions which have sharp or forcing possibilities. If you don't do this you will regress.

However there are compensations in this task. Great pleasure can be had in discovering combinations, or in working through the combinations of others. Some are real works of art which will give pleasure throughout the ages. We all know how worked up a player can get when going through such combinations. It is said that Alekhine sometimes got so excited with the position that he jumped up from the board and ran round it 'like a hawk'. It was Alekhine too who when asked what were the qualities which made for success at chess stressed the need to know your own strong points and defects as well as those of the opponent and then added, 'Thirdly a player must have a higher aim than passing satisfaction. I see this aim in scientific and creative achievements which put chess on a par with a number of other arts.'

Chessboard Drama

Combinations can entrance us by their surprising turns and dramatic content. Here we find one of the most surprising moves ever played *(99)*.

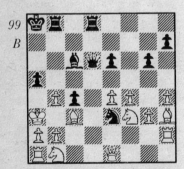

99
B

Koskinen–Kasman,
Helsinki, 1967

  1 ...   ♕×b4+!
  2 ♗×b4   ♖d2!!

Could you possibly imagine such a move with the rook putting itself en prise to five (!) pieces. All this with a sacrifice of the queen. Yet each one of the five captures leads to mate. The knights cannot take, nor the bishop because the rook at h2 is shut off and 3 ... ♘c2 mate follows. If the rook takes, the queen is shut off and there is mate by 3 ... a×b4.

  3 ♕×d2   ♘c2+!
  4 ♕×c2   ab mate.

A superb finish. Note that after 3 ♕×d2 the queen was blocking the defensive line of the rook at h2.

The striking and unexpected nature of some combinative blows produces entrancing impressions. One cannot but be delighted by the next finish, although the idea had already occurred in games by Marshall and Alekhine *(100)*.

  1 ♗×d5   cd
  2 ♘f6+   ♔h8
  3 ♕g6!!

Such a move, putting the queen en prise to two pawns cannot but excite the true chess artist. Yet it

Rossolimo–Reissman
Puerto-Rico, 1967

Kotov–Holmov,
Moscow Team Ch. 1972

cannot be taken—3 ... h×g6 4 ♖h3 mate, or, 3 ... f×g6 4 ♘×g6+. Black defends the vulnerable h7 square from afar.

3 ...   ♕c2
4 ♖h3!   1–0

How pleasant a feeling it is to play such moves. You get the feeling that you are creating something valuable which will attract the attention of thousands of chess fans.

The author has lived a long chess life and played a number of beautiful and tricky combinations, but his heart still beats faster when he is able to play a queen sacrifice *(101)*.

1 ♖×c5!   ♖×c5
2 ♖c2   ♖fc8
3 ♕b5!

Now if 3 ... ♖×b5 then first 4 ♖×c8+, then 5 ♗×a7. So Black must take the rook.

3 ...   ♖×c2
4 ♗×a7   ♖×a2
5 ♗c5!   1–0

White had only one move to save his bishop and stop the mate on c1.

The triumph of inferior forces, of the little man, as in Charlie Chaplin films, is a powerful device favoured by drama writers. It also produces a strong effect on the chess fan. The dramatic effect of many combinations and studies is based on this. Who can fail to admire the following piece when he sees it for the first time? Black has his whole army intact, White has just one little pawn *(102)*.

Moreover White promotes not to

the powerful queen but to a lowly knight. Yet then the mighty army is vanquished.

The following position was quoted round the world *(103)*.

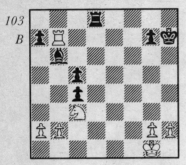

Ortueta–Sanz, Madrid, 1934

Black starts by occupying the 7th, always useful.

    1 ...   ♖d2

    2 ♘a4   ♖×b2!

The start of a brilliant combination based on pawn promotion.

    3 ♘×b2   c3

Now if 4 ♘d3 (the only square from which to catch the pawn) then 4 ... c4+ 5 ♖×b6 cd and one pawn queens.

    4 ♖×b6   c4!

Not 4 ... ab? 5 ♘d3. Black intends to queen the c3 pawn. If 5 ♘×c4 c2.

    5 ♖b4   a5!! *(104)*

An amazing position. Two doubled isolated pawns beat rook and knight.

    6 ♘a4   cb

    0–1

A quick glance at the following

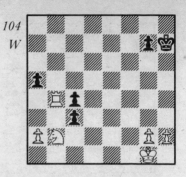

position, a study by Chekhover, is sufficient to convince one that White is hopelessly lost *(105)*.

The threat is ♖h2, winning the f2 pawn with White's king cut off. Then Black will penetrate with his king via f5. Resistance seems hopeless, yet here too David beats Goliath.

    1 ♔d1 ♖h2 2 ♔e1! ♖×g2 3 ♔f1 ♖h2 4 ♔g1 ♖h3 5 ♔g2 ♖h6 6 f3 *(106)*.

A surprising position in which a rook up is not enough to win. White will play ♔g1 and ♔g2 not letting the rook in at the rear. If ♖e6 then ♔f2 to stop ♖e1. Nor can the black

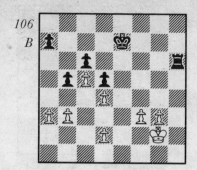

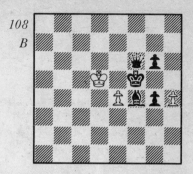

king penetrate anywhere. Finally if Black tries to win by sacrificing his rook on e4 after playing ♔f5 then the resulting pawn ending is only a draw.

Here is another triumph of miserly force over a whole army (*107*) It is a study by A. Kazantsev.

shown in the theatre and cinema, and here too there are examples of its equivalent in chess (*109*).

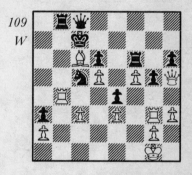

Mason–Winawer,
Vienna, 1882

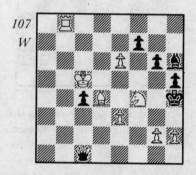

1 e7! ♕a3+ 2 ♖b4 ♕a7+ 3 ♔×c4 ♕×e7 4 ♘×g6+! f×g6 5 ♗f6+! ♕×f6 6 ♔d5+ ♔g5 7 h4+ ♔f5 8 g4+! h×g4 9 ♖f4+! ♗×f4 10 e4 mate (*108*).

Truly a beautiful demonstration of the greatness of spirit over crude inanimate force.

Cunning is another quality often

The first few moves of the combination are fairly straight-forward.

1 ♖×g5 hg 2 ♕h7+ ♘d7 (not 2 ... ♔d8 3 ♕h8+ ♔e7 4 ♕g7+ ♖f7 5 f6+ and White wins) 3 ♗×d7

At first sight 3 ... ♕×d7 seems forced, leaving the rook at b8 en prise after the exchange of queens.

3 ...   ♕g8!

Now it looks nothing like so simple to win, but . . .

4 &Rb7+!   &Kx b7
5 &Bc8+!*(110)* 1-0

110
B

In the next example, a composition by Konstantinopolsky, Black looks hopelessly placed *(111)*.

111
B

There is a threat of mate in two by &Qxh6+ and knight discovers check, or &Ng4 at once. In fact Black can win, though his various threatening moves do not appear to have enough time to come to fruition.

1 . . .   &Re1+!

Why?, the reader may wonder.

Only later will he realize that e1 has to be blocked as a potential flight square.

2 &Rxe1   &Qxc2+!!
3 &Kxc2 &Nd4+ 4 &Kb1 (4 &Kd1
&Nxb2 mate)
4 . . . &Nc3+! 5 bxc3 (5 &Ka1 &Nc2
mate)
5 . . . &Rb8+ 6 &Ka1 &Nc2 mate.

Continuing our analogy with the theatre and the cinema, we have chess positions that like ballet and opera are based for their appeal on the beauty of the construction.

112
W

I am always impressed by the cross-fire action of the line working pieces as in this study by Troitsky *(112)*.

1 c6 b2 (not 1 . . . &Be4 2 c7 &Bb7
3 &Bg2) 2 c7 b1/&Q (or 2 . . . &Bg6+
3 &Kd8 b1/&Q 4 c8/&Q+ &Ka7 5
&Qc7+ &Ka8 6 &Bg2+ &Be4 7 &Qc8
and mates since the &B at e4 is
pinned) 3 c8/&Q+ &Ka7 4 &Qc7+
&Ka8 5 &Bg2+ &Be4 6 &Qh7! *(113)*.

Black must lose his queen or be mated. The pattern of double attack on diagonals or file/rank is

113
B

sometimes known as the Maltese Cross.

A position from a Moscow Championship game *(114)*.

114
B

1 ... ♖a2+ 2 ♖e2 and the rooks were exchanged with a draw resulting. Yet Black could have won by 2 ... ♕e3!

A sword fight with blows from both sides is another favourite theatrical device; the analogy with chess is most dramatically seen in combinational complications. Positional play is the confirmation of generally accepted points, whereas combinational play is the denial of all that is obvious: the one underlines accepted values, the other causes the re-assessment of values.

Here is a study that I greatly admired when I saw it in Lasker's textbook, in my childhood *(115)*.

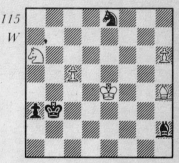

115
W

Study by Villeneuf-Esclapon

White wins as a result of blow and counter-blow, each of which is attack and defence as in a sword fight.

1 ♘b4 ♔×b4 2 h7 ♗e5 3 ♔×e5 a2 4 ♗e1+ ♔b3 5 ♗c3! ♔×c3 6 h8 = ♕ a1 = ♕ 7 ♔f4+ wins.

In this position *(116)* Black struck White a serious positional blow by 27 ... f5, a move based on very complicated combinative lines. Having analysed the position Petrosian did not take en passant, and after 28 f4 ♕d7 29 ♔f2 ♔f7 it ended in a draw. The main interest lies in the variation 28 ef ♖×e2 29 ♖×e2 ♖×e2 30 ♕f8+ ♔h7 31 f7. White has given up a rook to get a powerful attack.

There would follow 31 ... ♘f6 32 ♘e4!! de 33 ♗e7 ef! An

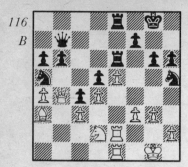

Petrosian–Bangiyev,
Moscow, 1973

unpleasant move to face. Petrosian saw this far, and could not find a winning blow. Thus if 34 ♕×h6+ ♔×h6 35 f8 = ♕+ ♔h7 36 ♕f7+ ♔h6 and it is only a draw, while 34 ♗×f6? loses to 34 ... f2+ 35 ♔f1 ♕h1+ 36 ♔×e2 f1 = ♕+.

However an hour after the game while still on his way home, the ex-world champion 'saw' in his mind's eye that there is 34 ♕g7+!! ♔×g7 35 f8 = ♕+ ♔h7 36 ♕f7+ ♔h8 37 ♗×f6 mate.

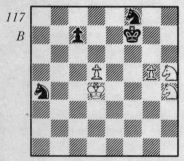

Sergeyev–Kotov,
Moscow Ch. 1935

In the position of diagram 117,

my opponent had an extra pawn, but Black has good drawing chances. During the actual game each player commented to his opponent that he was setting him a study to solve!

1 ... c6! 2 dc ♘e6+ 3 ♔e5 ♘×g5 4 ♘f4 ♔e7 5 ♘d5+ ♔d8 6 ♘f3! ♔f7+! 7 ♔e6 ♘b6!!

Now the last pawn falls and Black draws.

Art only becomes worthwhile and essential when it reflects actual life in some way. Chess is a form of abstract thought, but the chess pieces have long been used to form pictures from life.

Here are some examples. The author hopes that the reader will develop a taste for this sort of thing, since I must repeat that the development of a strong feeling for beauty in chess is a sign of appreciation of the unusual, which is an indication that your combinational vision is improving. This cannot but be helpful in competitive play.

White wins from diagram 118 in

an original fashion. There are many ways to force victory, but the author's solution is the most original by far.

1 f3+ gf 2 ed+ cd 3 ♗f5+ ef 4 ♖e6+ de 5 ♘f6+ gf 6 ♖d4+ cd 7 a8=♗+ ♕d5 8 ♗×d5+ ed 9 ♕e5+ fe 10 ♘g5 mate *(119)*.

♘×g4 ♔h7 (at no stage can Black allow d8=♕+) 5 ♘ef6+ ♔g7 6 ♘e6+ ♔f7 7 d8=♘+ ♔e7 8 c8=♘ mate *(121)*.

121
B

Here is a chase as in a Western cowboy film *(122)*.

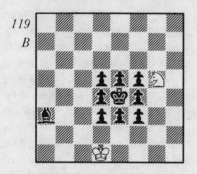

119
B

The author called his composition 'The Iron Cage of Tamerlane'.

122
W

1 ♖h3+ ♔g5 2 ♖h5+ ♔f4 3 ♖f5+ ♔e3 4 ♖f3+ ♔d4 5 ♖d3+ ♔c5 6 ♖d5+ ♔b6 7 ♖b5+ ♔c7 8 ♖b7+ ♔d8 9 ♖d7 mate.

Another chase *(123)*, but this time 'They got away'.

1 ♘g4+ ♔e7 2 ♘f5+ ♔d7 3 ♘e5+ ♔c8 4 ♘e7+ ♔b8 5 ♘d7+ ♔a7 6 ♘c8+ ♔a6 7

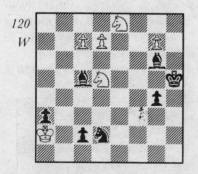

120
W

Korolkov called this position *(120)* 'Budyonny's Cavalry'. White wins by 1 ♘f4+ ♔h6 2 g8=♘+! ♔h7 3 ♘gf6+ ♔h6 4

123
W

♘b8+	♚b5	8	♘a7+	♚b4	9
♘a6+	♚c3	10	♘b5+	♚d3	11
♘b4+	♚e2	12	♘c3+	♚f2	13
♘d3+	♚g3	14	♘e4+	♚g4	15
♘e5+	♚f5	16	♘g3+	♚f6	17

♘g4+ and so on from the start.

The conclusion for the reader to draw from these fine examples is that chess combinations are a sort of dramatic work of art, full of tension and aesthetic content. It is for this facet of the game more than any other that millions of people throughout the world love chess.

Now that we have seen the romanticism of combinations we can settle down to their mechanism, and try to develop our eye for combinations by trying the exercises. A love for this is necessary in order to improve.

The Theory of Combinations

It is useful to master some concepts of the constituent parts of combinations. After a great deal of discussion in Soviet chess literature about the correct definition of a combination, it was decided that from the point of view of a methodical approach it was best to settle on this definition:—A combination is a forced variation with a sacrifice.

This definition fits in well with earlier ideas. Thus Lasker wrote that 'By positional play a master tries to prove and exploit true values, whereas by combinations he seeks to refute false values . . . A combination produces an unexpected re-assessment of values.' Clearly what he has in mind here is the sacrifice which leads to the triumph in given circumstances of lesser forces over greater.

Or take this quotation from Botvinnik, 'What is the essence of a combination? From his first steps a player is taught the normal material values of the pieces. It is known that a rook is stronger than a knight, that a bishop is about equal to three pawns, and a bishop and two pawns is about worth a rook, and a queen is stronger than a rook and so on.

However there are positions where these relationships cease to apply, where, for example, a queen turns out to be weaker than a pawn. The path to such positions lies through the sacrifice'.

I must point out that the definition which we have adopted fails to include many fine combinations in which there were no sacrifices, but it is a handy definition for the purpose of instruction.

In order to clarify the constituent parts of a combination and what they consist of, it is best to examine a simple concrete example *(124)*.

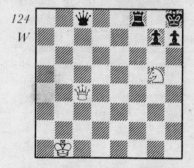

124
W

White delivers the well-known smothered mate by the following forced variation involving a sacrifice.

1 ♘f7+ ♚g8 2 ♘h6++ ♚h8 3 ♕g8+ ♖×g8 4 ♘f7 mate.

First of all what features of the position made the combination possible? The presence of two pawns blocking flight squares, the lack of space for the king that gives the mate its name.

Such factors are called in chess theory the motif of the combination, the reason for it arising, the special features which enable the sacrifice to be made so that a specified aim can be achieved.

As Lasker put it, 'The range of circumstances in which it is possible to presuppose the presence of a combination is very limited. The presence of such circumstances is the reason for the genesis of the idea in the master's brain'.

The next vital element of a combination is the final position which we are striving to reach. This position is called the theme of the combination. In our example, the theme position was the position when the king was mated and the name smothered mate is the name of this particular theme.

In order to reach the final position from the initial one, we have to make a series of moves which carry out the desired transformation. This series of moves that turn the initial position into the thematic one are called the means of the combination. In our example the means are the check on f7, the double check on h6, the queen sacrifice on g8 and finally the mating move to f7.

One important further condition has to be mentioned. In addition to the main features or reasons making a combination feasible, there are always subsidiary features. In our example the combination would not have existed if the queen was not at c4 (or e6) since Black could then meet ♘f7+ by taking the knight, and would be two pawns up. These subsidiary features have always to be taken into account when seeking a combination. They can be appropriately named the particular features of the position.

The Basic Themes

All possible combinations can be divided into three basic types, which can be further sub-divided as follows:—

Mating Combinations
1. Smothered mate
2. The 7th and 8th ranks
3. Verticals and diagonals.
4. Attack on weak points.
5. Drawing out the king.
6. Destroying the guard of the king.

Pawn Combinations
1. The 'quicksilver' pawn.
2. The pawn wedge.
3. The pawn phalanx.

The bad position of pieces
1. Double attack.
2. Trapping.
3. Pinning.
4. Line Closing.
5. Diversion.
6. Attraction.
7. Ambush.
8. Overloading.

Let us go through these sub-headings with one or two examples of each type.

Smothered mate

We have already seen one example of smothered mate, in its purest form, though there are other ways in which the defending king is forced by the attacker to surround himself by self-blocking units *(125)*.

125
W

Tal–Portisch,
Biel Interzonal 1976

White has given up a piece for the attack, the defender's knights are far away from the king.

34 ♕f7+   ♔h8
35 ♖d1   ♕c8
36 ♘g5!

Creates many threats e.g. 37 ♕h5 h6 38 ♘×h6! mating.

36 ...   ♗f6
37 ♘h6!

A fine blow which leaves Black unable to defend against smothered mate. If 37 ... ♖e7 38 ♕×e7 ♗×e7 39 ♘gf7 mate, and against other moves comes 38 ♕g8+ ♖×g8 39 ♘f7 mate.

The 7th and 8th ranks

Interesting complications occur here using the lack of defence of the back two ranks *(126)*.

28 ... ♗b5! 29 ♕×c7 ♗×d4+
30 ♖f2 (otherwise the ♖ at f1 is

Kaklauskas–Kiselev,
Vilnius, 1976

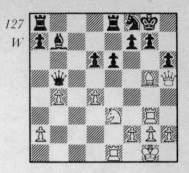

Torre–Lasker, Moscow, 1925

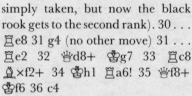

Tal–Olafsson, Las Palmas, 1975

simply taken, but now the black rook gets to the second rank). 30 . . .
♖e8 31 g4 (no other move) 31 . . .
♖e2 32 ♕d8+ ♔g7 33 ♖c8
♗×f2+ 34 ♔h1 ♖a6! 35 ♕f8+
♔f6 36 c4

Black now went wrong by 36 . . .
♖a1+ letting the king slip away to
h3. The simple 36 . . . ♗h4! wins
since there is no perpetual check
e.g. 37 ♕d8+ ♔e5, or 37 ♕h8+
♔g5 38 f4+ ♔×g4 39 h3+ ♔f5 40
b3 f6 and mate on a1 follows.

Attacking rooks are particularly
fearsome when supported by a
bishop on the long diagonal. A
typical theme then is the 'windmill'
(127).

1 ♗f6! ♕×h5 2 ♖×g7+ ♔h8 3
♖×f7+ ♔g8 4 ♖g7+ ♔h8 5
♖×b7+ ♔g8 6 ♖g7+ ♔h8 7
♖g5+ ♔h7 8 ♖×h5 ♔g6 9 ♖h3
♔×f6 10 ♖×h6+ 1–0

In diagram 128 White has carelessly weakened his back row.

1 . . .   ♕f4!!
2 ♖e7!

Trying to save himself by a
counter blow. If 2 ♕e2 ♖×e4, or 2
♕e1 ♗×f3 with obvious advantage
to Black. Now Black must not
accept the queen by 2 . . . ♖×d2 as
White gets two rooks for the queen
by 3 ♖×e8+ and 4 ♘×d2.

2 . . .   ♖f8!

Very strong, despite its modest
appearance. If 3 ♕e2 ♗×f3 4 gf
♕g5+ winning a rook, or 4 ♕×f3
♕d6! and the back row mate
threat wins the rook again. 3 ♕c1
also loses—3 . . . ♗×f3 4 gf
♕×f3 5 ♖d2 ♕g4+ 6 ♔h1 ♕g5

and once again Black wins material.

The weakness of the back two ranks are sometimes exploited by the help of a passed pawn *(129)*.

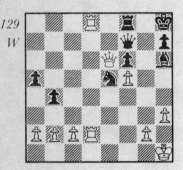

129
W

Ljubojević–Milicević,
Yugoslavia, 1974

1 ♖2d7!   ♕×e6
Not 1 ... ♘×d7 2 ♕×f7 ♖×d8
3 ♕e7, nor 1 ... ♕h5 2 ♕×f6+
♔g8 3 ♕×e5, nor 1 ... ♔g8 2
♖×f8 ♕×f8 3 ♖c7! and 4 ♖c8.
2 fe   ♘×d7
(2 ... ♔g8 3 e7! ♘×d7 4
♖×f8+ ♘×f8 5 e8=♕)
3 e7!   ♔g7
4 ♖×f8   1–0

Verticals and diagonals

In diagram 130 White makes elegant use of the weakened b1/h7 diagonal.
1 ♖f6!
Blocking the f7 pawn to prevent a freeing advance f5. Black cannot take the rook since 2 e5 forces mate.
1 ...   ♔g8
2 e5   h6

130
W

Fischer–Benko, USA Ch. 1963/4

3 ♘e2!   1–0
If the knight retreats then 4 ♕f5 mating on the diagonal, and 3 ... ♗×f6 loses to 4 ♕×h6.

Weak Points

131
W

Spassky–Korensky, Sochi, 1973

In diagram 131 Black has weak points at f7, g7 and h7. First of all White presses on g7, then transfers the attack to the others.

1 ♗×g7! ♔×g7 2 ♕f6+ ♔f8 3 ♖hf1 ♖c7 4 ♘×d5 .ed 5 e6! ♕×a2 6 e7+ ♔g8 (6 ... ♖×e7? 7 ♕h8 mate) 7 ♕×f7+ ♔h8 8 c8=♕+ and Black soon resigned.

Drawing out the King

Here sacrifices are used to winkle the king out from his comfortable quarters to the centre, or even into the enemy camp, where he duly perishes *(132)*.

Bakulin–Sokolov, USSR, 1973

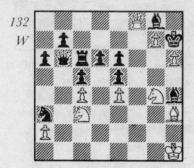

Melikov–Shakhnazarov, USSR, 1974

1 ♕×g8+! ♔×g8 2 ♘f6+ ♗×f6 3 ♗×e6+ ♔h7 4 g8=♕+ ♔×h6 5 ♗f5 ♗g7 6 ♕h7+ ♔g5 7 ♕g6+ ♔f4 8 ♕g4+ ♔e3 9 ♕e2+ ♔d4 (after 9 . . . ♔f4 the king is driven back to be mated on h6—10 ♘d5+ ♔g5 11 ♕g4+ and 12 ♕g6.) 10 ♘b5+!! ab 11 ♕d2+ ♔×c4 12 ♗e6+ mates.

Destroying the Guard

Logically enough the removal of the king's defenders enables the attacking pieces to do their worst *(133)*.

1 ♗×h6! gh 2 ♖g3+ ♔h8 3 ♕d2 ♘g8 4 ♖×g8+ ♔×g8 5 ♕×h6 f5 6 ♕g6+ ♔h8 7 ♖c3!

Bringing up the reserves. The possibility of such reinforcements

has always to be taken into account when analysing variations.

    7 . . .   ♖f6
    8 ♕h5+   ♔g7
    9 ♗×f5!

A further destruction. If 9 . . . ♖×f5 10 ♖g3+ ♖g5 11 ♖×g5+ ♗×g5 12 ♕f7+ and mates next move.

    9 . . .   ♖g8 10 ♖g3+ ♔f8 11 ♖×g8+ ♔×g8 12 ♕h7+ 1-0.

Pawn Combinations

Here we see the use of a passed pawn or passed pawns, or advanced pawns generally which are used actively. The squares on which they operate, or on which they rush forwards to promote, are normally weaknesses in the defender's camp.

The quicksilver pawn

A careful watch has to be kept on passed pawns or potential passed pawns lest they slip forward quickly *(134)*.

White had failed to do this here by his last move 45 ♔f5–g6? when

Ree–Zaitsev, Sochi, 1976

45 e6! should win. There followed:
45 ... h4 46 gh ♗b4! 47 e6
(or 47 ♗×b4 g3 48 e6 gf 49 e7
f1 = ♕ 50 e8 = ♕ ♕g2+! 51 ♔h6
f2 and gets a second queen) 47 ...
g3 48 e7 ♗×e7 49 fg ♗b4! 50 ♗f2
♗c5 51 ♗e1 f2 52 ♗×f2 ♗×f2
0–1.

The pawn wedge
Here too the mechanism is simple.
Exploiting the lack of control by the
pieces at one point a pawn pushes
forward into the enemy camp and
helps create mating threats (135).

Ivanović–Popović,
Yugoslavia, 1973

1 h6+   ♔h8
2 ♗e6!!

This puts the black bishop en
prise, but it cannot move as then 2
♕d4+ mates. Nor can it be defended —2 ... d5 3 ♕e5+. If 2 ...
♕×e6 then 3 ♕f8+ ♕g8 4 ♕f6+.

The pawn phalanx
A united pawn mass can be very
hard to cope with, especially if far
advanced. In some cases it is
possible to make considerable
sacrifices in order to get such a
phalanx (136).

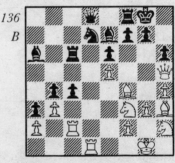

Cheremisin–Chumak, USSR, 1975

1 ...   cb!
2 ♖×c6   ba
3 ♘d2

White transfers his pieces to the
Q-side to cope with the enemy
pawns, but fresh sacrifices make the
phalanx even more dynamic.

3 ...   ♘c5!
4 ♖×a6   ♘×a6
5 ♘b3   ♘c5
6 ♘×c5   ♗×c5

7 ♗f1   b3
8 ♗c4   ♛d4!! *(137)*.

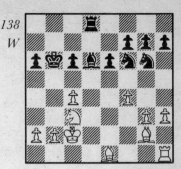

138
W

Karpov–Sergievsky,
Kuibyshev, 1970

137
W

The pawns are so strong that Black does not worry about his queen.

9 ♗×b3 a1 = ♛ 10 ♖×a1 ♛×a1+ 11 ♔g2 ♖b8 12 ♗×h6 ♗×f2 13 ♗f4 ♛g1+ 14 ♔h3 ♖×b3 15 ♛g5 ♖×g3+! 0–1

The Bad Position of Pieces
Various defects in piece placing can be exploited by combinations.

The Double Attack
The double attack or fork is learned by the beginner quite early on. It is based on some geometrical motif linking certain pieces which lets them be attacked simultaneously so that at least one of them must fall. Such combinations are very common, since the fork can be carried out by every unit from pawn to king *(138)*.

     1 c5+!

Forking king and bishop. If 1 . . . ♔×c5 2 ♗f2+ ♔b4 3 ♗b6 and mates, or 2 . . . ♔c4 3 a3!

threatening 4 b3 or 4 ♗f1 mate.
     1 . . .   ♗×c5
     2 ♘a4+   ♔b5
     3 ♔b3!

Mate threatens by 4 ♗f1. Black has to give up the exchange. 3 . . . ♖d3+ 4 ♗c3 ♖×c3+ 5 ♘×c3+ ♔a5 6 ♘a4 ♗f2 7 ♖c1 and Black soon resigned.

Trapping
In this case the active side uses his men to surround an enemy unit and forces it to be given up for a weaker piece *(139)*.

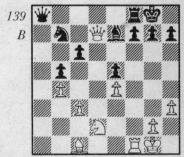

139
B

Karaklajić Bely,
Hungary–Jugoslavia, 1957

1 ... ♛c8! 2 ♛×e7? (He should exchange queens) 2 ... f6! 0–1. There is no defence to the threat of 3 ... ♖f7.

Pinning

This is another feature that the beginner soon learns: sacrifices can be made to bring about a decisive pin. Note that every unit can be pinned except the king. Here is a combination on the theme of pinning *(140)*:

1 ♘×e4!   ♘e×e4
2 ♖×e4   ♘×e4
3 ♖×e4   ♛×e4
4 ♘g5!

White has given up two rooks for a knight in order to pin the rook at g7. Now the attacked queen must move while defending against the smothered mate at f7.

4 ...   ♛g6
5 ♛×h7+!   ♚×h7
6 ♘f7 mate.

When a king is stuck in the centre, the action of rooks and bishops can lead to decisive pins *(141)*.

Kotov–Kalmanok, Tula, 1931

This is a possibility in the game which did not actually occur.

1 ♛g7 ♖f8 2 ♖×d5 ed 3 ♘f6+ ♗×f6 4 ♘g6+ ♗e7 5 ♛×f8 mate.

Always bear in mind that a pin is not necessarily a permanent feature: there may also arise some possibility of forcibly breaking a pin by a combinative stroke.

Line Closing

This feature occurs frequently, and is sometimes banal, but here is a spectacular example *(142):*—

White has a clear win, and such

Silich–Rokhlin, USSR Ch. 1929

moves as 1 ♕f8+ or 1 ♔h2 would win without difficulty. White decided to win the queen.

    1 ♖f8+   ♔h7
    2 ♗e4+

The losing move, brilliantly refuted. White could still win by 2 ♕e4+ ♗×e4 3 ♗×e4+ ♖gg6 4 ♗×g6+ and 5 ♖×c8.

    2 . . .   ♕f5!
    0–1

The queen occupies the critical point at the intersection of various files, ranks and diagonals. As the reader will see, White has no defence.

143
W

Lloyd–Moore, London, 1879

This position *(143)* saw an equally fantastic move. Black's pieces are ready to deal with any discovered check from the rook at h3 by blocking with ♖h6, or capturing the checking rook.

    1 ♕e6!!

Occupying the intersection point of the h3/c8 diagonal and the sixth rank. If 1 . . . ♗×e6 2 ♘f5+ and 3 ♘e7 mate, if 1 . . . ♘×e6 or 1 . . .

♖×e6 then 2 ♘g6+ and 3 ♖h8 mate. Other moves do not parry the threatened discovered check.

Diversion

If often happens that a piece is firmly posted on a square where it blocks our approach to the king or hinders the execution of our intentions. Then it may be worth a great deal of material to divert it from its post *(144)*:

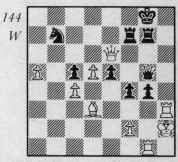

144
W

Johansson–Rey, Postal, 1935

The check on e8 is obvious but then 1 ♕e8+ ♖f8 and 2 ♖h8+ gets nowhere—2 . . . ♔×h8 3 ♕×f8+ ♖g8 with a further obstacle. The diversion of the defending queen is called for to provide a follow-up to this sequence!

    1 ♖×g4! ♕×g4 2 ♕e8+ ♖f8 3 ♖h8+ ♔×h8 4 ♕×f8+ ♖g8 5 ♕h6 mate.

Attraction

Sometimes our task is not to divert a unit from a vital square, but to attract it to a square so that we can profit from it *(145)*.

145
B

Gendel–Sushkevich,
Moscow, 1956

Black has the initiative on the K-side, and wishes to profit from the pinned f- pawn which makes the bishop at g3 an object of attack.

  1 ...   Rhg8
  2 Rd3   Rab8!

There was the slow 2 ... Ng5, but this innocent move is much stronger, driving the queen to a square on the third rank not guarded by the bishop at c4.

  3 Qc3   Rxg3+
  4 Rxg3   Rg8!
  5 Rxg8   Qxc3
     0–1

From diagram 146 Black attracts the rook onto a vulnerable square while gaining time for his bishop to deliver a blow.

  1 ... Bc7 2 Rf6 (2 Rd7? Bh2+) 2 ... Bd8 3 Rd6 Be7 4 Rb6 Qxb6! 5 Qxb6 Bc5+ and Black duly won.

146
B

Lasker–Ragozin, Moscow, 1935

The Ambush

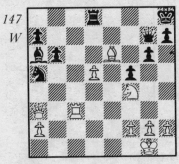

147
W

Furman–Smyslov, USSR Ch. 1948

At first sight, in diagram 147, Black has no problems, but a quiet move just one square long changes the assessment.

  1 Qb2!   Nc4

Black could find nothing better than this in view of the threats 2 Nxg6+ hg 3 Rh3 mate, or 2 ... Qxg6 3 Rg3+. If 1 ... h6 then 2 Rc7! Qxb2 3 Nxg6 mate.

  2 Nxg6+ Qxg6 3 Rxc4+ Qg7 4 Qxg7+ Kxg7 5 Rc7+ Kf6 6 f4 and won easily.

This is just one example of an

ambush, a frequently recurring feature, though the term itself is more frequently used in chess composition: it is defined in the 1964 Soviet 'Chess Dictionary' as the positioning of a long ranging piece behind its own or an enemy piece, whose movement opens up the action of the ambushing piece on to a certain square or along a certain line. Here is another illustration *(148):*

Barcza–Bronstein, Moscow, 1959

1 ... ♘×d3 2 ♕×f5 ♘×e1! (The rook and knight now form the ambush with the threat of mate by 3 ... ♘f3++.) 3 ♔f1! ♘e2+! (3 ... gf 4 ♗×e1 prolongs it) 4 ♗c1! ♖×c1+ 5 ♔e2 ♘d4+ 6 ♔d2 ♘b3+ and taking the queen leaves Black two pieces up.

The Mind of a Grandmaster

Now we have to deal with the difficult process of the origin and realization of combinations. To this end we must work through, step by

Overloading

There are positions in which everything looks safe, but where the experienced eye will spot that a defending piece has too many functions to carry out and so is overloaded *(149).*

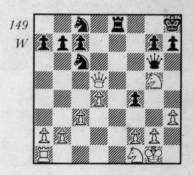

1 ♘f7+   ♔g8
2 ♘d6+   ♕e6

At first sight Black has coped. If 3 ♕×e6 ♖×e6 4 ♘×c8 ♖e8 recovering the knight at the cost of just a pawn.

However the queen is overloaded, guarding the rook and screening off the a2/g8 diagonal.

3 ♖e1!   ♕×d5
4 ♖×e8 mate.

Further cases of overloading will be seen in the exercises at the end of Part Two.

step, the thought processes of the player who discovers and carries out a combination at the board.

Certain dramatists allege that

the idea for an episode or a whole scene in their plays strikes them as a sudden flash of inspiration which can come to them in the most unexpected places, at the most unexpected time.

Something similar can happen to a grandmaster at the board, but it is not an accident, it has been prepared by the play leading up to that particular position. Even many moves before the actual combination arises he may have had a feeling, or even the certainty that a combination is latent. This thought is suggested by certain motifs in the position. For example if he sees a weakened long black diagonal, he will feel that it would be nice to find a way of exploiting this. Or if the opponent fails to make a bolt hole for his king, there will arise the desire to achieve a back rank mate.

One might say that the appearance of combinative motifs in a position provokes an urge in the player to seek a forcing line, a mood to play combinatively. The mood may change if the position becomes simplified, but in tense situations this mood is present to the maximum extent. In the majority of cases his search for combinations, even in sharp positions, is not crowned with success—the position turns out not to be 'ripe' for such a solution, but suddenly, in the appropriate circumstances, the player is rewarded for his unremitting effort by the 'explosion' of a brilliant combination.

Using the terms we have previously defined, we might say that by going through the motifs of a given position we choose a corresponding thematic position for them. Or, on the other hand, knowing that a certain theme is possible, say back row mate, we seek the appropriate means, the measures required to reach the desired goal.

Through Means to the Theme

In many cases, probably the majority of them, a combination arises in the mind in the process of going through various plausible lines of play. When we start the calculations, we do not know the sort of thematic position we are aiming for; it arises in our mind after careful study of the available motifs followed by examining various ways of playing, one of which becomes the means of our combination.

Let us imagine White's train of thought in diagram 150. We work on the assumption that he has come fresh to the position and so has to work it all out from the start, though in actual fact he has been sitting at the board for about three hours and his mind is already filled with the possibilities before him.

He would be working it out along these lines:—What do I have? His king is badly placed, but I still have

150
W

to exploit that. I have the d and f files, a strong knight at d4. Must hurry before he can slip away with the king to safety at b8. His last move was rook to e4 attacking the knight. Defend it by ♕f2? He'll go ♖d8. No, then I go ♕f6+ winning. So he'll go ♕g5 or ♕e5 centralizing, and then what do I have?

Wait a minute. What about ♘f5+? He has no choice, takes and I go ♖×f5. Then he can't take rook—mate on d6 by the queen. But he doesn't have to take. What do I have after ♕c6 or ♕c7? A piece gone. What about ♖f5 instead? Well we are playing for mate, so a rook down wouldn't matter if it's sound. If his queen moves then ♕g5+ with a powerful attack. Nor can he meet the rook sac by e5, since we go ♕g5+ ♔f8, ♘e6+. So he has to take the rook and I take on f5 with knight, check. Then his king is drawn forward.

But what if he doesn't take? Say ♕d6; but then I win the queen by ♖×f7+ ♗×f7, ♘f5+.

So he definitely has to take, and

then I must have something. An interesting position! So, 25 ♖f5 ef 26 ♘×f5+ ♔f6 (26 ... ♔e6 makes no difference) 27 ♖d6+. Two lines. Takes the knight or rook blocks. If 27 ... ♖e6 the win is easy: 28 ♕g7+ ♔×f5 29 ♗c2+ and now 29 ... ♔f4 30 ♕g3 mate, or 29 ... ♖e4 30 ♕f6+ ♔g4 31 ♗d1+ and mate next move. So there remains 27 ... ♔×f5. Then what did I see? Oh, yes! 28 ♕f3+ ♖f4 (28 ... ♔g5 and White wins simply, 29 ♕f6+ ♔h5 30 ♗d1+ ♖g4 31 ♕h6 mate) 29 ♕h5+ ♔e4 30 ♗c2+ ♔e3. Can he really get away safe from there? No, there's 31 ♖d3+ and wherever he goes 32 ♖d2+ and mate by 33 ♕e2. It's all there!

Just check once more. How do I stand on the clock? Ten minutes left. I'll check again. After all it's a question of a forced win, so time trouble won't matter too much.

That is the way it went in the actual game*. What can we say about the method of finding the combination? White stated the motifs—the bad king-position, the open files. Nor did he fail to notice the special features of the position—the bishop at e8 that made ♕d6 mate possible in some lines. The thematic position was quite unknown to White at the

---

*Tr. Note. Although the author does not state it, the game is Kotov–
   Yudovich, USSR Ch. 1939

start, yet there were several such positions—every mating position that arose. Thus White went through the means of the combination (or more accurately speaking he sought continuations that became the means) and saw that he could draw out the king into his own position and there give mate, so there were various thematic positions according to the way Black chose.

This was a typical example of finding a combination by the sequence motif—means—theme.

Here is another example of the same pattern *(151)*.

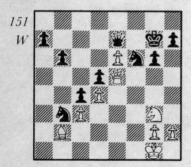

151
W

Botvinnik–Capablanca,   Avro, 1938

We shall again try to establish the thought process, and apologize to the ex-world champion if the way we depict it is less deep and quick than his method at the time. At least the device has teaching value.

So, White to move. The tension in the position indicates that there might be a forced way to win. What

motifs? Mainly the passed pawn at e6. Two moves forward and queens. Also my strong queen at e5, the distance of the knight at b3 from the scene of action. Removing the blockading queen would be desirable. The only way is ♗a3. What other use for the bishop which is otherwise dominated by the knight? Possibly 30 ♘h5+ gh 31 ♕g5+ ♔f8 and only then 32 ♗a3.

In any event the sacrifices at a3 and h5 clearly figure as possibilities. After ♕g5+ where would the king go? Makes no difference, since after ♕×f6+ the king must go to g8— ♔e8 allows mate in two by ♕f7+ and ♕d7. So ♔g8 and then either ♕f7+ and e7 or e7 at once. Clearly we get a new queen and the whole question is whether Black has perpetual check in the interim.

So 30 ♗a3 ♕×a3 31 ♘h5+ gh 32 ♕g5+ ♔h8 33 ♕×f6+ ♔g8 34 e7. Now consider the checks 34... ♕c1+ 35 ♔f2 ♕c2+ 36 ♔g3 ♕d3+ 37 ♔h4 ♕e4+ 38 ♔×h5 ♕e2+ 39 ♔h4 ♕e4+ 40 g4 and the checks have run out. Fine! (It was later proved that there was a win too by 34 ♕f7+ ♔h8 35 e7 ♕c1+ 36 ♔f2 ♕d2+ 37 ♔g3 ♕×c3+ 38 ♔h4 ♕×d4+ 39 ♔×h5 ♕e5+ 40 ♔g4 ♕e4+ 41 ♔h3 ♕e3+ 42 g3 ♕h6+ 43 ♔g2 ♕d2+ 44 ♔f2 and the pawn queens).

So a last check before playing 30 ♗a3. What if he doesn't take? Well he would be in a bad way with the pawn going to e7 at once, or after 30 ... ♕e8 31 ♕c7+ ♔g8 32 ♗e7 ♘g4 33 ♕d7 and Black can resign. Or 30 ♗a3 ♕xa3 31 ♘h5+ and now refusal by 31 ... ♔h6. Then 32 ♘xf6 ♕c1+ 33 ♔f2 ♕d2+ 34 ♔g3 ♕xc3+ 35 ♔h4 ♕xd4+ 36 ♘g4+! All clear!

Here again it was a case of having clearly expressed motifs. White then examined the means and came to the thematic position of the whole combination, which is promoting the pawn on e8.

The number of thematic positions in chess is practically unlimited. That is why the mating position cannot be foreseen in most cases from the starting point, and becomes clearer only after the motifs and means have been worked through.

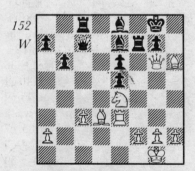

152
W

Engels–Consultants,
Ribeirato Preto, 1949

In diagram 152 we get various fine mating positions, but they are not the starting point of White's calculations, but at the end. The most refined chess genius could hardly hope to tackle it in the reverse order.

White has a strong attack, but how to mate? 1 ♖g3 should win but a forcing solution is more desirable. What are the motifs? The badly defended king, and as more specific features the concealed battery ♕g6/♗d3, and the pressure on the g-file.

So we have to work through the means. 1 ♖g3 and 1 ♘g5 are not forcing enough, but suddenly the idea of the attack on h7 leads to the inspired thought that 1 ♕h7+ may work. (Possibly for a combinative player such as Tal this queen sacrifice followed by double check would be the first idea to consider).

After 1 ... ♔xh7 (Forced, otherwise 2 ♕h8 mate) the battery opens fire by 2 ♘f6+. If 2 ... ♔xh6 3 ♖h3+ we find to our creative delight that it is mate in every variation, 3 ... ♔g5 4 ♖g3+ and 5 ♖g6 or 5 ♖g4 to follow.

Then we seek other thematic positions of mate if 2 ... ♔h8. By hard effort we find these too, though our previous examination of variations and discovery of thematic positions helps us in the search. Thus 2 ... ♔h8 3 ♗xg7+! ♔xg7 (or 3 ... ♖xg7 4 ♖h3+ and mate next move) 4 ♖g3+ and once again there are four squares to go to, but in each case the vindictive rook gives mate on g6 or g8.

If we work it out we will find that there were nine (!) different thematic positions in this combination. Such an abundance could not be coped with unless we started with motifs and means.

Through Theme to the Means

Any grandmaster can quote examples in which the road to discovery of a combination was different.

153
W

If we come 'cold' to diagram 153 we would quickly see its special features. If we had played for hours to reach it in an actual game, the motifs would be engraved in our mind. They are the open files and the presence of two advanced pawns. As a result the thought must arise, is it possible to promote one of them?

Remembering standard patterns, you consider 1 罝e8+ ♘xe8 2 d7 when often the pawn queens because of a double threat to queen on

e8 and d8. Here it isn't the case, given the bishop on d8 and the rook on b8.

Then we get the idea of 1 d7 at once, but it fails to 1 . . . ♘xd7 or 1 . . . ♔f8. However the idea of pawn promotion still persists. Then there comes the inspiration that d7 would work if it forked units on e8 and c8. So consider 1 罝c8 罝xc8 2 罝e8+ 罝xe8 3 d7. Wait though, can three enemy pieces not cope with one pawn? Black has 3 . . . ♘d6, but only a few seconds of dismay give way to delight when we continue with 4 dc=♕ ♘xc8 5 ab and finally promotion is forced.

Here the order was motif—theme—means. We considered the advanced pawns and then recalled the theme of a pawn on the seventh rank threatening a knight on the eighth. So the theme here was clear to us and preceeded the means. (I trust the reader would not have been surprised if such means had not existed. We have already stressed that for a combination to exist we had to have certain special factors as well as the presence of motif, means and theme).

Here is another example of the motif and theme becoming clear, with the difficulty lying in the search for the means to link the two (*154*).

At this point, and possibly earlier than this, White must have had the feeling that a back row mate could be 'on'—all three pawns are in

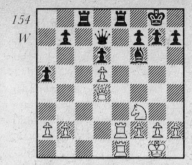

154
W

Adams–Torre, New Orleans, 1920

place denying the king a flight square off the back rank, while two pieces attack e8 and two defend it. Clearly a tense position. White can afford to put his queen en prise to the rook at c8 and to the queen at d7, as long as he does not do it along the a4/e8 diagonal.

Where should White's attacked queen go to? Clearly ♕g4 is possible; not ♕c4 as there is no threat and Black would just make a bolt hole or go 1 . . . ♖×e2. So 1 ♕g4 when Black cannot go 1 . . . ♖×e2 since he loses his queen and White's remaining rook is guarded. (Don't lose sight of the fact that White too has no flight square and so a potentially weak back rank).

Neither black rook can guard the attacked queen, so 1 . . . ♕b5 is forced. How then to keep the pressure on. 2 a4 looks fine, but wait, what about 2 . . . ♕×e2! and you are the one to be mated (3 ♕×c8 is met by the intermediate move 3 . . . ♕×e1+). Good thing that was spotted in time!

So 2 a4 fails. What else? 2 ♕c4 is a fine move now attacking the loose queen and closing the line of attack to the rook at e2. Fits in with the plan of diverting the defenders of ♔e8.

So 2 . . . ♕d7 is forced. Does that save him? Well, if we can go to c4 with impunity with the queen why not c7 too? Then the same considerations apply and he is forced to b5 again with his queen. We rest a moment and then take up the search again. His queen is at b5, mine at c7. Is 4 ♕×b7 a diversion of the queen? No, he has that 4 . . . ♕×e2 again. Can we do anything with that rook at e2? If his queen was on a4 we would have 4 ♖e4! threatening 5 ♕×c8 and then 6 ♖×a4 with a rook up.

But we can get the queen to go to a4 by 4 a4! His ♕×e2 doesn't work any more—our queen blocks his rook on the c-file. So 4 . . . ♕×a4 5 ♖e4 and now back again 5 . . . ♕b5. Now he isn't threatening ♕×e2, so we can go 6 ♕×b7 and finally his queen has no squares from which to guard e8. Check it again. 1 ♕g4 ♕b5 2 ♕c4 ♕d7 3 ♕c7 ♕b5 4 a4 ♕×a4 5 ♖e4 ♕b5 (Any alternatives? 5 . . . ♔f8 6 ♕×d6+ ♗e7 7 ♖×e7, or 5 . . . g6 6 ♕×c8 ♕×e4 7 ♕×e8+) 6 ♕×b7. Hooray!

This is the process then, by which the mind of a player, step by step, sees a combination, though at first he can only suspect that there is a beautiful possibility in front of him. Sometimes the suspicion cannot be turned into reality as the special features do not 'co-operate'. However fixing on a thematic position, studying the motifs, it is sometimes possible for the player to find the means to link the two. The creative thought of a player on the path motif—theme—means enables him to finally see the whole course of this magical process.

The grandmaster in his creative search can be compared to a weary traveller in the forest who is looking for the hut .where he will find warmth, comfort and rest. How should he find it? In one case he does not even know if there is such a hut, though his intuition and experience of life tell him that there could be. He tries this path and that. He may find it in the tangle of paths, or his search may finally prove to be in vain. Nevertheless he must seek it high and low!

Then there is the case where the traveller knows for sure that there is a hut. He has been in this place before and seen it. This time there are no paths, and he must fight his way through marsh, fallen trees and other obstacles. Yet there must be a path to the desired goal!

Learn from the World Champions

Once again we call upon the help of the world champions, and hope to develop our combinational vision by working through the thought processes behind their best efforts in this field.

Our helpers will work through the variations without moving the pieces on the board, and you must try to do the same. This method, which most closely approaches the conditions of competitive play, cannot be recommended too strongly. You should seize every opportunity to solve puzzles, studies, and 'find the continuation' quizzes in newspapers and magazines.

Here we will work through themes in the order in which we have already considered them. Our supposition about the way the champions discovered and worked through their combinations is based on their notes, and partly on the author's knowledge of the men and their methods.

155
W

Alekhine–Golombek,
Margate, 1938

The position of diagram 155 looks fairly level. If Black can get in h6 then he will soon follow up with the freeing move e5. However the presence of the knight at g5 and the absence of a pawn at f7 always suggests a check on the a2/g8 diagonal. How can this diagonal be opened?

Consider 19 d5!. If 19 ... ♘e7 (as was played in the actual game) then 20 de ♗×e6 21 ♖d1 ♕e5 (21 ... ♘d5? 22 ♘×e6 ♕×e6 23 ♕c4 and the pinned knight will be lost) 22 ♗×b7 and the extra pawn will win. (Back row mate!)

The combination comes after 19 ... ed 20 ♗×d5+! ♕×d5 21 ♖d1! and the queen has nowhere to go on the diagonal to prevent 22 ♕a2+, or 22 ♕b3+.

So the motif was present, and the means were found. However, we must stress that the means depend on a combination of circumstances. It needed only a small change in the position for the combination not to work. Let us imagine that White had an extra pawn at b3. Then Black would have been able to play 21 ... ♕b5 and after 22 a4 ♕b4 would still prevent ♕c4+.

Assessing the position of diagram 156 by the method which he had recently formulated, Steinitz would look for small advantages in White's position. Black has weak points at e6 and g7. White has possession of the c- and e-files, though not total control of them.

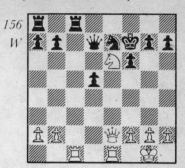

Steinitz–von Bardeleben,
Hastings, 1895

Black is a pawn up which is in the centre, but the king is subject to attack. The overall assessment gives White the advantage, so he has the obligation to attack upon pain of losing his advantage.

In Steinitz's days the theory of middle game play was not so far advanced as now, and Steinitz would not use the words motif, means and theme. From our point of view the bad position of the black king is an important motif for the following combination, which involves play on the back two ranks.

Consider 20 ♕g4 g6 21 ♘g5+ ♔e8. The presence of forced moves and the tension in the position suggest a combination. Try 22 ♖×e7+. Then capture by the queen allows 23 ♖×c8+. Or 22 ... ♔×e7 23 ♖e1+ with a powerful attack. Thus 23 ... ♔d8? 24 ♘e6+ and wins the queen by 25 ♘c5+. Or 23 ... ♔d6 24 ♕b4+ ♔c7 (24 ... ♖c5 25 ♖e6+) 25

♘e6+ ♚b8 26 ♕f4+ ♜c7 27
♘×c7 ♕×c7 28 ♖e8 mate.

So 22 ♖×e7+ wins? Wait, what
about 22 . . . ♚f8 with threats of
back row mate on c1? All four white
pieces en prise. White has to save
his queen and stop ♖×c1+. Try
the rook checks along the 7th rank.

23 ♖f7+ ♚g8. Now if 24 ♕f4
fg, or 24 ♕d1 ♕g4! So 24
♖g7+. Again the rook is not to be
taken. Black goes 24 . . . ♚f8, or 24
. . . ♚h8. Have a little rest and
consider both.

24 . . . ♚f8 loses to 25 ♘×h7+
and I take the queen with check.
So, 24 . . . ♚h8 25 ♖×h7+ ♚g8
26 ♖g7+ ♚h8 and now with the
pawn at h7 gone there is 27 ♕h4+
with a mating attack. Work it
out:— 27 . . . ♚×g7 28 ♕h7+ ♚f8
29 ♕h8+ ♚e7 30 ♕g7+ ♚e8 31
♕g8+ ♚e7 32 ♕f7+ ♚d8 (32 . . .
♚d6 33 ♕×f6+ mates) 33 ♕f8+
♚e8 34 ♘f7+ ♚d7 35 ♕d6 mate
(157).

157
B

So White can take on e7 and
force a brilliant win.

158
W

Alekhine–Molina,
Buenos Aires, 1926

Diagram 158 is from a simul-
taneous with clocks on eight boards.
Both sides need a square for the king
in view of possible back row mate.
So 24 h3, and if 24 . . . h6 then 25
♕c2 and after, for example, 25 . . .
♗f6 26 ♘e1 ♘e5 White gets a nice
endgame by 27 ♕×g6 with some
winning chances in view of superior
pawn structure. All very well, but
what about the fork 24 . . . ♘×b2.
Since Black has no flight square for
the king there is the idea 25 ♕×a7!!
Shades of Adams–Torre! Work
through the variations.

25 . . . ♖×a7 26 ♖×d8+ ♗f8 27
♗×c5 h6 28 ♖×f8+ ♚h7 29
♖dd8 The rook at a7 is en prise, he
must make room for the king with
gain of time by 29 . . . ♕b1+. Then
30 ♚h2 ♖b7. Then what? Ah, I
can cramp the king again by 31
♘h4. If 31 . . . g6 then 32 ♗d4 f6
33 ♗×f6 mating. So the thrust 31
. . . g5. White has a king driving
operation. 32 ♖h8+ ♚g7 33

♖dg8+ ♔f6 34 ♖×h6+ ♔e5 35
♖e8+ and mates—35 . . . ♖e7 36
♖×e7+ ♔f4 37 g3 *(159)*.

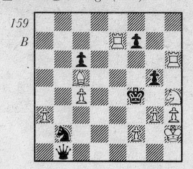

159
B

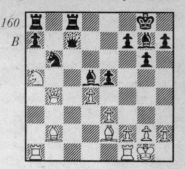

160
B

Goglidze–Botvinnik,
Moscow, 1935

Right, now the side variations if
he doesn't accept the queen offer on
a7. 25 ♕×a7 ♘×d1 26 ♖×d7
♘×e3 27 fe ♖×d7 28 ♕×d7
♗f8 29 ♘e5 with positional
advantage—queen checks get
Black nowhere. If 25 . . . ♖×d2 26
♖×d2 ♖×d2 27 ♘×d2 White has
the advantage again with that
passed a pawn.

Wait, he has 25 . . . ♗d6. Then I
have a lot en prise, while his queen
guards the bishop at d6. If my
queen moves the exchange is lost.
Ah, I have 26 ♕×d7 ♖×d7 27
♖×b2. The pin on the d-file to be
intensified by 28 ♖bd2, and the
back row mate is still on. He can try
to unpin by 27 . . . ♖d8 28 ♖bd2
♕f6 so that if 29 ♗×c5 ♗c7, but 29
♗g5 knocks that on the head.

Black sees the awkward placing
of White's pieces in diagram 160,
especially the bishops on the second
rank. This suggests the entry ♕c2
either now or after preparation. 20

. . . ♕c2 at once is met by 21 ♗d1.
So 20 . . . ♗f8 first, a good move in
itself to bring the bishop into action,
and try to drive the queen from the
defence of the bishop. If 21 ♕d2
♕c2 22 ♖fd1 ♕×d2 23 ♖×d2
♗b4 24 ♖dd1 ♖c2 achieving the
desired fork. 21 ♕e1 looks very
passive, and 21 . . . ♕c2 still creates
difficulties for White.

So 21 ♕b5 a6 22 ♕d3 e4 still
harrassing the queen. White has
two retreats. If 23 ♕d1 ♗b4 24
♖c1 ♕d7 with pressure, or 23 . . .
♕c2 and White has a very passive
position—24 ♗c1, or 24 ♗a3
♗×a3 25 ♖×a3 ♕b2 26 ♖a1
♖c2.

Or the retreat 23 ♕b1 ♕c2
when queens can't be exchanged
and if 24 ♗d1 then 24 . . . ♕×b1
25 ♖×b1 ♘c4! 26 ♘×c4 (26 ♘b3
♖ab8) 26 . . . ♗×c4 27 ♖e1 ♗b4
winning the exchange.

What about 24 ♗a3 as an
answer to 23 . . . ♕c2? He frees
himself by exchanging the passive

bishop. Then we get the forced 24 ... ♗×a3 25 ♖×a3 ♛×e2 26 ♛×b6. Then what? His back row looks weak. Yes, there is 26 ... ♖ab8 27 ♛d6 ♛×f1+! 28 ♔×f1 ♖b1+ 29 ♔e2 ♖c2 mate!

This was the variation that occurred in the game. It could be said that the combination was not forced from the initial position, but that by threats to enemy pieces Black worked towards a critical point where White went wrong and allowed mate. So it was a case of a motif leading through means to a position with other motifs and a thematic back row mate.

161
W

Petrosian–Balashov, Moscow, 1974

Black has slipped up in the play leading to diagram 161, ignoring the point stressed by his former teacher Botvinnik that the isolated pawn should not be allowed to advance to d5 in this sort of position.

So 15 d5! and behind the unblocked pawn the pieces come to life; he can't allow the capture on

e6, so 15 ... ed. Then 16 ♗g5 threatening h7. If 16 ... g6? 17 ♖×e7 ♛×e7 18 ♘×d5. So the only defence against mate is 16 ... ♘e4. Should White take then on e7? No, he recaptures with knight and the ♗b7 guards d5. Well there's nothing wrong with the simple 17 ♘×e4 de 18 ♛×e4 g6 19 ♛h4. What a fine position! How can Black defend? White has the e-file, the diagonals c1/h6 and a2/g8, while f7 and h7 are weak. No need to look further. Let him try and defend that!

These moves were made and Black chose here 19 ... ♛c7. Possibly 19 ... ♖c7 was stronger. White starts working it out again. Well my first move is clear. 20 ♗b3 to take on f7 with check and mate in two. How does he defend f7? If 20 ... ♗f8 21 ♗f4 and 22 ♘g5.

Black preferred 20 ... h5. White must have felt that after such a weakening move there must be something; g6 has been weakened. 21 ♛e4 suggests itself. He must go 21 ... ♔g7. Now does 22 ♗h6+ ♔×h6 23 ♗×f7 work? No, he has 23 ... ♖g8, or even 23 ... ♛d6. There must be something. Try it the other way round. Yes! 22 ♗×f7 ♔×f7 23 ♗h6 and after this quiet move he is faced with mate on e6, d5 or c4. He can't defend by moving the knight since then I have 24 ♘e5+. 23 ... ♖g8 fails too. So the only reply is 23 ... ♛d6. Then 24 ♛c4+ ♔f6. How can I get at the king there? 25 ☖ad1 and the queen cannot flee. He must offer the knight by 25 . . . ♞d4. Well no problems there. 26 ♕×d4+ ♕×d4 27 ☖×d4.

But that is nice, since there is still a mate threat on f4. If 27 . . . ☖c5 28 h4 ♝×f3 gf and Black can resign. The pinned bishop at e7 must be lost.

This is how the game went. White prepared the ground for a combination by a breakthrough in the centre that opened diagonals and files. At the start he had no idea of the final thematic position, but by working through the means he arrived at the position where the threat of ☖f4 mate was decisive.

Smyslov–Konig,
Radio match, USSR–Gt. Britain
1947

The earlier pawn sacrifice has left White with the advantage in diagram 162, since he has a concentration of forces round the enemy king. There is the open h-file, but 31 ♔g2, 32 ☖h1, 33 ♕h4 looks too slow. Three moves is too long since it would let Black organize a defence, and my own king is not too safe.

I must strike at his weakest point. He has a good defence built up on f7 and h7. The knight sacrifice on g7 looks right. Then I follow up ♞f5+ and the bishop attacks from h6 or f6. That looks logical.

(Of course Smyslov in his whole build-up would have seen that he was angling for a knight sacrifice on g7, but we are working on the basis that he has come 'cold' to the position, as the reader had done).

Now to work out the variations. 31 ♞×g7 ♔×g7 first. Obviously 32 ♞f5+ and he can take or move the king. 32 . . . ♝×f5 33 ef looks bad for him with the various discovered checks, such as ♝d8+. Still I have to work it out. Not 33 . . . f6 34 ♝e3+ and 35 ♕g8 mate. Nor 33 . . . ♞g6 34 ♕h5! quite apart from taking the knight. So 33 . . . ☖d4 attacking my queen is the best defence. I have to go 34 f6+ and the king cannot come forward—34 . . . ♔g6 35 ♝f4+ ♔×f6 36 ♕g5 mate. So back, 34 . . . ♔g8. Then 35 ♝f4+ ♞g6 (otherwise mate on g7) 36 ♕×g6+ finishes him.

No, wait. Does it finish him? He has 36 . . . ♔f8. I might have a follow-up, but 'might' isn't good enough. How often do people hope that something will turn up, and the king slips away. So what happens after 36 ... ♔f8? 37 ♗h6+ ♔e8. Now 38 ♕×c2 is bad—38 ... ♖×c4 39 ♕×c4? ♗×f2+ winning my queen. Still there is 38 ♕g8+ ♔d7 39 ♗×f7 and the attack is powerful.

Where else has he in answer to 34 f6+? If 34 ... ♔h7 35 ♗f4! ♘e6 36 ♕h5+ ♔g8 37 ♔h2 and the rook check at g1 decides.

So capturing the second knight is hopeless. Refusal? 31 ♘×g7 ♔×g7 32 ♘f5+ ♔g8. There are many ways of following up, but 33 ♗f6 looks simple and decisive. Threats are 34 ♘h6+ or 34 ♕h4. For example 33 ... ♖d6 34 ♘h6+ ♔h7 35 ♕h4 ♖×f6 36 ♘×f7+ ♔h5 37 ♕×h5+ ♔g7 38 ♕h8+ ♔g6 39 ♕h6 mate. So it looks as if the knight sacrifice wins after its acceptance.

Now, if he refuses. 31 ♘×g7 and he can try 31 ... ♗×f2+. Then 32 ♖×f2 ♕×c4 33 ♘e8 ♘h7 34 ♘f6+ ♘×f6 35 ♗×f6 and he will have to give up the exchange on f6. Then the attack with the exchange up should tell.

This variation actually occurred in the game, but Black preferred 34 ♘f6+ ♔g7 and then came 35 ♗h6+! ♔h8 (35 ... ♔×h6 36 ♘f5+ ♗×f5 and White mates by 37 ♘g8 or 37 ♖h2) 36 ♘×d7 ♕d4 37 ♘×e5 1–0.

How was the combination found? Yes, by the sequence motif—means—theme.

Larsen–Spassky,
USSR–Rest of World,
Belgrade, 1970

In diagram 163, White has just attacked the knight. Should I retreat? Then he would complete his Q-side development. I can sacrifice the knight by 12 ... h4 and after he takes my knight I get a powerful pawn on g3. Nearly all my pieces can back it up, while he has a set of undeveloped pieces on the other side. Moreover his queen is a long way away and cannot get over to the K-side in time. Plenty of motifs here. The pawn at g3 can go forward to promote by g2 and ♖h1.

So here we have a thematic position arising very soon, before the means are clear. Black envisages queening the pawn on g3, though he cannot yet see whether he will achieve this.

How will it work out? 13 hg (If 13 ♗×g4 ♗×g4 14 hg hg and then as in the main line, only Black is not a piece down) 13 ... hg 14

☐×h8. No, that looks quite wrong, since Black's rook will get to h1 and his queen to h4. Better to keep the rook on. Obviously not 14 ☐f1 g2 15 ☐g1 ♕h4+ 16 ♔d1 ♕h1. That fearsome pawn at g2. So 14 ☐g1, and then 14 . . . ♕h4. But why so slow? There is a quick way of finishing it. 14 . . . ☐h1! and he has to take (15 ♔f1 ☐×g1+ 16 ♔×g1 ♕h4 and mates) when 15 ☐×h1 g2. Now two lines. 16 ☐g1 or 16 ☐f1. First 16 ☐g1 ♕h4+ 17 ♔d1 ♕h1 18 ♕c3 since he must make room for the king. Then 18 . . . ♕×g1+ 19 ♔c2 ♕f2 and it's hopeless for White—say 20 ♘a3 ♕×e2 21 gf ♗b4 22 ♕×b4 ♕d3+ and the new queen at g1 mates. Second 16 ☐f1 when the simplest is 16 . . . ♕h4+ 17 ♔d1 gf=♕+ 18 ♗×f1 ♗×g4+ 19 ♗e2 ♕h1 mate.

Let us stress again that although the presence of many motifs could be seen by a strong player, and the thematic position of queening the g⌐ pawn, or attacking with its help (no flight square at f1) was also clearly seen, it might have turned out that the means did not exist to link the two. What does one do in such a case? Never mind, just keep on playing! Perhaps later in the game the combination may prove feasible. Even if not, there is no reason to despair. How many games are played without there being a combination. There are other delights in chess!

Another case of an advanced pawn working like a piece and creating havoc in the enemy camp *(164)*.

164
W

Tal–Suetin, Tbilisi, 1969

Black hopes to exploit the Q-side weaknesses which he created by capturing the knight at c3 with his black square bishop, but where is he going to hide his king? I can already open fire at it with all my pieces mobilized by 16 f5, when he must take since fe mustn't be permitted. So 16 . . . ef 17 ef ♘e5. Now 18 ♘e6! ♗×e6 19 fe. Castling is ruled out by mate on h7, so 19 . . . g6. If the queen goes to h3 he can castle or play f5, and if ♕h6 he still has f5. Wait, I can get a giant pawn on f7 by sacrificing the queen. 20 ♕×e5 de 21 ef+ and if 21 . . . ♔f8 then 22 ♗h6 mate. So he goes to the d-file and I have discovered check. If 21 . . . ♔d7 then 22 ♗f5++ ♔c6 23 ♗e4+ ♘d5 24 ♗×d5+ ♔d6 25 ♗×a8+ ♔e7 26 ♗g5+ ♔f8 27

♖d8+ and it's over, or 21 . . . ♔d8 22 ♗f5+ ♘d5 23 ♗g5+ and he can resign.

Smyslov–Botvinnik,
Match-Tournament, 1941

In diagram 165 a mass of pawns plays the main role, but the play is very sharp since the opponent has the same trump. The first moves are obvious:—50 . . . b2 51 ♗a4 c3. Now the bishop at d3 has come into action to stop White's a6. White goes 52 ♖b3 and the knight is brought over to the main action by 52 . . . ♘e2. White will play to exchange bishops so that his own pawns can advance. 53 ♗b5 ♗×b5 54 ♖×b5 ♘d4. The threat of ♘c2 forces the further exchange. 55 ♗×d4 ed. Black has achieved a lot—three passed pawns against two, but who gets in first?

After a short rest carry on with the calculations. 56 a6 ♖×b6 (otherwise the pawns are unstoppable) 57 ♖×b6 d3. This is a critical position. Can White do

anything with his extra rook on the K-side before the pawns sweep home? Obviously not 58 a7 d2 59 ♖g1 c2 and wins e.g. 60 ♖b7+ ♔h8 61 ♖b8 c1=♕ 62 a8=♕ ♕×g1+ 63 ♔×g1 d1=♕+ 64 ♔g2 (64 ♔f2 ♕d2+ 65 ♔f1 b1=♕+ etc.) 64 . . . ♕e2+ 65 ♔h3 ♕×f3+ wins. Or 60 ♖×b2 c1=♕ 61 ♖b7+ ♔h8 62 ♖b8 ♕×g1+ etc.

So what can White do? Ah, there is a tricky line—58 ♖g1 d2 59 ♖×f6. Now the careless 59 . . . c2 concedes a draw to 60 ♖f7+ ♔h8 61 ♖f6! ♔h7 62 ♖f7+ and perpetual check. 61 . . . ♖c7 would even lose—62 ♖h6+ ♖h7 63 a7. So be careful!

Is there a win there? Yes, by defending the second row. 59 . . . ♖c7 stops the check at f7 and the pawns will win.

So there were motifs for the combination, Botvinnik worked through the means and came upon a thematic position in which three advanced pawns overcome a rook. The game actually finished 59 ♖×f6 ♖c7! 60 ♖fg6 d1 = ♕! 0–1, but not 60 . . . c2? 61 ♖6g5 with a draw.

Diagram 166 is a famous example in which Alekhine played a long combination on the theme of forking. We remind readers of our advice to try and work through examples mentally, without moving pieces. If you can do this here, you have already made great

166
B

Reti–Alekhine, Baden Baden 1925

progress in developing your combinational vision. If you cannot work through all the complicated variations at sight, do not worry. You still have a way to go, but practice will make perfect.

Now let us work through it. The first move is obvious, 1 . . . ♘×e2+ and the king must go to h2, since 2 ♔f1 is met by 2 . . . ♘×g3+ 3 fg ♗×f3 4 ♗×f3 ♖×f3+ 5 ♔g2 ♖8a3 6 ♖d8+ ♔h7 7 ♖h1+ ♔g6 8 ♖h3 ♖fb3 and the threat of mate on the back two rows forces White to abandon his knight; or 2 ♔g2? ♗×f3+.

White's pieces look badly placed. An unharmonious mass on the K-side and the offside knight at b7, which could be exploited by getting the bishop on to the h1/a8 diagonal.

There is the forcing move 2 . . . ♘e4 when 3 fe is bad—3 . . . ♘×d2 with win of material. Both rooks are attacked, so I am surely winning. Wait! He has the tricky 3 ♖c4! Nice! Then 3 . . . ♘×d2 4

♘×d2! and I have nothing e.g. 4 . . . ♖d3 5 ♘c5 ♖×d2 6 ♗×a8. So consider 3 . . . ♗×f3 4 ♗×f3 ♘×d2. No, he has the alternative 4 ♖×e4! ♖×e4 5 ♗×f3 and Black might even lose.

Such tricky lines show the need for real care. Need I be looking to take his rook? 3 . . . ♘×f2 removes the threat to my rook, and threatens 4 . . . ♘×h1 and if 5 ♔×h1 ♗×f3 with check. So he will go 4 ♗g2, and the position loses some of its tension. How can Black win? Just a pawn up with such a relation of forces would not win an endgame. He could give up a knight for a pawn with a theoretical draw. Something forced has to be looked for instead.

Clearly I must attack and 4 . . . ♗e6 fits the bill. His rook is en prise, a knight check on g4 becomes possible, followed by discovered check—his king cannot go to the back rank in view of my ♖a1+.

Where will his rook go? If 5 ♖b4 ♘g4+ 6 ♔h3 then 6 . . . ♘f6+ 7 ♔h2 ♘e4 8 ♖d8+ ♖×d8 9 ♘×d8 ♘2×g3 and Black is two pawns up. The same variation applies if 5 ♖c7.

Why look at passive moves by the rook? He will play 5 ♖c2 attacking both knights. Then there must either be a forced win, or I will have to play the long boring endgame with two pawns against one on the K-side with only minimal winning chances.

So 5 ♖c2 ♘g4+ 6 ♔h3 (again 6
♔h1 ♖a1+) 6 ... ♘e5+ 7 ♔h2
(Not 7 ♔h4 ♖a4+ and mates).
Now taking on f3 with knight is just
an exchange. If I take with rook on
f3 he clearly won't recapture but go
8 ♖×e2. Wait, then I have a
forcing variation with him finishing
with his rook on f3 and I get the
forking move ♗d5 to hit ♖f3 and
♘b7.

It runs 7 ... ♖×f3 8 ♖×e2
♘g4+ 9 ♔h3 (Yet again the back
rank is forbidden to him). 9 ...
♘e3+ 10 ♔h2 ♘×c2! 11 ♗×f3
♘d4 12 ♖f2 ♘×f3+ 13 ♖×f3
♗d5! *(167)*.

167
W

Yes, that's it. The rook must
move and cannot guard the knight.

Yet again a motif, here the cut-
off knight at b7, was combined with
the idea of a fork on the h1/d5
diagonal, and examination of
various forcing lines provided the
means to link the two.

In diagram 168 White has
obvious plusses in his better

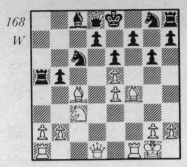

168
W

Alekhine–Chajes, Calsbad, 1911

development and the chance to use
various open lines, notably the d-
and f-files. Getting a knight to d6
with a catastrophe for Black on f7
would be fine, but the immediate
capture on b5 (with knight or
bishop) loses two pieces for a rook in
view of his queen check on b6. If his
knight were on b4 and I had an
open b-file, the capture on b5
would be feasible since ♖b1 then
piles up pressure on the pinned
knight on b4, so:

1 b4! ♘×b4 2 ♘×b5 ♖×b5 3
♗×b5 ♕b6+ 4 ♔h1 ♕×b5 5
♖b1.

Now the threat is 6 a3, and Black
must move his queen to one of three
squares—a5, c5 or c4—still
guarding the knight. 5 ... ♕a5 6
♗d2 wins a piece. 5 ... ♕c5 6 ♖c1
and the bishop at c8 falls. Or 5 ...
♕c4 6 ♕a4. So queen moves don't
save him. Try 5 ... ♗a6 so that if 6
a3 ♕×f1+.

White has to move his queen up
in order to rule out the capture on

f1. Right, there is 6 ♕d6 putting the pressure on. Then if 6 . . . ♘e7 there is 7 ♕×b4 ♕×b4 8 ♖×b4 ♗×f1? 9 ♖b8+ winning the rook at h8. Can Black try slipping away with the queen? If 6 . . . ♕c6 then 7 ♖×b4 ♕×d6 ed ♗×f1!? 9 ♖b8 mate. What else? Make room for the king by 6 . . . f6. But then I can simply go 7 ♖fc1 and the knight is lost.

The game ended 6 ♕d6 f6 7 ♖fc1 ♕d3 8 ♖×b4 g5 9 ♖d4 ♕b5 10 a4 ♕b7 11 ♖c7 ♕b1+ 12 ♖d1 1–0.

Fischer–Gligorić,
Havana Olympiad 1966

Castling on opposite sides implies a pawn storm against the king, but in diagram 169 a4 and b4 are hard to fit together. Black in his turn has g5, h5, and g4. So it is better to attack the black king by the plan ♗f4, ♖c1 and d5 when Black will almost certainly have to take the pawn, opening lines against c7.

So 11 ♗f4! though this gives

Black tempi in playing his own attack—11 . . . g5 12 ♗g3 h5. Must get the break going, so 13 d5 cd 14 ♖c1. Now 15 ♘×d5 is a grave threat, and if 14 . . . de then 15 ♘a4! ♕×d1 16 ♖×c7+ ♔b8 17 ♖c8+!! ♔a7 (17 . . . ♔×c8 18 ♘b6 mate—pretty) 18 ♗b8+ ♔a8 19 ♘b6 mate *(170),* yes really pretty!

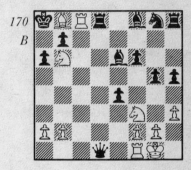

Since 14 . . . de doesn't work the only defence must be 14 . . . ♗d6. Try 15 ♘a4 ♔b8 16 ♘c5 ♕e7 (taking on c5 is bad since I will crunch in on c7) 17 ♘×a6+! ba 18 ♘d4 ♗d7 19 ♕b3+ ♔a7 and now the crunch on c7 again—20 ♖×c7+ ♗×c7 21 ♗×c7. Then if 21 . . . ♕c5 22 ♕e3! and he loses queen or rook, or 21 . . . ♗b5 22 ♘c6+ ♗×c6 23 ♕b6+ and mate next move.

Conclusion:— 11 ♗f4 is right and Black cannot play his own pawn storm in time.

The game actually went 11 . . . ♘e7 12 ♖c1 ♘g6 13 ♗g3 ♗d6 14 ♘a4! ♗×g3 15 fg ♔b8 16 ♘c5 ♕d6 17 ♕a4 and after the error 17

... ♔a7 White won by 18 ♘×a6!
♗×h3 19 e5! ♘×e5 20 de fe
21 ♘c5+ ♔b8 22 gh e4 23
♘×e4 ♕e7 24 ♖c3 b5 25 ♕c2
1–0.

offer? The threat is 2 ... ♖×g2+
and 3 ... ♕f2+ mating. Look at 2
♕×c5 ♖×g2+ 3 ♔h1. Then 3 ...
♖×h2+ 4 ♘×h2 ♕×e1+ and
soon mates. Or 2 ♘bd2 when the
simplest is 2 ... ♕g4 3 g3 ♕h3.

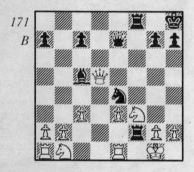

Amateur–Steinitz, London, 1869

Alekhine–Tylor, Margate, 1937

In diagram 171 Black has
excellently placed pieces, and could
take on e3 if White had no knight at
f3—1 ... ♗×e3 2 ♖×e3 ♖f1
mate. That means the knight has a
vital function and any piece could
be put en prise to it. Try 1 ... ♕h4
so that if 2 ♘×h4 ♗×e3. Now 3 h3
♖f1+ 4 ♔h2 ♗g1+ 5 ♔h1 ♘g3
mate (Note that this mate is exactly
the same as in the previous
example, showing how there is
nothing really new!) or 3 g3 ♖e2+
4 ♔h1 ♖×e1+ 5 ♔g2 ♖g1+ 6
♔h3 ♘f2 mate. That suggests the
need for a flight square at h4, so 3
♘g6+ hg 4 g3 ♖e2+ 5 ♔h1
♖×e1+ 6 ♔g2 ♖g1+ 7 ♔h3
♘f2+ 8 ♔h4 ♖f4+! 9 gf ♖g4
mate, or 9 ♔g5 ♖g4 mate.
Can White refuse the queen

A tense position *(172)* with both
kings in some danger. The knight
sacrifice at g5 suggests itself. He
cannot take since he loses the
queen, but the counter stroke 1 ...
♗×f4 looks nasty. So 1 ♘×g5
♗×f4 2 ♕c3+ and the bishop
cannot block because of 3 ♘f3+ or
3 ♘f7+. The king has no good
move (2 ... ♔g8 3 ♘f7+ ♗×g3 4
♕h8 mate, or 2 ... ♔g6 3 ♘h7+!
♗g5 4 ♘×f8+). So he blocks with
a rook. 2 ... ♖5f6 is bad, 3 ♘f7+
♗×g3 4 ♖×g3+. Hence 2 ...
♖8f6 3 ♘e4+! ♗×g3 4 ♖×g3+
♔h8 *(173)* (4 ... ♔f8 5 ♕b4+
mates

5 ♕×f6+! ♖×f6 6 ♖g8+ and
his queen is lost.

The tension on the adjoining
diagonals a1/h8 and a2/g8 in

173
W

diagram 174 is very great. White has to cope with the snag that his king is in the corner where it is susceptible to a back rank mate or to ♛×g2 mate.

174
W

Euwe–Thomas, Hastings, 1934

The attacked queen has to move and still has to keep on the second rank or the g-file to stop Black's diversionary 1 . . . ♜×f7. Clearly 1

♛g5 is best, threatening mate on f6.

The obvious reply is 1 . . . ♛d4 when 2 ♜d2 looks strong, as if 2 . . . ♛g7 3 ♛×d8! winning, but there is the fine reply 2 . . . ♜d5! Then 3 ♜×d4 ♜×g5, or 3 ♛h6 ♛g7. If 3 ♛×d5 ♛×d5 4 ♜×d5 ♝×d5 and it is Black who is winning.

So the ♜d2 idea doesn't work. Then there comes a fine idea instead—break the communications between Black's queen and his rook. 2 ♝d5! Now Black is unable to simultaneously guard his f8 square and the long black diagonal. If 2 . . . ♜×f2 then 3 ♛×d8+ ♚g7 4 ♛g5+ ♚f8 5 ♛g8+ ♚e7 6 ♜e1+ and 7 ♝×b7. Or 2 . . . ♛g7 3 ♜×f8+ ♜×f8 4 ♜×f8+ ♛×f8 5 ♛e5+ and 6 ♛b8+ mating.

So 1 . . . ♛d4 loses to 2 ♝d5. Has Black any other first move? Try 1 . . . ♜d6. Then the same idea 2 ♝d5 works again since if 2 . . . ♜×f2 3 ♛g8 mate.

In closing this section, we stress again that regular training of combinational vision is needed. When studying combinations and trying to solve puzzles with such finishes, think in terms of motif, means and theme.

Exercises

Now try to solve Diagrams 175–182 using the same technique. The detailed answers are at the back of the book.

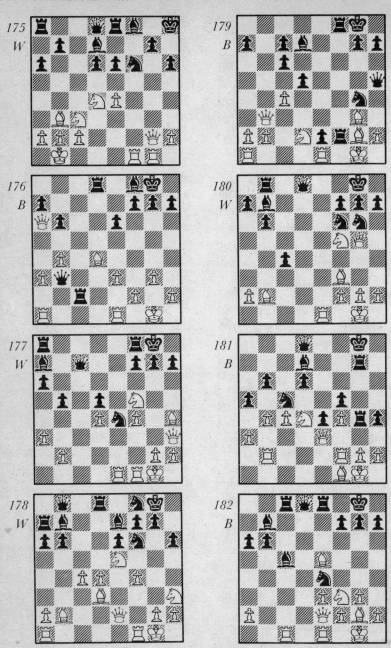

4 Calculation and Practical Play

The Calculation of Variations

The ability to calculate variations rapidly and accurately is the third of the basic attributes of a chess master: lapses in this respect can cancel out in a moment the efforts of hours. That is why you may come across top class practitioners who do not assess positions well enough, or are not dab hands at combinations, but you will never come across one who calculates variations badly.

This topic is dealt with thoroughly in the book 'Think like a Grandmaster', so here we restrict ourselves to a summary of the main points and then develop the theme with examples from the leading grandmasters.

The first important point is the order in which we think of moves. When we are setting out to calculate various variations from a given position, we must first establish clearly in our minds all the possible candidate moves in this position. If we fail to do this and get engrossed in one line of play, we may quite fail to see what might be the main line.

Once we have established all the candidate moves, we then proceed to work out the variations arising from them one by one. The question of what order to tackle them in is a matter of taste. Some players like to look at the hardest lines first and only then dispose of the easy ones. Others prefer to do it the other way round.

All possible variations may be depicted in the form of a tree of analysis in which the variations and sub-variations are represented by the branches and boughs of the tree.

The main thing to master is the rule that during a game you must go along each branch once and once only. No going back, no repeating yourself! Wandering to and fro through the branches of the tree leads to loss of time and that scourge of practical players-time trouble.

To achieve such self-control takes great effort, but the results are well worth it. Learn to trust your brain. It is only in very exceptional positions that a grandmaster will check and re-check the same line, and this when it is particularly complicated. As a rule he does not wander aimlessly through the branches.

Then we must recall the important piece of advice that we call Blumenfeld's Rule. It often happens that a player carries out a deep and complicated calculation, but fails to spot something elementary right at the first move. In order to avoid such gross blunders, the Soviet master B. Blumenfeld made this recommendation:– When you have finished your calculations, write down the move you have decided on on the score sheet. Then examine the position for a short time 'through the eyes of a patzer.' Ask whether you have left mate in one on, or left a piece or a pawn to be taken. Only when you have convinced yourself that there is no immediate catastrophe for you should you make the planned move.

There are various sorts of the tree of analysis according to the nature of the position we are dealing with.

Here are some examples: (see the drawing)

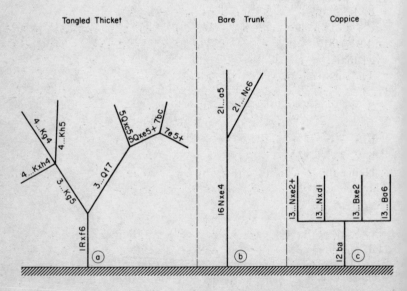

Capello–Kotov, Malta, 1976

Just as Black had to do the move before, White here *(183)* has to work through the variations to answer the question, can White take on f6? The first moves are clear: 1 ♖×f6 ♔×f6 2 ♕×e8 bc 3 ♕f8+. Now there are two candidate moves 3 . . . ♔g5 and 3 . . . ♕f7 which we examine in turn. I. 3 . . . ♔g5 4 h4+. Now there are three candidate moves which we examine in the order a. 4 . . . ♔×h4; b. 4 . . . ♔g4 and c. 4 . . . ♔h5.

a. 4 . . . ♔×h4 5 ♕h6+ ♔g4 6 ♘d3 ♕f7 7 ♕h3+ ♔g5 8 ♕e3+ ♔h5 9 ♘×c5 dc 10 bc with slight advantage to White.

b. 4 . . . ♔g4 5 ♕f6 h6 6 ♘d3 forcing mate.

c. 4 . . . ♔h5 5 ♕f6 h6 (5 . . . ♔h6 6 g4 ♕c8 7 ♔g3 and mates by 8 g5+ and 9 ♕f3) 6 ♘d3 cb 7 g4+! ♔×g4 8 ♘f2+ ♔h5 9 ♕f3+ ♔×h4 10 ♕g4 mate.

The answer is that 3 . . . ♔g5 is bad.

II. 3 . . . ♕f7! 4 ♕×d6+ ♔g7. Now there are two candidate moves:

a. 5 ♕×c5 cb 6 ♕c2 ♕f4+ and Black wins.

b. 5 ♕×e5+ ♕f6 6 ♕×f6+ ♔×f6 and now two possibilities:

b. 1. 7 bc ♖×c3 8 ♘e2 ♖e3 9 ♘g3 ♔e5 and wins.

b 2. 7 e5+ ♔×e5 8 ♘d3+ ♔d4! and wins.*

Hence the conclusion that the rook capture on f6 does not save White. The tree of analysis is depicted on the drawing as (a).

Tr. Note. In fact the analysis has to be taken further—9 ♘×c5 cb 10 d6 b1 = ♕ 11 d7 and now not 11 . . . ♕b6? 12 d8 = ♕! ♕×d8 13 ♘e6+ winning, nor 12 . . . ♔×c5 13 ♕×b6+ ♔×b6 14 ♔g3 winning, but 11 . . . ♕b8+ and 12 . . . ♔×c5 winning.

Petrosian–Kupreichik, USSR Ch. 1976

Here *(184)* we have the straight line sort of continuation with hardly any diversions or off-shoots.

16 ♘×e4 ♕×e4 17 ♗d3 ♕b4+ 18 ♕×b4 ♘×b4 19 ♗×h7+ ♔h8 20 ♗b1+! ♔g8 21 ♖c4 a5 (or 21 ... ♘c6 22 ♗h7+ ♔h8 23 ♗c2+! ♔g8 24 ♖ch4 g6 25 ♖h8+ ♔g7 26 ♖1h7+ ♔f6 27 ♖×f8) 22 ♗h7+ ♔h8 23 ♗f5+! ♔g8 24 ♖ch4 g6 (24 ... f6 25 ♗g6!) 25 ♖h8+ ♔g7 26 ♖1h7+ ♔f6 27 ♖×f8 gf 28 ♖hh8 and wins.

This is shown as (b).

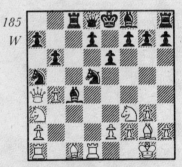

Sveshnikov–Kupreichik, USSR Ch. 1976

At this point in this game *(185)* both sides had to consider this way of complicating matters—12 ba ♘c3 13 ♕c2 and now there are four main lines:–

a. 13 ... ♘×e2+ 14 ♔h1 ♗a6 15 ♕b2 with advantage to White.

b. 13 ... ♘×d1 14 ♕×d1 with advantage to White.

c. 13 ... ♗×e2 14 ♖d2 with advantage to White.

d. 13 . . . ♗a6 14 ♕b3 ♘×e2+ 15 ♔h1 ♖c3 16 ♕a4 ♘×c1 17 ♘b5 with great complications which cannot be assessed with any great accuracy.

This type of position produces a coppice—see (c).

Now let us follow our principle of taking examples from the world champions.

Fischer–Najdorf, Varna Olympiad, 1962

In diagram 186 White has in mind to play 12 ♖e1. Black has quite a number of replies which have to be considered—I 12 . . . ♖g8 II 12 . . . e6 III 12 . . . h5 IV 12 . . . ♘d7 V 12 . . . ♗×g2 VI 12 . . . dc VII 12 . . . e5. Seven candidate moves in all! Is there any move not counted here which might be played? No, so White settles down to each in turn.

I 12 . . . ♖g8 13 ♖×e4! de 14 ♕h5 ♖g7 (14 . . . ♖g6 15 ♕×h7 ♖g7 16 ♕×e4 ♖a7 17 ♘f5 or 17 ♗f4) 15 ♘f5 etc.

II 12 . . . e6 13 ♕h5 ♗g6 14 ♕×d5 ♕×d5 15 ♗×d5 ♖a7 16 ♗f4 ♖d7 17 ♘×e6 fe 18 ♗×e6 ♘c6 19 ♖ac1.

III 12 . . . h5 13 ♖×e4 de 14 ♕b3! ♕×d4 15 ♗e3 with a winning attack for White.

IV 12 . . . ♘d7 13 ♘c6 ♕c7 14 ♗×d5 etc.

V 12 . . . ♗×g2 13 ♔×g2 dc 14 ♕f3 ♘d7 15 ♘f5 ♖g8+ (15 . . . e6 16 ♖×e6+! fe 17 ♕h5 mate) 16 ♔h1 e5 (16 . . . e6 17 ♕c6 threatening 18♖×e6+) 17 ♗e3 and despite being two pawns down White has an overwhelming position.

VI 12 . . . dc which is comparatively best—13 ♖×e4 ♕d5 14 ♕f3 e6.

VII The game continuation 12 . . . e5 13 ♕a4+ ♘d7 14 ♖×e4! de 15 ♘f5! ♗c5 16 ♘g7+ ♔e7 17 ♘f5+ ♔e8 18 ♗e3 ♗×e3 19 fe with a decisive attack.

Smyslov–Euwe, World Ch. Match-Tournament, 1948

Smyslov had sacrificed a pawn to reach this position *(187)* and now played 14 ♕e4! with these possible variations:

I 14 . . . ♕e6 15 ♖d6 ♗×d6 16 ♕×c6+ ♔e7 17 ed+ ♕×d6 18 ♕e4+ ♕e6 19 ♕h4+ f6 20 ♕g3 attacking the pawns at c7 and g7.

II 14 . . . ♕b7 15 ♘c3 ♖b8 (or 15 . . . ♗c5 16 e6 ♗×e6 17 ♘e5) 16 e6! with the sub-branches:

a. 16 . . . ♗×e6 17 ♘g5 ♘d8 18 ♖×d8+ ♔×d8 19 ♘×e6+ fe 20 ♕×e6 ♗e7 21 ♗g5! threatening 22 ♖d1+.

b. 16 . . . fe 17 ♘g5 ♘d8 18 ♖×d8+ ♔×d8 19 ♘f7+ ♔e8 20 ♘×h8 with material advantage.

III 14 . . . ♘b4 15 ♗g5 and again the sub-divisions:

a. 15 . . . ♗c5 16 ♘a3! ♗b3 17 ♖dc1 ♗f8 18 ♘×b5—crushing.

b. 15 . . . c6 16 ♖d8+ ♕×d8 17 ♗×d8 ♖×d8 and White has the advantage.

IV 14 . . . ♘e7 (the move actually played) 15 ♘a3! c6 (15 . . . ♗b3 16 ♖d3 ♗e6 17 ♘×b5 ♗f5 18 ♘×c7+) 16 ♘×c4 bc 17 ♕×c4 ♕b7 18 e6! f6 19 ♖d7 ♕b5 20 ♕×b5 cb 21 ♘d4 with great advantage.

Ravinsky–Smyslov, USSR Ch. 1944

From diagram 188 Black sacrificed a pawn by 25 . . . c4! based on these variations:

A 26 ♗×c4 ♘g4, and now

I 27 ♖e2 ♖d3! 28 ♗×d3 ♖×c1+ 29 ♔g2 ♖c3 with nasty threats e.g. 30 ♕d1 ♕×f2+ 31 ♖×f2 ♘e3+ 32 ♔g1 ♘×d1 33 ♖d2 ♗c5+ 34 ♔f1 ♘f2 35 ♔e2 ♖×a3 with a pawn up.

II 27 ♖c2 ♖d7, then a. 28 h3 ♘×f2 29 ♖×f2 ♗c5 30 ♖e2 ♕c7 forking c4 and g3, or b. 28 ♗f1 ♖dc7 29 ♖d2 (or 29 ♖ec1 ♗×a3!) 29 . . . ♖c3 strengthening the pressure.

III 27 ♖f1 ♖d3! 28 ♗×d3 ♖×c1.

B 26 ♖×c4 ♘g4, and now

I 27 ♕c2 ♖×c4 28 ♗×c4 ♘×f2 29 ♕×f2? ♗c5

II 27 ♖e2! ♖×c4 (or 27 . . . ♗c5 28 ♕c2) 28 ♕×c4 ♗c5 29 ♕c2 ♕×b5 30 h3 and White has repulsed the immediate threats.

C 26 h3 (The move made in the game, but it is inferior to 26 ♖×c4). 26 . . . c3 27 ♕b3 ♗c5 28 ♖c2 ♖d2! 29 ♖×d2 cd 30 ♖e2 ♗×f2+ 31 ♔g2 ♖c3! and Black has a winning attack.

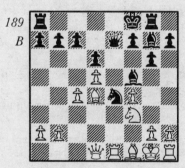

189
B

Corzo–Capablanca, Havana, 1913

In diagram 189 Black played 15 . . . g5! with the following possibilities:

A 16 ♘×g5 ♗×d4+ 17 ♕×d4 ♘×g5! 18 ♖×e7? ♘h3 mate.

B 16 fg ♘×g5 and now:

I 17 ♖×e7? ♘h3+ 18 gh ♗×d4 mate.

II 17 ♘×g5 ♗×d4+ 18 ♕×d4 ♕×e1.

III 17 ♗×g7+ ♖×g7 18 ♘×g5 ♕×g5 with advantage to Black.

C 16 ♗d3 gf and again Black has the advantage.

D 16 ♗×g7+ (the move played in the game) 16 . . . ♖×g7 17 ♘d4 ♗d7 18 f5 (18 ♗d3 is better) 18 . . . ♕e5 19 ♕d3 ♖e8 20 ♘e6+ fe 21 fe ♖×e6! 22 de ♗c6 23 ♕f3+ ♕f4! and Black finally won.

Alekhine–Koltanowsky, London, 1932

In diagram 190 White played 22 ♘×c7! based on the following calculations after the forced 22 ... ♖×c7 23 ♖×d6:

I 23 ... ♗×b3? 24 ♕×f6+ and 25 ♖×b3 winning easily.

II 23 ... ♘d4? 24 ♘×d4 etc.

III 23 ... ♕c4 24 ♘×c5!

IV 23 ... ♘d8 24 ♖f3 ♖f7 25 ♘×c5 and wins.

V 23 ... ♗f7 24 ♖×f6! ♘d4 25 ♘×d4 cd 26 ♕×c7 ♔×f6 27 ♖f3+ and wins.

VI 23 ... ♖e8 24 ♘×c5 ♘d8 25 b4 ♘f7 26 ♖×e6.

VII 23 ... ♔f7 24 ♖f3 ♔e7 25 a4 ♕b6 26 ♖×e6+ ♔×e6 27 ♘×c5+ ♔d6 (or 27 ... ♔f7 28 ♕×f6+ ♔g8 29 ♕e6+ etc.) 28 ♕×f6+ ♔×c5 29 ♖c3+ ♔b4 30 ♕d6+ wins.

VIII 23 ... ♗c4 (Black's choice in the game) 24 a4! ♕×a4 25 ♘×c5 ♕b5 26 ♕×f6+ ♔g8 27 ♘d7! ♖d8 28 ♖f3 ♕b4 29 c3 ♕b5 30 ♘e5! ♖dc8 31 ♘×c6 1–0

Black plays a combination in diagram 191 to destroy the enemy K-side based on the following variations:

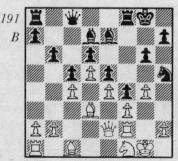

Alega–Alekhine, Paris, 1914

18 ... ♗×g4!! 19 fg f3! and now:

I 20 ♕e3 ♕×g4+ 21 ♔h1 ♗h4! 22 ♗d2 ♘f4 23 ♕×f3 (23 ♖×f3 ♕g2 mate) 23 ... ♘×d3! and wins easily.

II 20 ♕d1 ♕×g4+ 21 ♔h1 ♗h4 22 ♘e3 ♕h3 23 ♗f1 ♘g3+ 24 ♔g1 ♘×f1 25 ♕×f1 ♗×f2+ 26 ♕×f2 ♖f4! and Black should win as White loses the pawn at e4 in addition to the other losses already suffered.

III 20 ♕c2! ♕×g4+ 21 ♔h1 ♗h4 22 ♘e3 (22 ♗e3 g5! and then the g-pawn will be advanced further) 22 ... ♕h3 23 ♗f1 ♘g3+ 24 ♔g1 ♘×f1 25 ♘×f1 (25 ♖×f1? f2+ 26 ♔h1 ♗g3) 25 ... ♗×f2+ 26 ♕×f2 ♕g4+ 27 ♘g3 h5! and Black ought to win.

IV 20 ♖×f3 (as in the game) 20 ... ♕×g4+ 21 ♖g3 ♖×f1+ 22 ♔×f1 ♘×g3+ 23 hg ♕×g3 24 ♕e3 ♖f8+ 25 ♔e2 ♕g4+ 0–1.

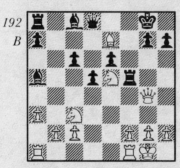

Yudovich–Botvinnik, USSR Ch. 1933

Let us try and re-establish the course of Botvinnik's thoughts in diagram 192.

I have gone wrong somewhere and the position is difficult for me. If 15 ... ♕×e7 then he will play 16 ♘×c6 ♕c7 17 ♘×a5 ♕×a5 18 ♕d4 with an excellent position. What about 15 ... ♕c7 with two pieces en prise? Perhaps I shall get the chance to exchange on c3 before recapturing a piece, and that would ease the position. What moves does he have? 16 ♘×c6, or 16 f4. Possibly also 16 ♖ae1 and then there is 16 ♗d8! Is that all? Yes, that seems all, so consider each in turn.

I 16 ♘×c6 ♗×c3! 17 bc ♕×c6 and the chances favour me. Black would have an excellent position, and White's extra pawn plays no part in it.

II 16 f4 ♕×e7 and the c6 pawn is safe because of 17 ... ♕c5+.

III 16 ♖ae1. That leads to a complicated game, for example:

  a. 16 ... ♖×e5 17 ♗d8 and White wins at least the exchange.

  b. 16 ... ♗×c3 17 bc ♖×e5 18 ♗d8! ♕d6 19 ♗f6 and Black can resign.

c. 16 ... ♗a6 17 ♘d3 ♕×e7 18 ♕×f5 and Black can resign.

d. 16 ... ♕×e7 17 ♘×c6 ♕c7 18 ♘e7+ ♕×e7 19 ♕×f5 and wins.

No, wait a moment! There is something wrong here. There is 16 ♖ae1 ♗×c3! 17 bc ♕×e7 18 ♘×c6 ♕g5! when I don't lose the exchange, and the weak pawns on White's Q-side deprive him of any chance of victory.

That leaves the fourth candidate move:

IV 16 ♗d8! ♕×d8 17 ♘×c6 ♕c7 18 ♘×a5 ♕×a5 19 ♕d4. I am a pawn down and stand badly.

What move should I choose then? Take on e7 at once or ♕c7? I will play the latter. If he finds 16 ♗d8! it will merely produce the same variation as if 15 ... ♕×e7, but I will force him to think a bit longer and he will have to solve additional problems.

In the actual game White did find 16 ♗d8 ♕×d8 17 ♘×c6 ♕c7 18 ♘×a5 with advantage.

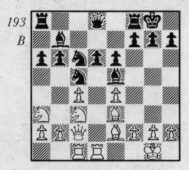

193
B

Karpov–Olafsson, Amsterdam, 1976

Before playing 15 ♖ac1 *(193)* the world champion worked through these variations arising after 15 ... ♗×c3 16 ♕×c3 ♘×e4:

A 17 ♕b3 and now:

a. 17 ... ♘c5 18 ♗×c5 bc 19 ♕×b7 wins.

b. 17 ... ♖b8! and Black has a sound position.

B 17 ♕d3! and now:

I. 17 ... ♘e5 18 ♕d4 ♘d7 19 f3 e5 20 ♕d3 ♘dc5 21 ♗×c5 ♘×c5 22 ♕×d6 with advantage to white.

II. 17 ... ♘b4 18 ♕b3 a5 19 ♘b5 and now:

a. 19 ... ♘a6 20 ♘×d6 ♗×d6 21 ♗×b6 ♕g5! attacking g2. Hence White does better to play 20 ♗f4.

b. 19 ... d5 20 ♗f3 dc 21 ♖×c4 ♗d5 22 ♖×e4! and White wins.

After solving each exercise, draw the tree of analysis for each one.

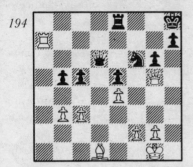

White intends 35 ♗e2. Which variations must he take into account?

Can Black take on h2? Back up your conclusion by variations.

White has just captured on g6 with his bishop. Confirm the soundness of this by variations.

Can White continue 14 e5? Work out the possible variations. Bear in mind that it is a complicated position and that the variations are intricate.

Work through the variations involved in the move 29 ♖g6.

Time Trouble

The two players sit down to play a game in a competition in a good mood, full of hope for the outcome, calm and confident. However the clocks tick away and moods change. One player becomes inspired by chances of victory, the other sits there under the threat of defeat. Now there is no question of their former equality and sense of well-being.

The change in atmosphere is noticeable in the state of the players, the position on the board and the state of the clocks. As a rule the player who stands worse is also worse off for time.

Then we get the last hour of play when the evil genie of time trouble hangs like a fearful apparition over the game. This evil genie has ruined thousands of games and fine creative ideas, has decided the fate of top titles: who amongst us has managed to keep calm when the flag is lifted by the minute hand and yet there are still several moves to make?

Time trouble pitilessly persecutes ordinary players and world championship contenders alike. Can it be cured, and if it can't, then how should you play with a hanging flag? The answers to these questions are of great practical importance.

The thinkers and the swift reaction players

The masters and grandmasters can be divided into three groups—the inveterate time trouble merchants, those who sometimes get into trouble, and those for whom the phenomenon is a very rare occurrence.

It is no secret that, for example, Geller is often at odds with his clock, and this applies just as much to Bronstein, Reshevsky, and Browne. On the other hand many experienced players fear time trouble and try hard to avoid it. There are a few grandmasters who almost totally exclude it: in this regard Karpov comes to mind. His speed of thought is so great that often his opponent's flag falls when he himself, even in the toughest top games, has a great deal of time in hand.

What is the reason for this? Obviously it is to be explained in terms of his natural ability, character, good nerves and most of all by the perfection of his 'thinking apparatus'. This apparatus has been so keyed up by much practice of analysis and play that it works perfectly under the most trying circumstances.

How to avoid time trouble

However even those who get into time trouble can get out of this habit. To do this they have to learn to discipline their thoughts, and develop the right way of thinking about variations. A great help in economizing on time is the right choice of opening and a knowledge of all the possible finesses in the line. If you can play the first ten to fifteen moves in just as many minutes, you can be in a state of bliss for the rest of the game. If, on the other hand, Bronstein thinks for forty minutes about his first move, then time trouble is inevitable.

There is an opinion that practice in lightning games can help. Obviously if you are practised in blitz play you may find it easier to find the right decision in a time scramble, but this is not an invariable rule. Some specialists at blitz lose their way in a scramble, and on the other hand some poor lightning players cope well in time trouble. The best example is Botvinnik, who never liked playing fast games, but always managed well when short of time.

So prepare well for the opening, and having saved time in that way do not lose it back again by wandering to and fro along the branches of the tree of analysis. That is the way to get out of the painful clutches of the clock.

Reference to time trouble as a justification for mistakes has long been condemned by the best players. In his notes to his game with Tylor at Nottingham 1936 Alekhine wrote about one of his moves, 'A horrible mistake, and the fact that White was in severe time pressure, in my opinion, is as little justification for it as the claim by a law-breaker that he was drunk at the time of the offence. The inability of an experienced master to cope with his clock must be regarded as just as serious a fault as an oversight'.

Calmness—the Paramount Consideration
The reader is entitled to advice on how to play in time trouble. What is it that guarantees success at such a point? First and foremost, be self-possessed and keep calm. If you can remain cold-blooded and do not make any impulsive gestures, if you can restrain your clenched fingers from reaching out to the pieces, you will greatly improve your chances.

When I was a young man I was a games demonstrator at the 1936 Moscow International tournament. The game between Flohr and Capablanca made a deep impression on me. The former world champion played inaccurately in the opening, lost the exchange for a pawn, and then blundered away the pawn as well. By move thirty his position was critical *(199)*.

Flohr–Capablanca, Moscow, 1936

It is not hard to see that White should win. He only had to play 30 ♖c7 for example and Black is hopelessly placed. However Flohr went 30 ♗g4 which let Black complicate.

30 ...	♞×g4
31 hg	♚g6
32 ♖d1?	

Lets slip his last chance to keep the advantage by 32 ♖c7, when the threat of 33 ♖×b7 ♛×b7 34 ♛f5 mate makes Black's defence difficult.

32 ...	♗a6
33 ♛f5+	

Trying to rule out any tactical tricks by exchanging queens, but in the endgame White's winning chances disappear completely.

33 ...	♛×f5

34 ♖×f5 ♖e4 35 ♖f3 ♖×g4 36 ♚f2 ♖e4 37 ♖e3 ♖f4+

38 ♖f3	♖e4

Not hurrying to win the pawn at f6 which would give White's pieces more freedom.

39 ♖d2	♚g5
40 b3	h5

The players carried on moving even though the forty moves laid down in the time limit had been reached. The point was that Flohr had stopped writing the moves down since he was in bad time trouble, while Capablanca did not feel that he should stop the blitz play. What if his opponent who had already gone wrong should make another mistake?

41 ♖e3	♖f4+
42 ♖f3	♖e4
43 ♚g3	h4+
44 ♚f2	♗b5

At this point Flohr finally took a breather and offered a draw. His winning chances were long gone—the time trouble had played a nasty trick on him. It is curious that on Capablanca's score sheet all the moves were written down in calligraphic handwriting.

Exploiting the opponent's time shortage
It is well known that it is advisable to drum up complications if the opponent is short of time, since he will not be able to work it all out in time. This is especially worth trying if the opponent has a totally won game (*200*):

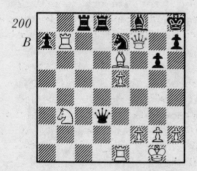

200
B

Reshevsky–Kotov, Candidates T. Zurich, 1953

Here I realized that my position was hopeless, but decided to play on his chronic time shortage. Reshevsky had already played a number of moves at blitz speed, and on each occasion had made ridiculous little jumps in his seat. This had exasperated me, and my next move is explained not only by my desire to exploit my last chance, but by my very nervous state.

Unexpectedly I put my queen on e2. If his rook goes to f1 then I have 35 ... ♖d1. Reshevsky realized this straight away and nearly lost his head.

His flag was quivering, but by a great effort he found the right answer. 35 ♕×f8+ forced me to resign at once.*

Well, all right, it hadn't worked, but it was a fine idea. I am firmly convinced that this was my only chance and I was obliged to take it!

Do we have the right to exploit the opponent's time shortage in this way? Is it ethical to try and trick in some way or other a player who has lost his head and sometimes all self-control? The best answer I can give is from the

---

Tr. note. In fact Kotov played on to beyond 40 moves before resigning.

'juridicial' point of view. At the start of the game each player is given $2\frac{1}{2}$ hours for 40 moves, on average $3\frac{3}{4}$ minutes a move. This 'treasure' must not be squandered. Then, on the other hand, there is no doubt that a player who plays quicker than the rate laid down runs some risk of making more mistakes than his deeper thinking opponent.

So the player who has used his time to the full has tended to think the position out better. Why then should we 'take pity' on the opponent who has used his time well to make a big step forward towards beating us? By the logic of the struggle we not only have the right but also the obligation to make use of his time trouble and put the maximum difficulty in the way of his finding the best moves.

The commonest misconception in such circumstances is to play quickly. Inexperienced players argue that if they take their time over moving, the opponent will use this time to work out all the variations and find the best answer. Such a policy of blitz play evens up the chances and can lead to gross blunders.

The best way to exploit the opponent's time pressure is to . . . conduct the game as if there were no time pressure at all. Of course you cannot be unaffected by the situation to some extent, but you must try to sit calmly at the board and work out your moves just as if the game was only starting. This is the most unpleasant thing for the opponent who is under pressure himself, but sees that you are ignoring his time pressure. This must be discouraging for him.

It is particularly important to maintain your imperturbability in positions where you stand better or in an even positional struggle. Here haste is out of the question. As I have indicated, there are cases where the attempt can be made to bamboozle, but this is only where you stand worse. If you can't see any good way to equalize then some form of unexpected shock move can be useful, even if it is unsound. This was the case with my ♕e2 move in a hopeless position against Reshevsky.

There is also the 'series of moves' technique used to baffle the opponent. You think out some unexpected line of play and spend a considerable amount of time on the process. The opponent is looking at the position during this period too, but it is hardly likely that he will work out as deeply as you can the consequences of this line. You after all have made up your mind to consider this alone, while he has to look at a range of other possibilities. Most likely many of the finer points of the line will escape his notice, since the introductory move is unexpected.

Once you have worked out all the consequences you play your moves at lightning speed. In the given circumstances the chances of success are high.

Cabalistic signs

The competition player is forbidden the use of reference material and mechanisms which might help or speed up his calculations. The only thing at his disposal is the score sheet and the 'time-trouble types' mark this up with all sorts of cabalistic signs which in their opinion help them to get out of time trouble.

I have seen many of these efforts on the sheets of my opponents and colleagues. The commonest is the 'mile-post sign'. After the 8th move they mark 30 m.; after the 16th 1 hr. and so on to the 40 with half an hour for each 8 moves. The intention is fine, but the implementation is pretty often poor. Such specialists in time trouble sit there using up their last quarter of an hour and they have only made twenty moves, sometimes less.

Then again some people try to cope with just the last ten moves. They are reconciled to getting into time trouble, and mark up the sheet in the reverse order so that opposite move 40 is written 1, opposite 39 is 2, 38–3, and so on. Then they have the count down to zero as in the launching of cosmic rockets.

They claim this gives them an instant sight of how many moves have still to be made, but not much good comes of it. Once time trouble arrives, any form of writing is forgotten in the rush to find a move and play it. Sometimes you will even see a player counting on his fingers. I have known players set up ten captured pieces by the side of the board and take one from the set after each time trouble move made. An unreliable method, and it is not clear whether the judge should permit such juggling.

Should any of these methods be imitated? Certainly not! I feel they not only don't help, but can hinder. I repeat that the only way is good preparation, proper analysis of variations, confidence in yourself and calmness. This is the way to play logically and accurately, the only way to use your time properly.

Anti Time Trouble Training

A universal remedy cannot be proposed since the fault is the product of so many different factors, but a significant reduction can be achieved by certain prophylactic measures.

Training in the calculation of variations has already been mentioned. Try to find a complicated position which is unknown to you and has been analysed by a strong player. Put a clock by the board and allow yourself and 'the opponent' three or four minutes before the flag drops. Try to play the position out working out the variations for each side. Then compare the lines you found with the annotations. By gradually reducing the time allowed you will get some practice at playing complicated positions with a hanging flag.

For particularly bad sufferers we can recommend play in special training events with the aim of avoiding time trouble. It is important to learn how to control your thoughts so that you do not waste time, but make up your mind without excessive timidity or doubts.

Botvinnik's Advice

It is particularly useful to read Botvinnik's comments, 'I tried as far as possible to rid myself of time trouble. Generally speaking you cannot be wholly rid of it, and this would be unwise. During a game there are moments when you have to examine the position scrupulously, you have to spend 20–30 minutes thinking it out and then make the remaining moves to the control at a quicker rate. This is "normal" time trouble and I do not intend to avoid it.

But it often happens that a player wastes valuable time at the board—he analyses variations which can be seen in advance as unsuitable, or he cannot drag himself away from a tempting but disadvantageous line. I have taught myself to use time economically, and reached a satisfactory solution to the problem sometimes even by reducing the standard of my play. There is no other way. How else can you accustom yourself not to waste time?!'

Then he adds this valuable advice, 'I long ago advised our masters who systematically get into terrible time trouble of a way of combatting this fault . . . You have to play training games in which your attention is directed primarily at the clock and not the standard of play or the result, and then continue these exercises until you have worked up the habit of using your time properly, of managing to work out all the necessary variations. I think that 90% of sufferers from time trouble would be cured by this method, with the one exception, naturally, of those who are "incurably ill".'

The Three Fishes in Action

The self-improvement process in a player has some similarities to the learning process of a musician. At first the student has to learn the correct handling of his instrument, then various exercises improve his technique and the suppleness of his fingers. Parallel with this is the study of the classical heritage of the great musicians, all those pieces which the performer will ultimately have to play on stage.

So too with the chess player. As he improves his positional understanding, his eye for combinations, and his technique of calculation, the
future master needs practice under the competitive conditions which will
test his application of these techniques.

All the rich variety of middlegame positions can be reduced to three
main groups:– positions in which we have the right and duty to attack;
positions in which we have to defend; and positions which are level,
characterized by lengthy manoeuvres. In each group the application of the
'three fishes' is decisive.

Attacking

As Steinitz stressed, the player with the advantage must attack, choosing
the opponent's weakest spot as his object of attack. Depending on the
circumstances this weak spot may be the king position, the centre or the
Q-side. We will examine first the attack on the king.

This is the most effective form of attack which follows up the main aim of
the game—to mate the enemy king. We consider three types in order:– the
attack on the uncastled king, the attack when the kings are castled on
opposite sides, and the attack when both kings are castled on the same side.

A lack of urgency or an opening mistake can lead to a failure to castle
when such a measure was called for. Then the other side can start
immediate play against the king or some other suitable object. In many
cases the result is a failure ever to reach safety with the monarch. Books on
the Sicilian Defence in particular abound with examples of this sort. The
attacker must spare no effort to exploit this situation. Here is one example
(201).

Kotov–Kalmanok, Tula, 1931

This position arose from a French Defence 1 e4 e6 2 d4 d5 3 ♘c3 ♘f6 4 ♗g5 de 5 ♘xe4 ♗e7 6 ♗xf6 gf 7 ♘f3 ♘bd7 8 ♗c4 c6 9 ♕d2 b6.

Black is lacking in development, but given the two moves ♕c7 and ♗b7 would succeed in castling on the Q-side. White takes immediate measures to stop this by threatening 11 ♕g7 and so forces Black to retreat a developed piece.

10	♕h6!	♗f8
11	♕f4	♗b7
12	0-0-0	h5
13	♔b1	♗e7
14	♕g3!	

The same idea, threatening the pawn win by ♕-g7-h7.

14	...	♘f8
15	♖he1	f5
16	d5!	

Now there is a direct way to finish off the king in the middle. Black has been kept so busy that he has not been able to remedy the chief defect in his position.

16	...	cd

Not 16 . . . ed 17 ♘f6 mate, nor 16 . . . fe 17 de threatening the queen as well as 18 ef mate.

17	♗b5+	♘d7
18	♘e5	

Black now played 18 . . . ♕c7, and lost quickly; if 18 . . . ♗c8, we have reached a position examined earlier in the book as diagram 141.

The main rule in playing against an uncastled king is that the attacker should initiate an immediate clash so as to prevent the defender developing and getting the king into safety. Do not be frightened of sacrifices to open lines against the king, though work out the consequences carefully.

Opposite side castling is normally a sign of sharp play, since each side can then advance a pawn storm against the enemy king without weakening the pawn cover of his own. An attack by pieces alone is a rare occurrence in such cases, and the following questions therefore naturally arise:– Who will get in first with the pawn advance, will one side be forced onto the defensive so that his pawn advance will merely prove to be weakening? Of course this does not mean that a few defensive moves on your king's side may not prove advisable.

It may prove advisable too to advance pawns against a potential castled position even before the enemy king has left the centre, both to act as a disincentive to castling and to be ahead of the opponent in the wing pawn race.

Remember that it takes several moves to get the pawns advanced so that line opening is inevitable, and we must therefore try to calculate the consequences as carefully as if in playing a combination, especially as such an advance normally means burning your bridges behind you.

The speed and effectiveness of the line opening advance is greater when the defender has made some pawn advance on that side, or when our advance is made with gain of time by attacking enemy pieces en route.

The position of our pieces must be considered, since a pawn storm cannot win on its own. If our pieces are far away some other method of play may be called for. All these considerations must be weighed before deciding on the pawn storm.

1 d4 f5 2 e4 fe 3 ♘c3 ♘f6 4 f3 e3 5 ♗×e3 e6 6 ♗d3 ♗e7 7 ♕d2 b6 8 ♘h3 ♗a6 9 0–0–0 ♗×d3 10 ♕×d3 ♘c6 11 ♘f4 ♘b4 12 ♕e2 0–0 13 ♔b1 ♕c8 14 a3 ♘bd5 15 ♘c×d5 ed *(202)*

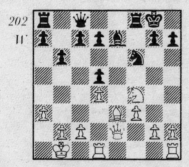

Kotov–A. Polyak, Moscow v Ukraine, 1937

White argued that his pieces are better placed to get at the king once lines are opened than Black could, but recognised that his advance a3 made line opening easier for Black. However with a stable centre and well placed pieces, the plan of a storm seemed sound. The position offers about equal chances to both sides.

    16 g4   ♕b7
    17 h4   b5
    18 ♕d3!

General considerations are not enough in such positions. Exact calculations indicated to White that when he advanced h4–h5–h6 Black could reply g6 when a knight sacrifice on g6 would be possible. The queen move is also a useful defence against Black's plan of opening the b-file since if now 18 . . . b4 then 19 a4 and 19 . . . b3 is ruled out.

              18 . . .   ♘e8?

A reasonable idea—to get the knight away from the advance of the pawns, but the advance itself could have been held up by the simple 18 . . . ♗d6 intending to take White's important knight.

              19 h5   ♖f6

We have said that the consequences of a pawn storm ought to be calculated as precisely as if it were a combination. Here are some of the lines worked out by White here in the event of 19 . . . ♗g5 which he considered the best method of trying to stop the pawns coming forward.

20 h6! and then:

a. 20 . . . ♗×h6 21 g5 winning.

b. 20 . . . ♗×f4 21 hg ♘×g7 22 ♕×h7+ ♔f7 23 ♗×f4 winning.

c. 20 . . . gh 21 ♘e6 de 22 ♗×g5 with a decisive attack.

d. 20 . . . ♖×f4 21 ♗×f4 ♗×f4 22 hg ♘×g7 (22 . . . ♘f6 23 ♕f5) 23 ♕×h7+ ♔f7 24 ♖h5 winning.

20	g5	♖d6
21	♕f5	b4
22	ab	a5
23	g6	♘f6
24	h6! *(203)*	

203
B

An impressive looking clash of pawns which forces open lines for the pieces to get at the king.

              24 . . .   hg

              25 ♕×g6   ♗f8

25 . . . ♘e8 26 h7+ ♔h8 27 ♕×d6 and 28 ♘g6 mate.

              26 h7+   ♘×h7

Equivalent to resignation, but if 26 . . . ♔h8 White mates in five by 27 ♕f7 ♘×h7 28 ♖×h7+ ♔×h7 29 ♖h1+ etc.

27 ♕×h7+   ♔f7
28 ♕f5+ ♔g8 29 ♘g6 ♖f6 30 ♖h8+ ♔f7 31 ♘e5+ ♔e7 32 ♕×d7 mate.

By far the most frequent case of attack on the king is when both sides have castled short. We have already seen examples of a piece attack in such cases e.g. Karpov–Polugayevsky (Diag. 48) Lasker–Capablanca (Diag 85) and a number of others. The method used is to concentrate as much force as possible on that side of the board and use weak points there to force a way home. More complicated cases occur when a pawn storm is involved, or intuitive sacrifices are played.

The advance of pawns in front of your own king to help in an attack is a risky business, which can only be justified if the centre is firmly closed and the opponent is not in a position to play some counter blow there.

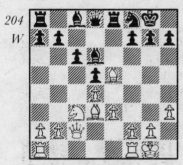

204
W

Ryumin–Kan, Moscow, 1936

In the position of diagram 204 White argued that the centre was safe from a counter strike and so he was justified in playing up his pawns to help in the attack.

14 f4! f6 15 ♗×d6 ♕×d6 16 ♖f3! ♗e6 17 ♔h1 ♖e7 18 ♖g1 ♖ae8 19 g4 ♗f7 20 ♕f2 ♔h8 21 h4! (Bold play, justified by Black's inability to force open the centre effectively). 21 . . . a6 22 f5 c5 23 ♘e2 cd 24 ed ♕b4 25 ♘f4 ♖e1 26 ♖g3 ♖×g1+ 27 ♖×g1 ♕e7 28 g5 fg 29 hg ♕e3

Black has finally succeeded in doing something active in the centre, but in the interim White's forces have become so strong that White's attack gets home even without queens on the board.

30 ♕×e3 ♖×e3 31 ♔g2 ♗c8 32 ♔f2 ♖e7 33 ♖c1 ♗c6 34 ♔f3 ♖f7 35 ♔g4 ♖c7 36 ♘e6 ♘×e6 (36 . . . ♖c8 was better) 37 fe ♔g8 38 ♔f5 ♔f8 39 ♔e5 g6 40 ♔d6 ♖e7 41 ♗×a6 ♔e8 42 ♗d3 1–0

What can happen if mass pawn advances are made in front of the king with an unstable centre is clearly shown here, where White's position crumbles quickly *(205)*

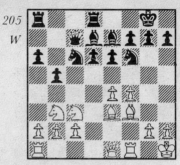

205
W

Vajda–Kotov, USSR–Hungary, 1949

14	g4	b4
15	♘e2	e5
16	f5	d5!

The appropriate counter stroke in the centre. If 17 ed e4! 18 dc ef 19 cd fe 20 ♕×e2 ♖×d7 there is nothing left of White's attempt to attack and his position is gravely weakened.

17	g5	♘×e4
18	♗×e4	de
19	f6	♗f8
20	fg	♗×g7
21	♕h4	

Black has little trouble repulsing this unjustified attack.

21 . . .   ♘e7

22 ♘g3 ♘g6 23 ♕h5 ♕c8! 24 ♕e2 ♗g4 25 ♕f2 ♗f3+ 26 ♔g1 ♘f4 and White soon resigned.

As the reader has already seen the successful conduct of an attack often involves sacrifices, which as a rule are based on exact calculation, if not to the very end then at least to the point where it is clear that adequate compensation is achieved.

However, there are cases in actual play where sacrifices are based on intuition rather than calculation, where the judgement and experience of the player tell him that the offer is worthwhile even though he cannot prove this. Such sacrifices are rare and there are players who never make them, who will only sacrifice if they can satisfy themselves that the offer is quite sound.

There are positions, however, where such an intuitive sacrifice is the only way to victory. Some would argue, why take the risk and still settle for a draw rather than get involved in the complications. It all depends on one's character, and attitude to chess.

Take an example from the greatest exponent of these sacrifices to see what entrancing complications can arise from such play *(206)*.

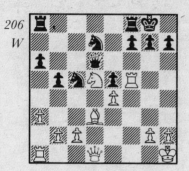

Tal–Pasman, Riga, 1954

White decides to go in for a line involving the sacrifice of two pieces to back up his attack on the king, believing in his instinct.

19 ♕g4 g6 20 ♖af1 f6 21 h4! ♔h8 22 ♖5f3 f5 23 ef!? ♕×d5 24 fg ♖×f3 25 g7+ ♔g8 26 ♗×h7+ ♔×h7 27 ♖×f3 ♘e4!

Black transfers his pieces quickly to the beleaguered king and the tension grows every move.*

28 h5 ♘df6 29 ♕g6+ ♔g8 30 h6 *(207)*.

*Tr. note. Tal has recently indicated 27 ... ♕e6! as the refutation e.g. 28 ♕h5+ ♕h6, or 28 ♖f5 ♘f6 29 ♕g5 ♘ce4.

This was the position Tal had in mind when giving up the two pieces, believing that the two far advanced passed pawns supported by queen and rook would generate strong threats to the enemy king. Tal has often played such double-edged lines disregarding the fact that subsequent analysis found holes in a number of them.

| | 30 . . . | ♖a7 |

Black already goes wrong. He could get a draw by 30 . . . ♘h7 e.g. 31 ♖f8+ ♘×f8 32 gf=♕+ ♔×f8 33 ♕g7+ ♔e8 34 h7 ♕d1+ 35 ♔h2 ♕h5+ with perpetual check.

| | 31 ♔h2! | |

A quiet move that leaves Black quite lost.

	31 . . .	♖e7
	32 ♖h3!	♘h7
	33 ♖d3	♕a8
	34 ♕×e4!	

The queen is diverted from the defence of the back rank and White's new queen helps in a winning attack.

34 . . . ♕×e4 35 ♖d8+ ♔f7 36 g8=♕+ ♔f6 37 ♖d6+ ♔f5 38 ♕g6+ ♔f4 39 g3+ ♔e3 40 ♖d3+ ♕×d3 41 ♕×d3+ 1–0

Among the many questions which the mind of the master has to resolve is whether to play a sacrifice. There are cases where it is obvious that he shouldn't, or that he should, but chess like life has many facets and such an ideal case is pretty rare. How much time is taken up in considering those unclear situations where he is tormented by doubt!

In those cases where analysis cannot answer the question, the player has to rely on intuition and experience; often he asks himself whether such a sacrifice has occurred before in similar situations. There is also the point that he may be able to reach his aim by quieter lines. The decision also depends on style and character. Some players are bold enough to go for a sacrifice even when calculation of the variations convinces them that it is dubious.

Then there is the opposite situation where a player works out that the sacrifice would give him a good game, even a win, but does not play it since a quiet line is just as effective and does not involve so much emotional upset. I remember a case where Capablanca worked out an impressive combination, but then chose to make a simple move in answer to which his opponent resigned at once!

Karpov too is well known for his rational approach to the game. We have given one example (diagram 48) where the press room experts 'recommended' an exchange sacrifice, but he took a simpler line. Does this

mean that he avoids sacrifices entirely? Not at all! When the offer of
material is the quickest way to victory, he will sacrifice even if it is not
entirely cut and dried and he has to rely partly on intuition.

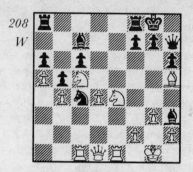

Karpov–Spassky, Candidates Match, 1974

Diagram 208 is a position from the decisive 11th game of the match that
took him to the final. He has the better position and 25 f4 or 25 ♘d2 would
leave him with the better of it. Instead he boldly sacrificed a bishop,
though the consequences could not be wholly clear at this point.

25 ♕f3!

The threat of 26 g4 trapping the bishop at h3 forces Spassky to accept
the sacrifice.

25 ...	f5
26 ♘c3	g6
27 ♕×c6	gh
28 ♘d5!	

White has only a pawn for the piece given up, but the knight move
produces an abundance of threats, such as ♖e7 or ♖e6 as well as various
knight moves not to speak of the bishop en prise at c7. Black's extra
material does not make itself felt.

28 ...	f4
29 ♖e7	♕f5
30 ♖×c7	♖ae8
31 ♕×h6	

The attack has brought White material advantage and Black could
already resign.

31 ...	♖f7

32 ♖×f7 ♔×f7 33 ♕×f4 ♖e2 34 ♕c7+ ♔f8 35 ♘f4 1–0

In deciding whether to sacrifice or not there are side-issues which can indicate one way or the other. These include the character and style of the opponent, the situation of the tournament or match in which you are involved, the state of the clocks, and the possible effect on colleagues in a team match.

A sacrifice may be more effective if played against a quiet player than one delighting in complications. You yourself may be one or the other. If you must go for a win, a sacrifice may well be indicated, but there are situations where a draw would suit you. Complications are best avoided in time trouble, unless you stand badly: of course if your opponent is badly short of time a sacrifice by you, even if not totally sound, has good chances of success.

Particular factors are involved in team competitions. Here the game is not just your personal responsibility since the course of the game will be followed with concern by your team mates. In such cases the spirit of collectivism has to be considered.

Let us assume that you have played a correct piece sacrifice. Only you know the fine points of your concept; to your colleagues it might seem that you have just lost material. Then they will start getting worried and this can affect the overall score. That is why, for example, in Soviet teams playing in the Chess Olympiads there is a strict though unwritten rule. You have to play in such a way that the rest of the team does not get concerned about your position. Even the greatest adherents of sacrificial play subordinate themselves to this consideration.

A large number of games are decided by assuming the offensive in the centre or the Q-side: in such cases sacrifices are less common; both piece pressure and pawn storms are suitable devices. When pawns advance in such cases they do not necessarily open lines, but the advance may also free space for the pieces to manoeuvre in.

The reader has already seen examples of various sorts of offensive in the centre, and on the Q-side; often pressure on the Q-side grows into an attack on the king. Such a transfer of the attack from one wing to the other occurs frequently in practice.

The important strategic postulate behind such play on both wings is that the pressure on one wing alone can be defended against adequately by the opponent, especially when the active side has no entry points for his pieces. In this case it is important to initiate action on the other side of the board. This stretches the defender's resources in having to move his pieces this way and that, especially if he lacks manoeuvring space. At some point the defender will not regroup in time and so suffer loss. Many games have been played in accordance with this strategical idea.

Defending

When a player gets an inferior position he is forced to defend, as indicated by Steinitz. The first essential is to realize the moment when your are required to adopt the defensive role and give up all ideas for the time being of winning. Many players recognize this too late, and start taking the necessary measures when it is already very hard to save matters. The author of this book, must, alas, be counted amongst this number—there you are sitting back and taking it easy when the enemy is already at the gates!

This feeling for danger is a most valuable asset, part natural and part acquired by practice. Karpov and Petrosian have such a sense of danger to a high degree. To achieve such a sense demands not just general understanding of the game, but also strong will power and self-control.

Once you have recognized that you are in some danger you must mobilize yourself to create the maximum difficulties for the opponent, put obstacles in his way and so hope to slow down the pace of his assault. It is at that point that you can start thinking of seizing the initiative again.

Passive defence demanding calm nerves and sticking power. There is also the policy of exchanges, especially of our passive units for active enemy ones, with the long term aim of reaching an endgame that will be easier to draw. This is particularly the case with rook and pawn endings or opposite coloured bishop endings. Of course this pre-supposes that the defender has a high level of endgame technique and knows how to play these endings which have a marked tendency towards a drawn outcome.

'Attack is the best form of defence' is a slogan that applies in many spheres of activity, chess included. If you choose the exact moment to counter-attack, it can have great psychological effect, so we advise the reader to take plenty of time over his choice of when to play the appropriate counter blow.

We must stress that preparing such a counter strike when under pressure is a difficult art, but the reader must try to master it. Counter attacking moves as a rule are very striking and enrich chess no less than the finest combinations. That is why players who have mastered this art have always been so highly thought of.

Level Positions

The position from which the game starts can be considered as fairly level. In the course of play one side often gets the better of it while the other side is forced to defend. However in many games the equilibrium is not disturbed and the players manouevre in accordance with Steinitz's precept, trying to upset the balance in their favour. If no mistakes or inaccuracies are made, then level positions keep on producing even chances for each side.

However the same methods of applying the three factors of chess mastery apply, though the effects they produce may well be in more subdued tones than when one side is bending the other to his will. For the same reason, play in such positions tends to be more exacting than when the aim is clearer. To recognize the crucial moment when a chance is presented is not easy and the only guarantee against failure is the overall and move-by-move assessments which we mentioned in Part One.

209
W

Alekhine–Feigin, Kemeri, 1937

Assessment indicates that diagram 209 is fairly level, though Black has weak points at b6, d6 and f6. There are some drawbacks in his piece position too, but the possession of d5 is valuable for him.

Alekhine's aim in his subsequent manoeuvring is easily understandable. He will try at all costs to drive an enemy knight from d5 so as to cramp Black. Also he will try to block the Q-side by a4–a5. Finally the position of the pawns at h6 and g6 may enable White to weaken the K-side further by the advance of the h-pawn to h5.

Black in his turn must try to prevent these threats directed against his weaknesses, and aim to avoid being more and more cramped for space.

	16 ♖fe1	♛d7
	17 ♗h2	

Removing the bishop from attack after Black's ♘d5, and freeing f4 for the knight transfer ♘c3-e2-f4.

17 ...   ♘fd5

18 ♘e2 ♖fd8 19 ♘f4 ♗f5 20 ♘×d5 ♘×d5 21 ♗c4! ♗e6 22 a4! ♖ac8 23 ♗b3 ♛c7

24 a5

White has achieved one of his aims, and Black should fight this blockade by b6, but he restricts himself to attempts to make use of the weakened b5 square.

	24 ...	♛d7

25 ♗a4 ♛e7 26 ♗g3 ♜c7 27 ♗b3 ♛d7 28 ♗h4 ♜b8

	29 ♗a4	♛c8

Typical slow manoeuvring play. White has achieved something in that the rook at b8 is not well placed, but this is not a great achievement and White continues his process of 'feeling out' the enemy position.

	30 ♖ac1	♜c4

Here is where 30 . . . b5 was necessary. Now White gets the chance to cramp Black's pieces.

	31 ♗g3	♝f8
	32 h4!	♞f6

Otherwise h5 would weaken the K-side seriously.

	33 ♗b3	♜×c1
	34 ♖×c1	♛d7
	35 d5 *(210)*	

Now the position can no longer be called level. White has cramped the enemy pieces which can no longer cope with White's pressure.

	35 ...	♝f5

36 ♛b4 ♝e4 37 ♛d4! ♛f5 38 ♞d2 ♝×d5 39 ♗×d5 ♞×d5

	40 ♞e4	

The time has come to exploit the advantage. There is a threat of 41 ♛×d5 and 42 ♞f6+ as well as the capture on d6.

	40 ...	♝g7

41 ♞×d6 ♛e6 42 ♛d2 ♞f6 43 ♛c2 b6? (Speeds up his defeat, but even after the superior 43 . . . ♞h5 44 ♗h2 b5 45 ♞×f7 White has the advantage) 44 ♛c7! ♞d7 45 ♞×f7 ♜f8 (45 . . . ♛×f7 46 ♖d1 winning) 46 ♞d8 ♛f6 47 ♖d1 1–0

The Opening

The exacting reader of this book whose aim is to know how to become a grandmaster may wonder at the amount of attention given to the middle game compared to the opening and endgame. Our answer is that in these phases of the game we get the same struggle of the pieces, of plans, tactical blows and combinations, though the first and last parts of a game do have their special features.

However there are incomparably more books available on the endgame and opening than the middle game. As a result, understanding of the middle game has greatly lagged behind those phases of the game where memory and learning now play such a big part.

We can discern four different attitudes to the opening depending on a player's tastes and character.

1. The wide reader: Talk to some young masters and they will overwhelm you with reference to a mass of variations, complete with references to games, who played what and when, what the world champions said about it. This is not just a specialist in one opening, but a walking encyclopedia who knows nearly all openings, remembers all the variations in the specialist works of theory.

Can he be called an expert in the openings? Strictly speaking, no. If you dig deeper, you find that he spouts out the variations without feeling the finesses of the position. Yet how much time goes on the study of these books and magazine articles! Such a player hardly has the time to study the basic theory of the middlegame and other aspects of chess.

This approach cannot be recommended; it is sure to lead to impoverishment of your play. How often have I met such sorry experts. Out of their band has come not a single player of top class.

2. The 'ideas' man: He is the direct opposite of the wide reader. He bases himself on a knowledge of the ideas of this or that opening, though he may not know concrete variations. He simply knows which piece to place where, which part of the front to give his attention to.

This approach is the one that grandmasters tend to have towards the end of their careers, when they lack the effort or the stimulus of ambition to make them work through current analysis of openings that they may have been keenly interested in in their youth.

So in opening the game, especially with an erudite opponent, such a player will play 1 ♘f3 2 g3 3 ♗g2 then fianchetto the other bishop and avoid any sharp opening fight. His argument is that he understands the position better than his opponent and it is in his interest to get to the middle game as soon as possible, avoiding all risk of falling into some sharp prepared line.

Look at many of the games of Smyslov and Bronstein to see that they never agree to set their foot on some path thoroughly worked out in modern analyses, but with which they are unfamiliar. The same applies to other veteran grandmasters.

3. The opening theoretician: Only a few current or previous grandmasters deserve or deserved this title. Their names figure in series of opening works, in regular articles in chess magazines. They are dangerous opponents, especially if you fall into one of their pet lines. However there are also cases where someone has found a hole in their published analysis and used it against them so that one might say, 'Those who live by the sword shall perish by the sword.'

It is hard to follow their example, there are only a chosen few who can devote themselves to such unremitting effort. However their knowledge can be regarded as an ideal in respect of a few openings that a player should specialize in. Follow their example of deep study in your favoured lines, not with the aim of perpetuating your name in chess history but so as to deepen your understanding and have the confidence to play this and other stages of the game into which there may well be a carry-over effect.

4. The world champions: Once again let us learn from their example. Straight away one can say that there were no 'widely read' types among them, except perhaps Euwe, and towards the end of their careers they nearly all turned to an 'ideas' approach. But the world champions were great connoisseurs of the openings that they did play, produced a lot of fresh ideas in them, sometimes shattering their opponents with an unexpected discovery.

What practical advice can be given, how should one proceed? The best answer seems to be, 'Learn a little about everything, and everything about one thing'. True, this is work enough for a lifetime, but it gives a guide to the problems posed by the expansion of knowledge and information.

You should choose two or three openings which you intend playing regularly in your games, and study them deeply. At the same time try and have some knowledge of the other openings. It might come in useful and the ideas found there might be applicable to your basic arsenal.

First of all consider the problem of playing with Black, which is always harder in view of the initiative which White enjoys in the early stages. Settle on one opening to adopt against 1 e4 and one against 1 d4. The choice must depend on your tastes, character and experience.

Then you have to decide whether you are basically going to be a 1 e4 player, or a 1 d4 player. In either case there is much to be studied in view of the wide choice of replies by Black.

I must admit that there is a risk of being too limited in this approach, but the overall aim must be to keep your opening play in harmony with your play in the later parts of the game. To make considerable advances in your opening play without being able to follow this up in the rest of the game is pointless.

Practical experience has shown that the more players get involved in studying theory from the many books available the more they run the risk of missing the elementary, of not seeing the wood for the trees. Even very strong players get so engrossed in a pet variation that they forget to check whether they are developing their pieces quickly and on the right squares, whether they are getting the king away from the dangers of an open centre.

Of course every rule has its exceptions, and knowing when you can make, say, three moves with a knight in a row is part of overall mastery. It is useful to remember that such cases of 'breaking' the elementary rules given in beginner's books often arise when the opponent himself has made such errors first, and the need to punish him for it demands concrete reaction.

Particular care should be taken over pawn moves since such moves cannot be taken back, and a weakness resulting from a bad pawn move is a permanent one.

While busy with development and pressure on the centre it is a useful guide to bear in mind the overall strategic aim of that particular opening you have adopted, so that you may be consistent in following up the aim.

Only in the case of forced variations should there be a need to go delving in opening books. Understanding general ideas and a mastery of the three fishes should give you the confidence to solve any opening task posed to you. Certain grandmasters keep an opening file, a collection of those variations which he will need during actual play, his own favourite lines. Such a file is handy and easily transportable so that it can be taken to a tournament. The reader may care to draw up such a file and notebook of his own, which will help him in preparing for his games.

The Endgame

The three fishes of chess mastery apply just as much here as to the opening or middle game, but the endgame does have its own specific features. First consider the transition to the endgame and the need to take a calm look at the new situation that has arisen.

As Belavenyets has pointed out, the middle game tends to put us in an excited frame of mind. With sacrifices and combinations in the air each side is tensed up, but suddenly we have mass exchanges and after the 'poetry' of sharp combinational struggle we get the 'prose' of the endgame.

Since technique predominates in the ending, the player has to re-adjust his thoughts and his mood. There will be little scope now for brilliancy or tactics. If you can spare the time on the clock, it would pay to devote several minutes to calm down after the passion of the middle game, so that you will start examining the position in the correct way from the point of view of the endgame.

The most general rule one can state about this phase of the game is that there is no need to hurry. In the opening or middle game we are conscious of the need to carry out our ideas with due despatch, not to lose a tempo and so on. If you examine the games of the best endgame players, Capablanca, Flohr, Smyslov, Karpov, you will be surprised at the number of repetitions, the slow measured progress they make. If a pawn can go h2–h4, say, the grandmaster will often take his time and play h3 first and h4 later.

The reasons for this approach are:

1. Gaining time on the clock in view of the hourly control applying at this stage.

2. The chance to sink deeper into the position, to make slight changes and then assess what real difference they make.

3. Developing the right attitude of massive calm.

4. The psychological pressure exerted on the opponent, who is thus convinced that he is in your power while you play cat and mouse with him. It is very hard to play well under such pressure, which often induces mistakes.

In the ending, as a rule planning comes to take first place, and relegates the investigation of variations to second place—in some way a reversal of roles as compared to the middlegame. Schematic thinking comes first, as seen in the way Capablanca thought about this position *(211)*

211

Capablanca–Ragozin, Moscow, 1936

He wrote thus:— 'White's plan is to prevent the advance of the enemy c-pawn which might make his own pawn at b2 weak, and to control the whole board as far as the fifth rank. This is achieved by playing the king to e3, the rook to c3, the knight to d4 and the pawns to b4 and f4. When this has been achieved White will advance his Q-side pawns'.

Note—no variations! Nor does he worry about how much time the process might take. The main thing is the scheme, the formation that has to be reached.

The next special feature is the change in the role of the king. No longer does he have to skulk in the corner for his own protection, there is an open field before him. In fact the participation of the king is often the decisive factor and it could well be that nothing fundamental should be undertaken until the king's role has been determined and his best position taken up.

Exchanges give rise to the endgame, and in the ending exchanges are of paramount importance in accordance with the scheme 'What piece to exchange, what to leave on' *(212)*

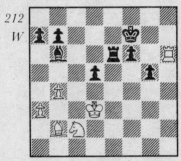

Alatortsev–Levenfish, Match 1940

White played 1 ♗d4 and Levenfish, a great master of the endgame, commented, 'The bishop had to be cherished like the apple of his eye, since in the struggle against passed pawns the knight is not a very suitable piece. The right move was 1 ♗c1 and if 1 . . . g4 then 2 ♗f4.'

In the actual game the knight could not vanquish the pawns and after 1 . . . ♔g7 2 ♖h1 ♔g6 3 ♗×b6 ♖×b6 4 ♘e3 ♖a6 5 ♖a1 f5 6 ♘×d5 f4 7 b5 ♖e6 8 ♖c1 ♖e5! 9 ♖c5 f3 10 ♘f4+ ♔f5 11 ♖×e5+ ♔×e5 12 ♘h5 ♔d5 the game ended in a draw.

The role of knowledge in the ending is nowadays very great in view of the extensive study that has been carried out of typical positions. The results have been summarized in a number of books, amongst which the series edited by Averbakh takes first place.

As a result many formerly unclear questions have been clarified and the technique of playing positions such as R+BP+RP v R, 2N v pawns, Q+P v Q and so on has been codified.

In fact theoreticians have gone further by classifying the correct methods of play in many varied endings such as R+P v R, all pawn endings and many queen endings. Is a grandmaster required to know all these analyses? Obviously not, but he does well to have an idea of their essential features.

One feature that the ending shares with the middlegame is the need to understand rather than to remember. What is the best way to train in endings? You are obliged to master the elementary examples such as the square rule for pawn endings, R+P on the 7th v R, consideration of the long and short sides of the passed pawn in rook and pawn endings. Then you have to consider those cases when a bishop is better than a knight or vice versa. After this you have to move on to endings with more material on the board. Once again we recommend the method of taking a position that has been analysed by a strong player: work through the moves yourself and compare your conclusions with the notes.

As an example of this sort of approach, we take an interesting ending of some length by Rubinstein *(213)*.

Faktor–Rubinstein, Lodz, 1916

First of all the assessment. White has weak squares at g4 and on the white squares generally. His pawn at e4 is weak and under threefold attack. Black's bishops are well placed, but he has the drawback of a doubled pawn which makes it harder for him to exploit his advantage.

Black's plan is to improve his piece position by putting his bishop on g6 or h7, and his knight on g4. Then he will try to exploit his well placed pieces by advancing the K-side pawns. In the long run further pressure will be applied to the weak pawn at e4 and the new weakness that will arise at f4. White's counter plan is based on advancing his e-pawn so as to divert Black from his plan.

	1 . . .	h5!

To fix the weakness at g4.

	2 c4?

A bad mistake robbing White of the chance to advance his e-pawn supported by a knight at c4.

	2 . . .	a5

Before preparing the opening of lines on the K-side, Black wants to close the other side. White goes along with this, though his only chance now was to keep open options of active play.

	3 a4	♔d7
	4 ♔f1	♗c6
	5 b3	♔c8

The lack of haste we spoke about as Black probes this way and that, psychologically as well as positionally.

	6 ♖e3	♗d7
	7 ♔g2	c6

Ruling out ♘d5 and preparing a possible retreat for the bishop if White plays a desperate e5 advance.

	8 ♘b1	♗c7
	9 ♘c3	♘h8

The start of the transfer to g4, but to keep up the pressure on e4 Black first gets his bishop to g6.

	10 ♖d3	♘f7
	11 ♖ed1	♗g4
	12 ♖1d2	♘h6
	13 ♗g1	♗b8!

A careful move to stop White getting any initiative e.g. 13 . . . ♗e6 14 ♘d5! cd 15 ed and 16 d6.

	14 ♗f2	♗e6
	15 ♖d1	♗f7
	16 ♗g1	♗g6
	17 ♘d2	♘f7

Where is the knight doing? Didn't we say it was needed at g4? Yes, but this manoeuvring helps to mask his plans so that the knight will reach g4 eventually with effect.

	18 ♖e1	♗h7
	19 ♔f3	♘h6

Why not g5 at once? Once again the motives are conspiratorial. Remember the classical phrase, 'The threat is stronger than its execution.' The point is that carrying out the threat removes some of the tension that the opponent suffers from as we keep him in suspense. This uncertainty can often induce panic.

20 ♗f2   ♘g4

21 ♗g1 g5! 22 ♖e2 gf 23 gf ♖g8! 24 ♖e1 ♖eg7

25 ♘e2

The threat was the unpleasant 25 . . . ♘h6 and 26 . . . ♖g4. Now comes another blow at the centre.

25 . . .   f5!

26 ef

(26 c5 ♗×e5! 27 fe ♘×e5+ 28 ♔e3 f4+)

26 . . .   ♗×f5

27 ♘e4 ♗×e4+ 28 ♔×e4 ♖e8+ 29 ♔f3 ♖f7 30 ♖dd1 ♖ef8

31 ♖f1   ♗×f4

There was no way for White to save this pawn; the end is near.

32 ♘×f4   ♖×f4+

33 ♔g2 ♖×f1 34 ♖×f1 ♖×f1 35 ♔×f1 ♘h6 and Black soon won with his extra pawn. (♘–f5–d4 etc.)

An examination of a couple of dozen endings like this one must produce a rise in the reader's ending play. Meanwhile try these exercises.

Exercises

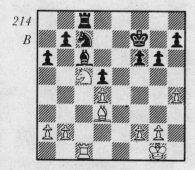

214
B

215
W

For each side work out which piece it is desirable to exchange and which to leave on.

Find White's correct plan and indicate the right piece formation to carry out this plan.

216
W

What does White's advantage consist of? Which exchanges should he aim for to enable him to realize this advantage? Indicate the winning plan for White.

218
B

What are Black's advantages and what plan should he follow? Indicate the moves following this plan.

217
B

What plan would you recommend to exploit the extra pawn?

219
W

White stands worse. Which piece should he leave on to help the defence and which should he exchange?

Final Words of Advice

In striving to play like a grandmaster one has to improve one's mastery of the three fishes, the three main components of play. To gain the grandmaster title however, more is demanded—practical results in international tournaments, so that approval will be given by the international ruling body FIDE.

Many people consider the competitive side a drawback which takes something away from the game as an art. Yet I feel the sporting element is the game's great advantage, which makes it popular amongst millions who do not play the game themselves.

The achievement of good results demands physical hardiness, strong nerves, endurance, calmness and the maintenance of a strict regime. As Alekhine put it, 'During a chess tournament a master must envisage himself as a cross between an ascetic monk and a beast of prey.' Fine words! A beast of prey towards the opponent, an ascetic in one's everyday life. Alas, Alekhine himself was not always an ascetic.

Botvinnik and other members of the Soviet School have worked out the right approach to preparation and sporting regime. About a month before the tournament a player should study the games of his opponents—no easy task. You should also try to get up to date with latest theory and study your own play. Alekhine stressed the last named point, and you often hear in all competitive activities the advice that if you want to be strong you have to be hard on yourself.

Opening preparation is also valuable, concentrating on those lines you intend playing in the event. If something that you do not know is published in one of these lines, you do well to try it out in two or three training games. The practice of using training games to get into trim has been widely used by a number of leading players, notably Botvinnik. On the other hand, other world champions have taken a sceptical view of training games on the grounds that they lack the stimulus of a real contest and so cannot be taken seriously enough. Not everybody can force himself to give of his best in such conditions.

A short time before the event begins, you should have a break to avoid boredom or staleness. Botvinnik said that he took a break about five days before the first round; I know of other grandmasters who make the break longer than that.

During the actual tournament you have to make an effort to keep calm and husband your strength. 'I try to play in a calm fashion not letting my nerves worry me, and it's not so easy to achieve this. You have to bear this in mind constantly during the game. Calmness is not just for show; my mind only works well when I keep calm, so I specially train myself to cultivate this quality' (Botvinnik).

In the 1946 Groningen tournament, the veteran grandmaster Bernstein reproached me for taking too much out of myself by playing to win in every game and creating sharp positions all the time. He warned me that my strength would give out before the end of the 19 round tournament.

He was right. I once checked up on my results in top class events and found that I had often lost my last round game; I was too exhausted to cope. Botvinnik too had difficulties in this regard; 'Earlier, as a rule, in almost all long tournaments I started off by garnering a lot of points, but then at the end could hardly "stick to the saddle". In the 12th–15th rounds I nearly always lost a game. It stands to reason that you must expend all your energy in that way. It is better to use it up in more even fashion so that there is no cracking up at the end, and the whole tournament will be less tense for you.'

When I played in top class tournaments, and later when I used to be captain of the Soviet team or chief judge of a tournament, I watched the routine of a tournament day that grandmasters maintained.

Only a few grandmasters have the habit of going to bed well after midnight and sleeping till noon—though you can't get to sleep straight away after a game. The majority of them had got into the habit of following Botvinnik's routine. In the morning after breakfast they would take a stroll for an hour, then do their preparation for the day's game. Then go on foot to the round, have supper after the game, and then to bed. No analysing adjourned games in the evening, though to be honest only Botvinnik himself could stop himself looking at them. I must insist though that you will save a lot of nervous energy if you don't look at adjourned games straight away. The main period of analysis of these should take place on the adjourned games day, but it is permissible to have a short look at them the morning after they are adjourned.

Folke Rogard, former President of FIDE, was once stressing that the factors of success at chess were not just good play and knowledge of the game, but good form and tiptop physical condition. He was interrupted by a reporter who objected that they were talking about chess not boxing.

The Swede had his answer ready: if you have to play for up to five hours a day, spend hours analysing adjourned games and openings and on top of that often sleep badly because of the great nervous tension, then you were undergoing a physical burden as great as any boxer had!

Our book is coming to an end. Whether you come to play like a grandmaster depends largely on you, your talent, character, persistence. I hope that working through this book will do you good, and if you make the grade I hope you will remember the contribution made by the author's advice.

Solutions to the Exercises

Diagram 32. Alekhine–Helling, Dresden, 1936.
Black has seriously weakened black squares, which give White a decisive positional advantage. He will aim at d6 with his knight after first exchanging the black square bishops. 17 ♗a3! ♗c6 18 ♕g4 ♖e8 19 ♘c4 (19 ♗×e7 ♖×e7 19 ♘c4 ♖d7 20 ♘d6 is possible, but White did not fancy the exchange sacrifice 20 . . . ♖×d6) 19 . . . h5 20 ♕f4 ♗g5 21 ♕g3 ♗h4 (21 . . . ♕×d4 loses to the sacrifice on g6 e.g. 22 ♗×g6 fg 23 ♕×g5 ♕×c4 24 ♕×g6+, or 22 . . . ♗f4 23 ♗×f7+ ♔×f7 24 ♘d6+ ♔f8 25 ♘×e8+ ♔×e8 26 ♕g6+ and 27 ♖ad1) 22 ♕e3 ♕d5? (22 . . . ♕g5 was better) 23 f3 ♗d8 24 ♘d6 ♖e7 25 ♗c5 1–0. The queen is trapped.

Diagram 33. Najdorf–Averbakh, Zurich, 1953.
White has weak pawns at a2 and c3 which are much weaker than the pair at a6 and b6. There is a gaping hole at c4 which Black can occupy with knight or rook. White has the inferior bishop.

White will hope to attack b6, but the pawn can move forward as well as be defended by the knight at c4. Note how Black transforms his advantages giving up his good bishop and ridding White of the pawn at c3 in order to penetrate with knight and rook. 21 . . : ♘c4 22 ♗e1 ♗×b4! 23 cb ♘a3 24 ♖b3 ♘b5 25 e3 ♖c2 26 a4 ♘d6 27 a5 b5 28 ♖c3 ♖ac8 29 ♖×c8 ♘×c8 30 f3 ♘e7 31 ♗f2 ♔f7 32 ♖b1 ♘f5 33 ♔f1 ♘d6 34 ♖b3 ♘c4 35 ♔g2 f5. White is in Zugzwang. If 36 f4 ♘d2 winning a piece; king moves lose the f3 pawn, rook moves lose the pawn at e3 or b4. White soon resigned.

Diagram 34. Kotov–Gligorić, Zurich, 1953
Black sacrifices two pawns to get a firm grip of the black squares, particularly e5. 11 . . . e4! 12 fe f4! 13 ♗f2 ♘d7 14 ♘g1 ♕g5 15 ♗f1 ♘e5 16 ♘f3 ♕e7 17 ♘×e5 ♕×e5 18 0–0–0 ♘f6 19 h3 ♗d7 20 ♗d3 a6 21 ♘b1! (To dislodge the queen by ♘–d2–f3. Black finds a superb reply) 21

. . . f3! 22 gf ♘h5 23 ♘d2 ♘f4 (Black threatens 24 . . . ♘×d3+ and despite the material superiority of two pawns it is White who is fighting to draw) 24 ♗f1 b5 25 h4 ♔h8 26 ♖g1 ♗f6 30 ♘b3 and White finally managed to draw.

Diagram 35. Botvinnik–Boleslavsky, USSR Absolute Ch., 1941.

'A positional mistake which increases White's advantage. White gets two pawn islands (Capablanca's term) while Black has three. Moreover the pawn at d5 can easily become weak. The question now is whether White will be able to exploit his slight advantage by piece play. After 14 . . . ♗e4 it would be almost level since the strong white knight at d4 would be compensated for by the bishop at e4' (Botvinnik). White went on to win in a long ending.

Diagram 36. Kotov–Steiner, USSR–USA, Moscow, 1955.

White has a marked positional advantage—the better pawn formation, weak white squares round Black's king, possession of the b1/h7 diagonal. White can open the g-file with decisive effect for his major pieces by g4–g5. 25 ♖f3! ♘d6 26 g4 ♖f8 27 ♔h1 ♔h8 28 ♖g1 ♕d8 29 ♖fg3 ♖d7 30 g5! ♘f5 31 ♗×f5 ef 32 gh gh 33 ♕g2 ♖df7 (Black defends against the threat of 34 ♖g7 which he can now meet with 34 . . . ♕e8 35 ♕g6 ♕e4+ 36 ♔h2 ♕c2+ 37 ♖g2 ♕×g2+! with advantage, but White has another entry possibility) 34 ♖g6! ♕e7 35 ♖g8+ 1–0

Diagram 37. Teichmann–Bernstein, St. Petersburg, 1909.

It looks about level except for the significance of the long black diagonal and the point f6. White plays to exchange black square bishops. 1 ♗h4! ♗d4+ 2 ♔h1 ♔g7 Now the king robs the bishop of g7, so 3 . . . ♗f2! ♗×f2 (3 . . . ♗e5? 4 f4) 4 ♖×f2 ♕a5 (to stop 5 ♕c3+) 5 ♕e2 f6 6 ♕b2 ♖f8 7 g4! h6 8 h4 g5 9 f4! gh 10 ♘×f6! and Black soon resigned, since 10 . . . ♖×f6 loses to 11 g5.

Diagram 38. Larsen–Najdorf, Lugano Olympiad, 1968.

Black has weak squares at e5 and c5 and weak pawns at c4, a6, e6, but this is outweighed by White's weak second row and the hanging position of his knight at d2 and pawn at e4. 1 . . . ♖8b2! 2 ♘×c4 ♖c2 3 ♕e3 ♘×e4 4 d5! ed 5 ♘b6 ♖×c3 6 ♕d4 ♕h5! (White's attempt to activate his pieces fails against the enemy concentration of force on his king) 7 ♕×d5+ ♔h7 8 ♕×a2 ♖×h3+ 9 gh ♕×h3 10 ♕h2 ♘f2 mate.

Diagram 39. Kotov–Bogatyryov, Moscow, 1935.

White's pawns hold the king in a grip and the weaknesses at f6 and g7 indicate an attack by ♘e4 or ♕e5. White's own king is badly defended too, but the passed d-pawn advance is decisive. 31 d6 N×f5 (otherwise 32 Qe5) 32 Ne4 N×e3+ 33 Q×e3 Qa4+ (to get queens off, otherwise 34 Qc3) 34 b3 Qd4+ 35 Q×d4 cd 36 Nf6+ Kh8 37 d7 Rd8 38 Kd2 and White wins by marching the king to e7 via d4.

Diagram 40. Capablanca–Vidmar, New York, 1927.

White has the two bishops, whereas Black's knight is not too well placed after f3, and it is not clear where it should go. B–e3–b6 is a nasty threat soon. Black can only hope to hang on for a draw by reason of the symmetrical pawn placing. 23 f3 Rfd8 24 Be3 h6 25 Red1 Bc6 26 Rac1 Be8 27 Kf2 R×d1 28 R×d1 Rc8 29 g4! White cannot yet play to win material by 29 Bb6 in view of the answer 29 . . . Nd7 and if 30 B×a5 Nc5. So he aims to dislodge the knight from f6 by h4, g5 and then follow up Rd5. 29 . . . Bd7 30 Bb6 Be6 31 B×e6 fe 32 Rd8+ R×d8 33 B×d8 Nd7 34 B×a5 Nc5 35 b3 N×b3 36 B×b4 Nd4 37 a5 1–0.

Diagram 41. Botvinnik–Levenfish, Moscow, 1935.

White has a formidable pawn centre and more space. Black is behind in development with the king still in the centre, so White can push forward there to open lines. 14 d5! Be7 (14 . . . cd 15 ed Be7 16 Bf4 0–0 17 de Qc6 18 ef+ R×f7 19 Kg1 with a pawn up, or 17 . . . Q×e6? 18 Re1 and 19 R×e7) 15 e5 Nb5 16 d6 N×c3 17 bc Bd8 18 Qd4 c5 19 Qg4 Rg8 20 Qe4 Rh8 21 Be3 and White finally won despite stubborn resistance.

Diagram 42. Kotov–Taimanov, Zurich, 1953.

Black's position looks quite reasonable, but he has one outstanding defect. His knight at a5 is badly placed and has little prospect of getting to a good square. White plans to exploit this by playing all his pieces to the K-side in order to work with an extra piece there. 19 Nh4 a6 20 a4 Qa7 21 Nf5 Bf8 22 Ne4 N×e4 23 B×e4 b6 24 Qd1 ab 25 ab Bd7 26 Qh5 Be6 27 Bf4 Nb3 (The start of an attempt to find some use for this piece. 27 . . . Nb7 loses to 28 N×h6+ gh 29 B×h6 B×h6 30 Q×h6 with a winning attack) 28 Qd1 Qa2 29 h4 Na1 30 h5 Nc2 31 Be5 Nb2 32 Bc7 Na3 33 Qg4 Qc1+ 34 Kg2 Nb1 35 Bf4 Nd2 (Losing a piece, but there was no hope left) 36 Qe2 1–0.

Diagram 43. Stahlberg–Kotov, Zurich, 1953.

  Despite the opposite coloured bishops White is lost—the bishop at d4 stands well, his opposite number is not supported, Black's king is more active. The pawn at f2 is an object of attack in which the pawn at g4 takes part. Finally White cannot exchange rooks. 48 Rh1 Re8 49 f3 b5 50 Kf1 bc 51 bc g3 52 Rh7 Rb8 53 Bb7 Be5 54 Kg2 Bf4 55 Rf7+ Ke3

56 f4 ♗×f4 57 ♖e7+ ♗e5 58 ♖f7 a5 59 a4 ♔d4 60 ♗d5 ♖b2+ 61 ♔f1 ♖a2 0–1

Diagram 90. Botvinnik–Sir George Thomas, Nottingham, 1936.

The stages are:– 1. Force the pawn from h7 to h5; 2. Win the pawn at h5 with the king; 3. Transfer the knight to f5 so freeing the king to come forward; 4. Retreat the knight to f1, then chase the enemy king into a stalemate position on a8, so that f2 is forced. This pawn is lost to the white king which comes back from c7 or c8.

45 ♘h5 ♔d8 46 ♘f6 h6 47 ♘g4 h5 48 ♘f2 ♔d7 49 ♔h4 ♔d8 50 ♔×h5 ♔e7 51 ♔g4 ♔e6 52 ♔g3 ♔d7 53 ♘h3 ♔d8 54 ♘f4 (There was the alternative method of sacrificing the knight on f3 to get a won pawn ending) 54 . . . ♔d7 55 ♘h5 ♔e6 56 ♘g7+ ♔d7 57 ♘f5 ♔c8 58 ♘d6+ ♔b8 59 ♘f5 ♔c8 60 ♔f4 ♔b8 61 ♔e5 ♔c8 62 ♔e6 ♔b8 63 ♔d7 ♔a8 64 ♘g3! (Not 64 ♔c7? f2 65 ♘g3 f1 = ♕ draw) 64 . . . ♔b8 65 ♘f1 ♔a8 66 ♔c8 1–0.

Diagram 91. Botvinnik–Unzicker, Oberhausen, 1961.

White has an active bishop, which he moves to its best possible position at f1. This lets the rook become active on the a-file, and then the king gets to the centre. 49 ♗f1! ♔g6 50 ♖c5 ♔h5 51 ♖×f5+ ♔×h4 52 ♖a5 ♖d7 53 ♔f2 ♖e7 54 ♔f3 ♘g6 55 ♗c4 ♘e5+ 56 ♔f4 ♘g4 57 ♖a6 ♔h5 58 ♗d5 ♘e5 59 ♗e4! 1–0 (It is Zugzwang—if 59 . . . ♘f7 then 60 ♗f3+ ♔h4 61 ♖a5!).

Diagram 92. Karpov–Pomar, Nice Olympiad, 1974.

White has the advantage with his active pieces—the bishop has good diagonals to fire along at the king, either a5/d8 or h2/b8, and the rook can get to the 7th and 8th ranks. Also White has more space and can activate his king, something which Black cannot do.

The plan is to provoke b6 which will finally imprison the black king on the back two rows. Then the bishop goes to the h2/b8 diagonal and the king comes up to the centre so that Black cannot successfully attack White's pawns. Finally White's pawns move forward to take part in an attack on the circumscribed king.

34 ♖f8+ ♔c7 35 ♗a5+ b6 36 ♗d2 ♘e4 37 ♗f4+ ♔b7 38 ♖f7+ ♔a8 (Not 38 . . . ♔a6 39 ♗b8) 39 ♖f8+ ♔b7 40 b4! ♖×g4 41 ♖f7+ ♔a8 (Here it was better to retreat to c8) 42 ♔c2 h5 43 a4 h4 44 ♔d3 ♘g5 45 ♖f8+ ♔b7 46 ♖b8+ ♔a6 47 ♗d2! ♖g3+ 48 ♔c2 1–0. There is no defence against the threat of 49 b5+ mating.

Diagram 93. Kotov–Pilnik, Stockholm Interzonal, 1952.

White has these advantages:– 1. All Black's pawns are on the colour of his bishop which thus lacks all mobility; 2. All White's pieces are active, whereas Black's skulk on the back two rows; 3. Black has two fixed weaknesses at a6 and f7.

The plan is to combine attacks on a6 and f7, notably by playing h5 at the right time, so that White will get his bishop to h5 attacking f7. 42 ♗e2 ♘b8 43 ♘d3 ♔e7 44 ♘e5 ♘c6 45 ♔b2!

This envisages ♘×c6 and ♖c1 to force a bishop ending that would be hopeless for Black after White gets his king to c5 and goes h5. Taking on e5 would leave the f7 pawn hopelessly weak.

45 . . . ♖b7+ 46 ♔c3 ♔d6 47 ♘×c6 ♖c7 48 ♔b3 ♖×c6 49 ♖f1 ♖c7 50 h5 gh 51 ♗×h5 ♖b7+ 52 ♔c3 ♖c7+ 53 ♔b3 ♖b7+ 54 ♔c3 ♖c7+ 55 ♔d2 ♖b7 56 ♖×f7 and White won with his extra pawn.

Diagram 94. Marshall–Capablanca, Match, 1909.

The position is about level. The logical sequel would be for White to advance his pawns by e4, ♔e3, f4, e5 so that he might possibly get attacking chances. Black would advance his pawn majority to get a passed pawn and divert White's pieces from the other side. In the game Black did this, White just ran on the spot: 16 ♖fc1 ♖ab8 17 ♔e4 ♔c7 18 ♖c3 b5 19 a3 c4 20 ♗f3 ♖fd8 21 ♖d1 ♖×d1+ 22 ♗×d1 ♖d8 23 ♗f3 g6 24 ♔c6 ♔e5 25 ♔e4 ♔×e4 26 ♗×e4 ♖d1+ 27 ♔g2 a5 28 ♖c2 b4 29 ab ab 30 ♗f3 ♖b1 31 ♗e2 b3 32 ♖d2 ♖c1 33 ♗d1 c3 34 bc b2 35 ♖×b2 ♖×d1 and Black duly won.

Diagram 95. Nimzovitsch–Capablanca, St. Petersburg, 1914.

White's plan is to consolidate his position and try to win with the extra pawn. Black's plan is to occupy the open files on the Q-side with his rooks, transfer the knight to c4 and exert general pressure on the enemy Q-side pawns. 1 . . . ♔e6 2 f3 ♘d7 3 ♗d2 ♘e5 4 ♔e2 ♘c4 5 ♖ab1 ♖a8 6 a4 (6 b3 is no better—6 . . . ♘×d2 7 ♔×d2 ♖a3 and the a2 pawn will fall) 6 . . . ♘×d2 7 ♔×d2 ♖c4 8 ♖fd1 ♖eb8 9 ♔e3 ♖b4 10 ♔g5 ♗d4+ 11 ♖×d4—otherwise the ♔-side pawns would be lost, but with the exchange up, Black soon won.

Diagram 96. Capablanca–Alekhine, Match, 1927.

The position is about level. Black plans to get maximum control of the white squares on the centre and on the Q-side. To this end he will play his knight from c5 to c4, exchange the knight at c3 and post his bishop on d5. This will give him many strong squares in the centre.

15 . . . ♘cd7! 16 ♗g3 (White should react by ♘–b3–a5 to keep a grip on c4) 16 . . . ♘b6 17 ♕b3 ♘fd5 18 ♗f3 ♖c4! 19 ♘e4 ♕c8 20 ♖×c4 (Another mistake. The accurate move was 20 ♕b1 continuing to struggle for the c-file and the c4 square) 20 . . . ♘×c4 21 ♖c1 ♕a8 22 ♘c3 ♖c8 23 ♘×d5 ♗×d5 24 ♗×d5 ♕×d5 25 a4 ♗f6 26 ♘f3 ♗b2! (Preparing the winning manoeuvre of advancing his e-pawn) 27 ♖e1 ♖d8 28 ab ab 29 h3 e5 30 ♖b1 e4 31 ♘d4 ♗×d4 32 ♖d1 ♘×e3! 0–1 Black wins a piece.

Diagram 97. Kotov–Stahlberg, Stockholm Interzonal, 1952.
Black has threats of breaking through with his well placed pieces. White will play for exchanges, or consolidate his position by transferring the bishop to f3. 23 ♗e2! ♘f6 (It was better to allow ♗×h5, since now Black starts to meet with difficulties) 24 ♗f3 ♗g4 25 ♗g1 ♗e3 (The move that gives the initiative to White. 25 . . . ♖e7 to double rooks was stronger) 26 ♗×e3 ♖×e3 27 ♗×g4 ♘×g4 28 h3 ♘f6 (If 28 . . . ♕h4 White has 29 ♘×d5 ♖×h3+ 30 gh ♕×h3+ 31 ♔g1 ♕g3+ 32 ♕g2) 29 ♕f2 ♖e6 30 ♕f4 White, glad that he has repulsed the enemy pressure only thinks in terms of a draw, whereas by the attacking line 30 ♖d3 intending 31 ♖g3 or 31 ♖f3 he would build up strong pressure that Black could hardly resist. 30 . . . ♕×f4 31 ♖×f4 Draw.

Diagram 175. Spassky–Petrosian, Match, 1969.
White has pressure on the g- and f-files, there are potential threats on the diagonals a2/g8 and b1/h7. 21 ♘f3 and 22 ♘h4 is slow. 21 e5 de 22 ♘e4 looks strong since if 22 . . . ♘×e4? 23 ♖×f8+ mating, or 22 . . . ed? 23 ♘×f6 g5 (else 24 ♕g6) 24 ♕h3 ♖e7 25 ♖×g5 ♗g7 26 ♖×g7 ♔×g7 27 ♖g1+ mating.
   So 22 . . . ♘h5 to guard g7. Then 23 ♕g6 ed 24 ♘g5! hg 25 ♕×h5+ ♔g8 26 ♕f7+ ♔h8 27 ♖f3 g4 28 ♖×g4 mating. The only defence remaining is 23 . . . ♘f4 24 ♖×f4 ef and now possible is the slow 25 c3 intending 26 ♗c2 and an early mate on h7. More decisive however is 25 ♘f3! (Not 25 ♘f5 ef 26 ♘g5 ♕×g5 27 ♖×g5 ♖e1 mate, nor 25 ♘d6 ♖e7 26 ♘4f5 ♗e8) 25 . . . ♕b6 (Only queen moves can affect the situation; if 25 . . . ♕a5 26 ♘f6 ♕f5 27 ♕×h6+! mating) 26 ♖g5! (Not letting the queen get to b5, which is the answer to 26 ♖g2 or 26 ♖g4. Not 26 ♘f6 ♕×g1+!) and now the threat is 27 ♘f6. The only way to stop it is 26 . . . ♕d8 and then 27 ♘e5 leaves Black helpless.

Diagram 176. Nimzowitsch–Capablanca, New York, 1927.
White's queen is far away from his weak K-side. Black intensifies the pressure by forcing doubled rooks on the seventh. 1 . . . e5! 2 ♗×e5 ♖dd2.

Now 3 ♖f1 ♕×e3! 4 ♗f4 ♖×f2! wins. Or 3 ♖f1 ♕d5 4 ♗d4 ♕h5 5 h4 (otherwise captures on f2 and h2) 5 . . . ♕f3 and again catastrophe on f2. White tried 3 ♕b7 ♖×f2 4 g4, but after 4 . . . ♕e6 5 ♗g3 ♖×h2! 6 ♕f3 (6 ♗×h2 ♕×g4+ 7 ♔h1 ♕h3 mating) 6 . . . ♖hg2+! 7 ♕×g2 ♖×g2+ 8 ♔×g2 ♕×g4 Black won.

Diagram 177. Tal–Najdorf, Leipzig Olympiad, 1960.
White has a concentration of forces on the K-side, but there is no breakthrough apparent after 1 ♕g4 g6, while suppressing the only defender by 1 ♖×e4 de and then 2 ♘×g7 loses to 2 . . . ♗×d4+ and 3 . . . ♗×g7. But 2 ♗f6! rules out this defence, and if 2 . . . gf? 3 ♕g4+ mates. Black has 2 . . . ♕b6 when the brilliant 3 ♕h6 loses to 3 . . . ♕×f6, but 3 ♗×g7 ♖fe8 4 ♗e5 yields a winning attack—4 . . . ♕g6 5 ♘h6+ ♔f8 6 f5! ♕g5 7 ♘×f7! ♔×f7 8 ♕×h7+ ♔f8 9 ♗d6+, or 6 . . . ♕c6 7 ♕h5.

Diagram 178. Botvinnik–Chekhover, Moscow, 1935.
Black has weak spots round the king, notably f7, and the pieces on the ♕-side do not defend the king. 22 ♘g5! is not even a sacrifice strictly speaking as after 22 . . . hg 23 fg the knight cannot move from f6 without allowing 24 ♘×f7 and ♕h5, ♕×e6 or d5 to follow. So 23 . . . ♘8d7. There is the straightforward follow-up 24 ♘×d7 ♖×d7 (24 . . . ♘×d7 25 ♖×f7 ♔×f7 26 ♕h5+ ♔f8 27 ♕h8+ ♔f7 28 g6+ ♔f6 29 ♕h4 mate) 25 gf ♗×f6 26 ♖×f6 gf 27 ♕g4+, but what about a grand assault by 24 ♘×f7 ♔×f7 25 g6+ with two main lines:

A 25 . . . ♔f8 26 ♕×e6 ♘e5 27 ♖×f6+! (27 de ♗c5+ 28 ♔h1 ♗×g2+ 29 ♔×g2 ♖×d3 is not good enough) 27 . . . gf (27 . . . ♗×f6 28 ♗a3+) 28 ♕h3 ♗b4 29 ♖e1! ♗c8 30 ♕h6+ ♔e8 31 de ♗×e1 32 ♕h8+ ♔d7 33 ♕g7+ ♔c6 34 ♕×f6+ ♔c7 35 e6 winning.

B 25 . . . ♔g8 26 ♕×e6+ ♔h8 27 ♕h3+ ♔g8 28 ♗f5 ♘f8 29 ♗e6+ ♘×e6 30 ♕×e6+ ♔h8 31 ♕h3+ ♔g8 32 ♖×f6! ♗×f6 33 ♕h7+ ♔f8 34 ♖e1 ♗e5 35 ♕h8+ ♔e7 36 ♕×g7+ ♔d6 37 ♕×e5+ ♔d7 38 ♕f5+ ♔c6 39 d5+ ♔c5 40 ♗a3+ ♔×c4 41 ♕e4+ ♔c3 42 ♗b4+ ♔b2 43 ♕b1 mate.

Diagram 179. Hewitt–Steinitz, London, 1866.
Black attracts the king to h3 into the firing line of the battery ♗d7/♘g4. 1 . . . ♖×g2+ 2 ♔×g2 ♕h3+! 3 ♔×h3 ♘e3+ 4 ♔h4 ♘g2+ 5 ♔g5 (or ♔h5) ♖f5+ 6 ♔g4 h5+ 7 ♔h3 ♖f2 mate. If 3 ♔g1 ♖f2! 4 ♕f3 ♖×f3 5 ♘×f3 ♘×h2 6 ♘×h2 ♕×g3+ 7 ♔h1 ♕f2 and 8 . . . ♗h3, or 6 ♗×h2 ♕×f3.

Diagram 180. Alekhine—Freeman, New York, 1924.

Taking on b7 will weaken Black's back rank and there are captures on g7 and f6 to be considered. 1 ♗×b7 ♖×b7 2 ♕×f6! (2 ♘h6+? gh 3 ♕×f6 ♕×f6 4 ♗×f6 is bad) 2 . . . ♕×f6 (2 . . . gf 3 ♕h6 ♕f8 4 ♖e8!) 3 ♖e8+ ♘f8 4 ♘h6+! ♕×h6 5 ♖×f8+ ♔×f8 6 ♕d8 mate.

Diagram 181. Keres–Petrosian, Bled Candidates, 1959.

The pawn wedge on g3 after 47 . . . ♖g3! 48 hg hg is strong with the threat of 49 . . . ♕h4. Rook and bishop must move from f2 and f1 to make room for the king. 50 ♖fd2 ♕h4 51 ♗e2 ♖h7. The point is the thematic back row mate after 52 ♔f1 ♕×f4+! 53 ♕×f4 ♖h1 mate. White has to make more room for the king by 52 ♗h5 ♖×h5 53 ♔f1. Then 53 . . . ♘d3 54 ♖×d3 ed 55 ♕×d3 ♕h1+ and 56 . . . ♕×g2+.

Diagram 182. Uhlmann–Smyslov, Moscow, 1971.

20 . . . ♘×f2 21 ♕×f2 ♗×f3 looks as if White has simply lost a pawn, but White has 22 ♗h3 so as to meet 22 . . . ♖a8 by 23 ♗×g7! which is unclear. Clearly Black does best to give up the exchange for powerful bishops. 22 . . . ♖×e5 23 ♗×c8 ♗c6. Then 24 ♗×a6? ♕d5, or 24 ♗h3 ♕e8 25 ♗g2 (25 ♖c3 ♗b4) 25 . . . ♖×e3 26 ♔h1 ♗×g2+ 27 ♔×g2 ♕e4+ 28 ♔h3 ♕e6+ 29 ♔g2 ♕d5+ 30 ♔h3 ♖e6! threatening mate and the queen.

Diagram 194. Fischer–Unzicker, Zurich, 1959.

1. 35 . . . ♘×e4? 36 ♕h6 ♖e7 37 ♕f8 mate; 2. 35 . . . b4 36 ♖a6 ♘×e4 37 ♕h4 ♕d5 38 ♗f3 ♕d3 39 ♖a7 wins; 3. 35 . . . ♕b6 36 ♖f7 ♘g8 37 ♕h4 h6 38 ♕g4 ♖d8 39 ♗×b5! with decisive advantage; 4. 35 . . . ♖b8 36 ♖f7 ♘g8 37 ♖d7! ♕f6 (or 37 . . . ♕×d7 38 ♕×e5+ ♕g7 39 ♕×b8 ♕×c3 40 ♕×b5) 38 ♕e3 ♕c6 39 ♖d5 and one pawn must fall; 5. 35 . . . ♖e7, as played in the game, 36 ♖×e7 ♕×e7 37 ♗×b5 ♔g7 38 ♗e2 and wins with the extra pawn.

Diagram 195. Fischer–Benko, Candidates, 1959.

14 e5 and now:– 1. 14 . . . ♘×b3 15 ef gf (15 . . . ♗×f6 16 ♘ce4) 16 ♗h6 with the threat 17 ♕g4+. 2. 14 . . . bc 15 ef ♗×f6 (15 . . . gf 16 ♗h6 f5 17 ♘h5 and ♕–f3–g3) 16 ♗×f6 gf (otherwise 17 ♕g4) 17 ♘e4 ♕f5 18 ♘×d6 and now either 18 . . . ♕c5 19 ♕g4+ ♔h8 20 ♕h4 ♕×d6 21 ♕×f6+ ♔g8 22 ♖ad1 ♕c5 23 ♖f3 ♖e8 24 ♖d8! ♗b7 25 ♖g3+ ♔f8 26 ♕h8+ ♔e7 27 ♕×e8+, or 18 . . . ♕g6 19 ♖f3 ♔h8 20 ♖g3 ♕h6 21 ♕g4 ♕g6 (22 ♕g8+ or 22 ♘×f7+ were the threats) 22 ♕h4 wins. 3. 14 . . . de, the hardest line and the one played in the game. 15 ♗×f6 and now three lines: a. 15 . . . ♗×f6 16 ♘ce4 ♕e7 (16 . . . ♕d4 17 ♘×f6+ gf 18 ♕g4+ ♔h8 19 ♖ad1 ♕×b2 20 ♘h5 ♖g8 21 ♖d8

and 22 ♕g7 mate) 17 ♘h5 ♔h8 (17 . . . ♗h4 18 fe and 19 ♕g4) 18
♘e×f6 gf 19 fe fe 20 ♘f6 and 21 ♕h5; b. 15 . . . bc 16 ♘e4
♕b4 17 ♕g4 ♗×f6 18 ♘×f6+ ♔h8 19 ♕h4 h6 20 ♘g4 threatening 21
♘×h6 with a powerful attack e.g. 20 . . . ♔h7 21 fe with 22 ♘f6+ or 22
♖f6 to follow; c. 15 . . . gf 16 ♘ce4 and now two further sub-divisions:–

A 16 . . . ♕c7 17 ♘h5! (Stronger than 17 ♕g4+ ♔h8 18 ♕h4 ♖g8)
17 . . . f5 18 ♘hf6+ ♔g7 19 ♕h5! ♗×f6 (19 . . . h6 20 ♖f3 ♖h8 21
♖g3+ ♔f8 22 ♕×h6+!, or 20 . . . fe 21 ♖h3 ♖h8 22 ♘e8+!) 20
♘×f6 h6 (20 . . . ♖h8 21 ♕g5+ ♔f8 22 ♕h6+ ♔e7 23 ♕h4 ♔f8 24
♘×h7+ wins) 21 ♖f3 ♖h8 (21 . . . ♗×f6 22 ♕h4+ ♔g7 23 ♖g3+ ♔h7
24 ♖h3 mates) 22 ♘e8+ ♖×e8 23 ♖g3+ ♔f8 24 ♕×h6+ ♔e7 25
♕h4+ and now either 25 . . . ♔f8 26 ♖h3! ♕d8 27 ♕h6+ ♔e7 28
♕g5+ winning the queen, or 25 . . . ♔d6 26 ♖d3+ ♔c6 (26 . . . ♔c5 27
♗a4 threatening 28 ♕f2+) 27 ♗a4+ ♔b7 28 ♗×e8 with a big material
plus.

B 16 . . . ♕d4 17 ♕h5! and there is no defence against the threat of 18
♕h6 and 19 ♘h5. The main variations are 17 . . . ef 18 ♘f5! ef 19
♖×f4 ♕×e4 20 ♖×e4 fe 21 ♕×a5, and 17 . . . ♘×b3 18 ♕h6! ef
(18 . . . f5 19 c3!) 19 ♘h5 f5 20 ♖ad1 ♕e5 21 ♘ef6+ ♗×f6 22 ♘×f6+
winning the queen.

Diagram 196. Euwe–Flohr, Match, 1932.
Black cannot take the pawn. 28 . . . ♕×h2 29 ♕f3 and now–:

a. 29 . . . ♕h6 30 ♕f6+ ♕g7 31 ♕×g7+ ♔×g7 32 ♗d7 ♖d8 33 e6
♔f6 34 e4! followed by ♖–f2–f7+.

b. 29 . . . h5 30 ♗e6 ♔g7 31 ♗f7! ♕h3+ 32 ♔g1 ♔h7 33 e6 with great
advantage.

c. 29 . . . ♔g7 30 ♕f6+ ♔h6 31 ♗f3! threatening g4–g5 mate. Now 31
. . . ♗c8 32 ♕f8+ ♔g5 33 ♕f4 mate, or 31 . . . ♕h3+ 32 ♔f2 ♕f5 33
♕×f5 gf 34 ♔e3 ♔g5 35 ♖c1 threatening ♖c1–h1–h5 and ♔f4, or 31
. . . ♕×g3 32 e3! ♖e8 (32 . . . ♗c8 33 ♕f8+) 33 ♖g2 ♕h3 34 ♔g1 and
35 ♖h2.

Diagram 197. Karpov–Cobo, Skopje Olympiad, 1972.
If 23 . . . fg 24 ♕h3 ♗d7 25 ♖f7! ♔×f7 26 ♕×h7+ ♔e8 27 ♕g8+
♗f8 28 ♖f1 ♔d8 29 ♕×f8+ ♗e8 (29 . . . ♔c7 30 ♕d6+ mates) 30
♗b6+ ♔d7 (30 . . . ♖c7 31 ♘c5 with decisive advantage) 31 ♖f7+
♗×f7 32 ♕×f7+ ♔c6 33 ♘d4 mate. Or 23 . . . hg 24 ♖e3 etc.

Diagram 198. Spassky–Bobotsov, Havana Olympiad 1966.
29 ♖g6! fe 30 d6 ♕f7 31 ♘d7 and now:–

a. 31 . . . ♗f5 32 ♖f6 ♕g7 33 ♕×g7+ ♔×g7 34 h6+ ♔h8 35 ♖f1 wins.

b. 31 . . . e3 32 ♖hg1 e2 33 ♖f6 and now a. 33 . . . ♖g8 34 ♖×f7 ♖×g1+ 35 ♔c2 ♗f5+ 36 ♖×f5 e1 = ♕ 37 ♖f8+ ♖×f8 38 ♕×f8+ ♖g8 39 ♕f6+ ♖g7 40 ♘c3! and Black has no defence against 41 h6 or 41 d7. b. 33...e1 = ♕+ 34 ♖×e1 ♕g7 (34... ♕g8 35 ♖g6) 35 ♕×g7+ ♔×g7 36 h6+ ♔h8 (36... ♔g8 37 ♘e7+ ♔h8 38 ♖×f8+ ♖×f8 39 ♘×c8 ♖×c8 40 d7 ♖d8 41 ♖×e5 winning) 37 ♖×e5 with a winning ending.

c. 31 . . . e3 32 ♖hg1 ♗f5 33 ♖g7 ♖g8 34 d7! winning.

d. 31 . . . e3 32 ♖hg1 ♖g8 33 ♘f6 e2 34 ♔d2 c3+ 35 bc ♕a2+ 36 ♔e3 winning.

Diagram 214. Levenfish–Kotov, USSR Ch. 1939

The position is almost level. Black has to keep the bishop on (It would not be bad to have a knight against White bishop, but this is hard to achieve). So 1 . . . ♘e6 to exchange knights was right. Instead there came 1 . . . ♘b5? 2 ♗×b5! ♗×b5 3 ♖c3 b6 4 ♘a4 ♖×c3 5 ♘×c3 with a favourable ending for White which he won—the d5 pawn is weak.

Diagram 215. Karpov–Polugayevsky, Candidates match, 1972.

White has the excellent plan of blockading the Q-side and then advancing his pawns there. This involves the moves a5, ♗e2, c4 and b2–b4–b5. 37 a5! ♖c6 38 ♗e2 ♔d8? (38 . . . ♘g6 was better) 39 c4 ♔c7 40 b4 ♘g6 41 b5 ab 42 cb ♖c2 43 b6+ ♔d7 44 ♖d2! ♖×d2 45 ♖×d2 ♖e5 (or 45 . . . ♖×e4 46 ♗b5+ ♔c8 47 ♖c2+ ♔b8 48 a6 ba 49 ♗×a6 ♖e8 50 b7 ♘e7 51 ♖e2 winning) 46 a6 ♔c6 47 ♖b2 ♘f4 48 a7 ♖a5 49 ♗c4 1–0

Diagram 216. Flohr–Bondarevsky, Moscow, 1939.

White's plus consists of the powerful knight at e5, but this alone is not enough for a win. White must manoeuvre to weaken the enemy position further. 1 a5! ♖c7 2 ♖h6+ ♗g6 3 ♖h1 ♗f5 4 ♖c1! An excellent manoeuvre threatening both b5 and a6. Black is forced to put another pawn on the colour of his bishop and lose all hope of active play on the Q-side. 4 . . . a6 5 ♖h1 ♖g7 6 ♖h2 (No hurrying!) 6 . . . ♖c7 7 ♖h6+ ♗g6 8 ♖h4! (To force e4 which will cover the transfer of the knight to c5) 8 . . . ♗f5 9 e4 de 10 fe ♗g6 11 ♖f4+ ♔e6 12 ♔e3 ♖g7 13 ♘d3 ♔d6 14 ♘c5 ♖e7 15 ♖f8 ♔c7 (To stop 16 ♖b8) 16 e5 ♖e8 (Black goes into a poor minor piece ending, but even with rooks on he was forced to remain passive. If 16 . . . b6 17 ♘a4 ba 18 ba and a6 is very weak). 17 ♖×e8 ♗×e8 18 ♔f4 b6 19 ♘a4 ba 20 ba ♗f7 21 ♘c5 ♗c4 22 ♔g5 ♗e2 23 ♔h6 ♔d8 24 ♔×h7 ♔e7 25 ♔g6 ♗f1 26 ♔f5 and Black soon resigned.

Diagram 217. Bogoljubow–Alekhine, Match, 1934.

Lasker wrote, 'All White's pawns are weak. Black can post his bishop on d6 and then advance the a-pawn in a threatening fashion. He follows up with the attack h6–h5–h4. White will have many difficulties in coping with the various problems which will arise, and will not be able to prevent the entry of the enemy king which will prove decisive'. No details, just the plan!

Diagram 218. König–Smyslov, USSR–Gt. Britain, 1947.
Black played 41 . . . g5! Smyslov comments, 'Finally the long prepared breakthrough comes. The fine point of the position is that White will not be in time to get in ♘g2 since his f2 pawn would be en prise. So he is faced with the dilemma: either allow Black an outside passed h-pawn after 42 hg fg, or concede a weak pawn at h4.'

There followed: 42 ♔e2 gh 43 gh f5 44 ♘g2 ♔e5 45 a3 ♗d6 46 b4 f4 47 f3 ♔d4 48 fe ♔×e4 49 ♘e1 ♔d4 50 ♔f3 ♔c4 51 ♔e4 ♔b3 52 ♘d3 ♔×a3 53 ♘c5 ♔×b4 0–1 (54 ♘×a6+ ♔b5 wins the knight).

Diagram 219. Boleslavsky–Smyslov, Leningrad, 1948.
White played 30 ♔f1 and lost. Smyslov writes, 'The right decision for White was 30 ♖d6 to force off rooks, and so reduce the attacking force of Black's pieces. After 30 ♖d6 ♖×d6 31 ♗×d6 f5 32 f4 ♔f7 33 ♔f3 White has a passive position, but it is quite sound, and he has drawing chances.'

Index of Names

References are to diagram numbers